Civic Activism Unleashed

The Carnegie Endowment for International Peace offers decisionmakers global, independent, and strategic insight and innovative ideas that advance international peace. Founded in 1910 as the first international affairs think tank in the United States, it is a global institution with centers in Beijing, Beirut, Brussels, Moscow, New Delhi, and Washington. Carnegie's network works together to provide analysis, shape policy debates, and propose solutions to the most consequential global threats.

The Carnegie Endowment for International Peace does not take institutional positions. Its scholars embody a variety of national and regional outlooks as well as the issues that transcend them. All views expressed in its publications are solely those of the author or authors.

Civic Activism Unleashed

New Hope or False Dawn for Democracy?

RICHARD YOUNGS

A Carnegie Endowment for International Peace Book

OXFORD
UNIVERSITY PRESS

Oxford University Press is a department of the University of Oxford.
It furthers the University's objective of excellence in research, scholarship,
and education by publishing worldwide. Oxford is a registered trade mark of
Oxford University Press in the UK and certain other countries.

Published in the United States of America by Oxford University Press
198 Madison Avenue, New York, NY 10016, United States of America.

© Oxford University Press 2019

All rights reserved. No part of this publication may be reproduced,
stored in a retrieval system, or transmitted, in any form or by any means,
without the prior permission in writing of Oxford University Press,
or as expressly permitted by law, by license, or under terms agreed with
the appropriate reproduction rights organization. Inquiries concerning
reproduction outside the scope of the above should be sent to the
Rights Department, Oxford University Press, at the address above.

You must not circulate this work in any other form
and you must impose this same condition on any acquirer.

Library of Congress Cataloging-in-Publication Data
Names: Youngs, Richard, 1968- author.
Title: Civic activism unleashed : new hope or false dawn for democracy? /
Richard Youngs.
Description: New York, NY, United States of America : Oxford University Press, 2019.
Identifiers: LCCN 2018030796 | ISBN 9780190931704 (pb : alk. paper)
Subjects: LCSH: Social movements-Political aspects. | Political
participation. | Social media-Political aspects. | Democracy. |
Democratization. | Civil society.
Classification: LCC HM881 .Y68 2019 | DDC 303.48/4-dc23 LC record available at
https://lccn.loc.gov/2018030796

ACKNOWLEDGMENTS

The author prepared this book under the rubric of Carnegie's Civic Research Network. He gratefully acknowledges the support of the Charles Stewart Mott Foundation, the Ford Foundation, and the UK Department for International Development for this ongoing project. The book benefited from input provided by Natalia Shapovalova, Graham Fowler, Jonah Belser, Emile Haeghebaert, and Thomas Carothers, in addition to the suggestions of anonymous reviewers provided by Oxford University Press.

CONTENTS

1. Introduction   3

2. The changing shape of civic activism   9

3. The spread of global protests   27

4. How effective have protests been?   52

5. New versus old civic activism: Rivals or allies?   70

6. Digital activism: Game changer or chimera?   82

7. Boon or bane for global democracy?   101

8. International support for civic activism   113

9. Activists at risk   129

10. Conclusion   146

Notes   159
Index   179

Civic Activism Unleashed

1

Introduction

Dramatic forms of civic activism have shaken global politics in recent years. The intensity, frequency, and geographical spread of large-scale protests across the world have reached unprecedented highs. Hardly a week goes by without a riotous protest breaking out somewhere in the world, whether Athens, Bangkok, Bucharest, Cairo, Caracas, Istanbul, Kyiv, Tehran, Tunis, or São Paolo. Civic movements have unleashed innovative forms of direct action against governments, sometimes tipping over into social violence or wider conflict dynamics. These trends have engendered widespread debate about the arrival of a new style of politics.

The emergent civic activism is not just about these high-profile protests but is also reflected in an increasingly dense network of civic organization. In India, village-level women's groups campaign against sexual harassment and caste discrimination. In Uganda, citizens coordinate a "walk to work" campaign to register their anger at stolen elections. In Ukraine, citizens organize to protect the country from Russian attacks. In Syria and Lebanon, community groups organize to provide humanitarian relief as conflict and instability intensify. In Iceland, activists mobilize to marshal popular input into a new constitution. In Spain, citizen circles form to plot a new economic and political course for the crisis-hit country. And in a very different ideological trend, nationalist and illiberal civic movements have risen in prominence across all regions.

An angry but also proactive citizenry—and in particular a youth disaffected and out of joint with its tumultuous times—has raised its head. Citizens seem to boil with rage at the injustices of corruption, repressive political elites, and the unmovable power of vested economic interests. Social media sites have in a few short years become mainstream forums that catalyze and amplify countless civic campaigns. And as all these elements of civic activism have intensified, so governments have responded by clamping down; the flip side of today's citizen empowerment is the more brutal repression meted out by many governments against civic activism.

Profound change is afoot within civil society in many countries. There is less certainty than a decade ago about what types of organization most typically represent civil society or about which forms of activism are most significant and effective. When diplomats and aid donors stress the importance of supporting civil society, they have mainly had in mind a certain type of formally organized, professional advocacy nongovernmental organization (NGO). But many of today's most vibrant forms of civic activism seem to be very different from the familiar NGO model, being self-consciously shapeless, indeterminate, and even nebulous in form, deed, and vision. This has sharpened debates over which kinds of civic activism are most conducive to shoring up good-quality politics.

Contentious issues

Such is the landscape that is prompting widespread discussion about the changing face of global civic activism. While these changes are of the utmost importance, the pictures that are painted of this civic landscape often leave crucial questions unanswered. In this book, I set out to shed light on three aspects of contemporary civic activism.

First, I investigate exactly *what kind of new civic activism* is emerging around the world. In what ways is this emergent activism really different from more established forms of civil society activity or from previous waves of protest? What issues does it focus on? Are the newer and older forms of activism at odds with each other or complementary? Is the new activism already peaking or set progressively to gain in strength? Are today's fast and furious protests a sign that democracy is in poor health or that it is working and adapting well? Are common patterns of civic activism emerging globally, or are there core differences, for example, between Western and non-Western activism? (See "Box 1.1: Terms and concepts.")

My second concern is to assess the *impact and effectiveness* of the new civic activism. Most specifically I uncover where large-scale protest has succeeded in its goals and where it has failed. I attempt to offer a systematic set of variables to help explain successes and failures across different cases of new activism. From this framework I draw an analysis of the challenges that activists face in moving "from protest to politics"—that is, from confrontational civic revolt to constructive involvement in mainstream political process. More broadly, the book probes whether the new activism is becoming more or less effective in its contribution to good-quality democracy.

The book's third concern is to examine the practical world of *international civil society support* and its relationship with the new forms of global civic activism. Taking a policy-relevant step that most assessments of civic activism eschew,

I assess the implications of the new activism for providers of civil society assistance. To what extent is civil society support keeping pace with changes to the civic sphere across the world? For many years critics have accused international civil society assistance of fostering an imbalanced "NGO-ization" of civil society. Is this criticism still fair, or have international organizations in fact begun to target new movements and alternative civic actors? What new forms and patterns of civil society assistance might best respond to the changing nature of civic activism? Is support from civil society assistance providers to emerging civic activism likely to be more or less difficult or sensitive than support to established NGOs?

The new civic era

I address the three core sets of questions by structuring the book in the following way. Chapter 2 presents an overview of emerging types of civic activism; my mapping of such organizational forms is the essential conceptual base from which the rest of the book proceeds. Chapter 3 then details one type of event closely associated with the rising wave of activism: the spread of large-scale protests in recent years. I separate a chapter on new organizational forms of civic activism from one on protests because these are interrelated but not coincident phenomena; protests can be one tool used by the new activism, but they are far from being its only avenue of expression.

Chapter 4 assesses the successes and failures of recent mass protests and tries to explain why some of these have achieved their aims while others have not. Chapter 5 examines the relationship between the old and new forms of civic activism and reflects on how these two styles of political action might best lock together in the future. I then delve in greater detail into the influence of digital technologies on civil society actors, assessing how the latest and incipient phase of online activism raises new questions about the good and bad sides of information communication technologies. A key chapter then assesses what all these features of emergent activism imply for the practice of democratic politics. In chapter 9, I explore international civil society support and whether aid donors have adjusted to the changing shape of civic activism. In my final chapter, I look at how governments around the world are now seeking to restrict civil society and assess what this implies for the new activism.

The book draws on a wide range of empirical evidence and original interview material. It also draws on the work of a project I help lead at the Carnegie Endowment for International Peace, namely, the Civic Research Network, which brings together a group of experts on civic activism from different parts of the world to explore how civil society activity is changing in their respective countries and regions.[1]

The book uncovers the emergence of a new civic era that has important yet varied implications for global politics. I classify how the new activism differs from the old but also uncover points on which the differences between them are less notable than their similarities: while civic activism is evolving, its roots in the past remain evident. I uncover a growing number of hybrid civic organizational styles that bridge leaderless movements and more deeply rooted membership organizations. And I identify nascent structures that might in the future combine the advantages of the new and the old activism. The emerging activism is intrinsically neither good nor bad for democracy; rather, it is one factor that is ushering in a different *type* of democratic practice. I suggest how all this matters for global politics: the international community has not yet changed its models of civil society support, and this is one factor holding the new civic activism back from reaching its full potential. I find that the new activism has certainly not run its course but argue that its future significance may be more subtle and nuanced than many have assumed.

> **Box 1.1 Terms and concepts**
>
> The book uses the term "civic activism" in a very broad sense, to mean forms of action carried out by civil society actors that are either formal or relatively informal in nature, and that can be organized or less institutionally structured. Civic activism in this sense includes but is not limited to the activities of so-called social movements; it includes but is not limited to the activities of professional, formally structured advocacy NGOs; and it includes but is not limited to mass protest. Part of my purpose in adopting this capacious definition is to explore the balance between these different dimensions of contemporary civic activism.
>
> As their distinguishing hallmarks, social movements are generally taken to involve sustained collective and conflictive action rooted in dense informal base networks and collective identities, while employing a range of tactics on a repeated basis. They are usually defined as being more loosely structured and less professionalized than NGOs.
>
> In recent years, social movements analysis has evolved to focus on a wider range of collective action and has acknowledged the need to examine social movements' relationship to other types of political actors.[2] In a similar spirit, I employ the term "civic activism" to denote a phenomenon that extends beyond social movements and captures very loose forms of activism that are not rooted in movementlike structures—loose forms of activism that are becoming one of the defining features of contemporary global politics.
>
> I also favor the term "civic activism" in order to distinguish my analysis from a focus within the democratization literature on certain types of traditional "civil society" organizations seen as key drivers of political change. In this way, I hope to help close the gap between social movement analysis and work on democratization and international democracy support—two strands of analytical work that have to date overlapped surprisingly little. I use the term "civil society" as and where it is appropriate to refer to a realm that includes but extends beyond purposively organized activism.
>
> My focus is on emergent *forms* of activism and an open exploration of the issues and identities that the new activism advances. I adopt this focus rather than approaching the topic through the lens of any predetermined stance within the long-standing debates over whether "civil society" as a concept is inherently constraining and neoliberal or should necessarily be radically counterhegemonic. Indeed, the book will show that the emergent

(continued)

> *Box 1.1* continued
>
> activism includes forms that are, in this sense, both moderate and less moderate in their aims and tactics.
>
> The book investigates and compares different types and levels of civic activism. It is concerned with protests, understood as large-scale citizen mobilizations in pursuit of certain political social, economic, or cultural agendas. While it is not my concern to single out a comparison between violent and nonviolent tactics, I do examine cases where new civic activism has involved, crossed over into, or ignited conflict. But the book also examines nonprotest forms of new activism. Such activism involves ongoing campaigns built around aims that are pursued in ways other than protest, and also distinct from professional NGO advocacy. It often revolves around a notion of self-help mutualism, defined as activism that seeks practical and positive solutions to citizen concerns and most commonly takes places on a micro scale within local communities and neighborhoods.
>
> I use the term "new civic activism" in a very specific sense. Social movement theorists have been debating the emergence of "new" social movements since the 1960s, referring to the postmaterial identities that have displaced organized labor. These issues are now part of mainstream civic activism and are no longer particularly new. Rather, I refer to "new" activism in the sense of innovations in civic organization and mobilization that have become more widespread in very recent years. The term often used among activists and analysts is "new, new activism" to distinguish today's fast-evolving activist forms. I acknowledge that current forms of activism have precedents in past patterns of mobilization; I do not assume that today's activism adopts forms entirely unseen in previous periods. Rather, I explore the ways in which it both differs from and resembles past patterns of activism.
>
> A significant part of social movement analysis seeks to explain collective behavior per se—with debates centring on whether this results from increased resources, new political opportunities, or evolving identities.[3] My concern is more specifically to identify very recent changes to the way global civil society organizes itself, what it aspires to achieve, and how it mobilizes. My chief concern is to explore how far there is a new vibrancy and fluidity to civic activism—a focus somewhat different to the long-running theoretical issues within the specialized social movement analysis field.

2

The changing shape of civic activism

This chapter maps the main kinds of civic activism that have emerged and gained traction in different regions of the world in recent years. Drawing out the most salient features of today's reshaped civic activism, it points not only to features that are new and important but also to aspects that are more familiar and less categorical or dramatic in their innovation. Today's emergent activism is the harbinger of a profound structural change to the civic sphere around the world. Yet the change it heralds is more multifaceted and fine-grained than much received wisdom assumes.

A reshaped civic sphere

There is widespread agreement that changes to civic activism are now so widespread as to invite a reconceptualization of civil society.[1] The International Civil Society Centre reports that a far wider range of different civic organizations is active today than previously.[2] The director of this influential agency writes that "the old world of civic participation is being replaced." The rise of new types of popular engagement indicates that "traditional civil society organizations (CSOs) are part of an old world that is about to be replaced by very different forms of civic participation.... The next generation of civic activists view traditional CSOs as the dinosaurs that will go down together with traditional politics." The spread of small, local organizations directly linked to citizens poses a challenge to the traditional NGO's role as intermediary between the state and local communities.[3]

Civicus, one of the largest and best-known international consortia of civic organizations, shares the conviction that activism is changing as citizens are now "engaging in ways that are instinctively inclusive, and embrace principles of solidarity and collective action."[4] Extensive consultations with activists show that there has been a gradual move away from a focus on formal civil society structures toward a focus on new civic *practices*—different types of resistance, different ways of "representing civic claims."[5] The director of one well-known and long-standing international NGO consortium admits in private, when talking of the "old" type of civil society body: "We have become part of the problem."

These shifts have not occurred overnight. Traditional interest-based politics began to break down as far back as the 1960s. In the 2000s, anticapitalist set-piece demonstrations morphed into antiwar protests linked to events in Iraq and Afghanistan, and these fed into subsequent antiausterity activism in many countries. In the 1990s and early 2000s, it was the formally structured advocacy NGO, campaigning on what became a familiar menu of rights questions, that was most prominent. Today, it is this form of NGO-based activism and structured advocacy that many activists refer to as the "old" civil society.

While informal and innovative forms of civic activism have been taking shape for many years, in very recent times they have moved into a new era. The change is not an absolute rupture from one form of activism to another form previously unseen at all; different forms of civic activism have coexisted and have been in constant evolution over long periods of time. Rather, the trend is one of gradation: even where many of today's civil society initiatives build upon civic forms that have been in gestation for some time, there are important shifts under way in the overall state of play in civic activism.

The political scientist Peter Mair famously wrote about the traditional form of civic organization being part of a "stakeholder politics" that is fatefully conjoined with the decline of political parties, and increasingly challenged by those looking for a "mass politics" of practical civic engagement.[6] Apparently underscoring his point, surveys reveal that people's confidence in NGOs has weakened in recent years in line with their declining trust in parties, media, and governments.[7]

The scale, pace, and geographical spread of today's expansion in civic activism are dramatic. Data from the International Social Survey Programme register a significant increase in citizens' involvement in different types of voluntary associations since 2004 over nearly fifty countries.[8] International IDEA uses five measures covering different components of democracy; the only one of these to register significant overall increase since 2012, and to do so across all regions, is a category of "civil society participation"—defined as the incidence of citizens' involvement in civic organizations.[9] The Varieties of Democracy Project also shows that indicators of citizen participation have risen by a greater margin than those of any other component of democracy, with most of this rise since 2010 taking place outside formal CSO structures.[10] With thousands of new initiatives of civic participation emerging around the world, a group of experts set up the open-source Participedia platform to collect information on this still-understudied trend.[11]

Civil society practitioners refer to a rise in "unconventional" activism. While this may not be entirely new, recent years have witnessed a peak of innovative activism and developments that push in qualitatively different directions. The eighty-seven-year old civic organizer Dolores Huerta, an icon among activists, says that "we are seeing a new dawn of resistance, a new dawn of movements."[12] Debates have opened up about the need for a new understanding of civic engagement. For years many saw this engagement as being in decline—a symptom of the "bowling alone" generation, to use the influential term coined by the sociologist Robert Putnam.[13] But the apparent revival of civic activism in remodeled forms seems to upend many of these assumptions.

The dynamics of civic innovation

If these are the general trends, what then is the precise shape of the civic activism that is adding new vibrancy to citizen engagement and challenging the primacy of formalized NGOs? The emergent civic activism involves a range of quite different dynamics and carries with it varied implications.

Informality. Today's most prominent forms of civic activism are typically diffuse and shifting in their organizational structures and membership. They link together different issue-based networks. They sometimes do not focus on attaining concretely defined aims but set themselves up to "counter power," remold social values, and create shared cognitive identities. They tend to reject standard forms of leadership. Symbolic acts of civic disobedience are a chosen modus operandi.[14] Economic crisis in many countries has brought forth a raft of campaigns motivated by concepts of nonhierarchical participation and "horizontality."[15] The recent trajectory of this civic activism has been about "heterogeneity" and a much stronger taming of formal institutional structures.[16]

Much contemporary civic activism tends away from the kind of social associational activity previously seen as civil society's main glue and toward a more postmodern concept of citizenship. Civic actors monitoring political decisions are ready to engage as and when they do not like particular policy decisions, and in turn periodically disengage. This results in a sporadic changeability that is very different from regularized and traditional NGO or political party work.[17] It denotes a significant change from work-based to community-based organization, and a shift from class to looser notions of community as the primary vehicle of social contestation.[18] Increasingly, citizen participation is more informal even than that which characterizes organized social movements.[19]

Scores of "citizen reporting initiatives" have, for example, sprung up around the world, with informal local groups exposing wrongdoing and corruption. Academic inquiry has begun to urge a shift away from the traditional understanding of civil society to a more expansive notion of informal "activist citizenship" or "citizenism" to capture the rise in informality.[20]

Contestation. Many contemporary activists say their distinction lies in a "swarm logic" of confrontation. They no longer believe in membership-based groups but in mobilizing a "swarm" of individuals around a certain campaign, local activity, or protest. They talk of a new wave of nonorganized resistance. The spirit of the times has been the rallying cry of *Indignez-vous!*[21]

The emerging activism reflects an altered understanding of adversarial politics.[22] Many observers believe that today's activism is intrinsically disruptive, and consequently rooted in malleable networks and coalitions rather than permanent movementlike structures.[23] This is expressed not only through dramatic, large-scale revolts but also through almost daily, low-key small events—what activists refer to as nano-protests that take the form of myriad types of contestation. Some writers argue that today's angry activism harks back to a spirit of classical anarchist movements, propelled by a destructive impulse against modernity.[24] In this view, today's activists are "rebels without a cause" who reject the need for solid, fixed organizational structures harnessed for clear, ideological, long-term goals.[25]

Self-help. If one strand of the new activism is about frustrated contention, another strand seems to encapsulate a very different spirit of constructive practicality. Indeed, some writers believe the fastest-growing strand of civic activism is that of "everyday" community-level self-organization.[26] This activism revolves around mutual self-help and volunteerism, along with the practical organization of alternative political, economic, and social solutions.[27] Greater heterogeneity is evident today as many activists engage in both contentious and more mundane, everyday practical activism.[28] One report characterizes the difference between old and new activism in terms of many newer groups being more practically "hands-on" and more temporary.[29]

This chimes with what the sociologist Ulrich Beck termed a shift from "politics with a capital P" toward "sub-politics" built around new forms of civic activity.[30] One writer alludes to a "resurgence of participatory culture ... an explosive revival of civic life, as people organize themselves to rebuild society from the bottom-up."[31] This involves people sharing resources and mutual assistance outside formal policy-making structures, often even using informal means of bartering to move outside the currency turmoil of recent economic crises. The number of cooperatives and other initiatives based on the principle of mutualism has increased many times over during the last five years. Examples include community shops that cut out middlemen suppliers; time-banking organizations in which members of a community exchange forms of practical help; free education initiatives, involving community members cooperating to deliver classes where local schools are threatened with closure; skill-swapping forums; and initiatives that claim back neighborhood streets for common usage. These all involve increasingly dense networks that mobilize for collective purposes around an ethos of solidarity-based civic participation.[32]

These community groups are not entirely new, but they are becoming more widespread. They are engaging more people who do not see themselves as politicized "activists," and they are bringing in more activists who previously would have gravitated toward the professional NGO sector.[33] A whole new practice has emerged of "communing"—a verb that sits at the heart of the new activism to denote a range of practices in which individuals advance shared community interests. The notion of "walk-in" civic groups has gained traction, with these functioning as community hubs for a range of local concerns. Organizations offering legal advice and support have become another staple feature of many local communities.

This is all driven by the notion of cocreating social enterprises; many new activists feel more confortable defining themselves in these terms rather than as "civil society" or "NGOs."[34] Informal clusters of people increasingly engage in networks of fablabs and hackerspaces to develop sustainable technology.[35] Environmental activism has also moved in this direction, with an increasingly significant focus on local communities organizing to preserve and manage natural resources.[36] The new activism recalls eighteenth- and nineteenth-century civil society, the era of local societies and mutualism, before the term become associated with professional, issue-specific advocacy NGOs.[37] Today's ascendant civic campaigns are "experiments in new forms of sociability," with dynamics that extend well beyond anything found in professionalized NGOs.[38] For some, the trend denotes a "second generation" of civic activism that is displacing the "first generation" professionalized NGO sector and is more concerned with the "citizen aid" of micro-organization.[39]

Localism and the city. In another crosscutting and associated trend, civic activism has shifted somewhat away from global campaigns to municipal politics. In the early 2000s, much focus was on initiatives like the World Social Forum that was convened as a meeting place for antiglobalization social movements. This and other such global initiatives struggled to gain traction, and many activists switched their focus to city-level issues.[40] Today, civic activism is closely associated with an emergent "right to the city" movement. This has risen up through neighborhood-level or even street-level organizations linked to municipal governance reforms. Activists have coined the term "fearless cities" to refer to the growth of self-organizing civic forums in a growing number of cities around the world. Initiatives in hundreds of cities have garnered public participation in very concrete day-to-day matters outside the channels of mainstream politics. Naples is an example of where new community movements took power at the municipal level. Linking such initiatives together is an incipient World Human Rights Cities Forum.

The sheer range of novel initiatives fostering citizen participation within cities and neighborhoods is staggering. These include the wider use of referenda on local issues, informal types of consultation to help decide such matters, new forms of local voting, the spread of neighborhood councils, and more sophisticated civic complaint mechanisms. The talk is of a new phase of municipal localism, in which citizens are involved more proactively in setting political agendas. Well over two thousand cities now have participatory budgeting schemes, involving significant numbers of previously unengaged citizens.

Rightist activism. Much of the new activism styles itself as either nonideological or progressive and keen to defend liberal human rights. However, a strikingly emergent strand of current activism has a right-wing or conservative identity in one form or another. Such right-wing activism is, of course, hardly unprecedented, but it has become notably more widespread in very recent times. While a great deal of attention has been paid to the rise of right-wing political parties, equally significant is the underlying rise in right-wing forms of civic activism. Civicus identifies the rise of conservative activism as one of the main global trends of 2017 and 2018.[41]

This ascendant right-wing activism spans a wide range of different identities and adheres to contrasting definitions. While in the early 2000s there was some analysis of violent "uncivil" CSOs,[42] a much broader type of mainstream conservative activism is now taking root. In some countries such activism is organized around nationalist causes, in others it is religious or primarily ethnic, in some it is antistatist or antiegalitarian, while in others it focuses on a less exclusivist notion of traditional community values. In many instances it adheres to and indeed purports to further democratic norms; in a smaller number of cases it embraces violence and menaces democratic politics. Despite the general spread of nonviolent activism, based on subtle forms of noncompliance short of protest, some new civil society actors deploy increasingly violent tactics.[43] Far-right civic groups may often be linked to far-right political parties, but they have looser structures and membership rules and may host the views of those whom rightist parties see as too extreme. Authoritarian values and illiberal politics today are not just the result of top-down regime actions but are also present in bottom-up civic activism.

Perhaps the most prominent strand of such activism is that rooted in the politics of religious identities. As we will see in the examples below, this is becoming more influential through Salafist networks in North Africa and the Middle East, and through orthodox groups in Israel, and has spread in parts of Asia, Africa, and some Eastern European societies. This religiously oriented activism can focus on very specific (what its proponents would classify as) moral issues, or it can take on a broader role of underpinning conservative political projects or regimes.

The more secular-nationalist strand of right-wing activism is more dominant elsewhere. Some of this nationalist activism involves a relatively benign civic patriotism and search for rooted identity; some of it shades into more aggressive intolerance. Ironically, many nationalist movements have been particularly successful in forging transnational links with like-minded groups.[44] Rising conservative civic movements typically mix elements of nationalist and religious identities; sometimes, however, these two strands of activism are strongly at odds with each other. The nationalist groups today often attract significant political and media attention even where they are modest in scale. Many of them have proved expert in the use of social media and innovative civic strategies, like running radio stations, film clubs, magazines, and fashion websites.[45]

In some instances, conservative activism pits itself more generically against what it sees as a liberal-progressive elite that includes most of the formal NGO sector. As we will examine in later chapters, some of the new right-wing activism forms an integral part of the much-debated populist wave, although some of it has little to do with populism. In general, conservative groups combine an often-imprecise pushback against globalism in its various forms with a loosely framed quest for traditionalism. The emerging conservative activism is rooted in a complex and varied mix of unease with economic globalism and dislike of cultural liberalism.[46]

In sum, far-reaching changes are afoot to the way that civic activists organize and mobilize. At the same time, it is clear that greater precision is required in analysing this new activism. Several dynamics are gaining ground. One core trend is toward structural informality; another is toward localism. Some new activism reflects a disparate spirit of contention; some of it rather embodies a notion of practical self-help. Some of it is determinedly leftist and progressive; some of it is radically rightist; some of it is avowedly non-ideological. Crucially, some of these different dynamics overlap with each other, while others appear to pull in quite different directions.

A global trend

Significantly, this proliferation of new civic activism is a global trend. A more fluid, informal and community-rooted activism is emerging in diverse contexts around the world. A rich and dense network of such initiatives has formed in Western countries, especially in response to economic crisis—"Box 2.2: Postcrisis civic activism in Europe" illustrates some of the most notable examples from Europe—but the new activism is equally present in other regions.

In the *Middle East and North Africa* (MENA) region, informal networks of students, bloggers, vocational groups and neighbourhood initiatives appeared in the years prior to the 2011 Arab revolts.[47] These revolts then crystallized a further shift away from an older generation of NGO leaders. The number of small organizations and citizen initiatives increased across the MENA region after 2011. Arab activists talk about a "post-NGO era" in which they have "moved from talking about civil society to talking about civic activism."[48] New civic initiatives have sprung up across the region to organize local communities in providing food, medical assistance, and vocational training. Young people are turning toward social entrepreneurship and what they term "social volunteering" that combines community organizing with locally based economic activity; this aims to make communities more resilient by circumventing dysfunctional government institutions.[49] Day-to-day forms of nonobedience and alternative social networks have grown in the region in the years since the dramatic protests of 2011.[50] More conservative religious activists have mobilized to push for stronger laws against blasphemy across the region in the wake of the Arab Spring.

Many examples could be cited. In Egypt, much civic momentum has come not from NGOs or politicized social movements but rather from a gradual coalescing of community-based functional groupings, like street vendors, doctors, and urban-renewal specialists. Community-level Nubian and Bedouin activism is a related and rising trend. As political restrictions have tightened in Egypt, activism has increased around so-called decentralized collectives that often overlap with conservative Islamist groupings—the latter increasingly returning to their local, apolitical roots.[51] In Syria and Lebanon, organizations have emerged to provide humanitarian relief within communities scarred by conflict, relying on crowdsourcing for operational funds and liaising through sporadic town hall gatherings. In rebel-held areas in Syria, "nonformalized civic groups" have sought to oversee local governance capacities.[52] The Sahem (Contribute) initiative has gathered Syrian citizens together to work on community-level governance issues with the aim of galvanizing more local involvement in day-to-day decisions; one community leader notes that this kind of activism has displaced what are locally referred to as "the elitist NGOs" that were the main civic actors before the conflict started in 2011. By mid-2018 the Assad regime's advance meant that most Syrian activists were now focusing on practical service delivery and reconstruction functions within very localized community structures.[53] In Lebanon, activists have increasingly distanced themselves from formal civil society organizations, as these are often linked to the patronage of political families and notables.[54]

In Palestine, new types of civic organizations are detaching themselves from the parameters of two-state peace talks and organizing for de facto local autonomy from Israeli influence—this activism contrasting with formal NGOs' main aim of supporting the Palestinian Authority in diplomatic negotiations. New cultural movements and forums have commenced in Gaza as an attempt to move civic activism away from the power struggle between Hamas and Fatah political factions. In Libya, kinship groups have become more important, as NGO-type

Box 2.1 Turkey

Turkey is a particularly instructive example of the trends in civic activism. Professional NGOs have grown exponentially in Turkey since the early 2000s. The country now has over 100,000 registered organizations, run by an expanding professionalized staff. Yet newer forms of movements have gradually come to the fore, with young people moving repeatedly from one issue campaign to another, using ad hoc methods and organizational forms. The so-called Gezi Park protests of 2013 signaled an apparent acceleration of this trend. Only a tiny percentage of the protestors were members of an NGO or any other civic or political organization. The protests gave birth to a series of public assemblies, known as forums, that consciously rejected formal and hierarchical structures of traditional civil society initiatives.[55]

The political divide between the ruling AK Party and opposition forces has begun to infect and dominate the civic sphere. The government and state institutions have supported a more conservative-Islamist strand of activism, in tune with and loyal to President Recep Tayyip Erdoğan's broad political project. Religious charities and similar bodies are a fast-rising and protected area of civil society in today's Turkey. For their part, paramilitary nationalist groups like the Ottoman Hearths, the AK Hearths, and the People's Special Operations deploy a neo-Ottoman discourse and violent, militia-style tactics.[56]

Other activists have moved to low-profile, small, and flexible citizen self-help initiatives.[57] The overall political situation has pushed them away from political activities and toward issues like urban renewal and development. Formal organizations focused on human rights and democracy represent a smaller part of Turkish civil society today. Many CSOs continue to meet without active campaigning, simply to keep their groups together in "wait-and-see" mode. Some of the Gezi forums still exist, although they have fractured as differences have emerged over whether more permanent NGO-like structures are necessary.[58]

A social incubation center was set up in 2014 to capture Turkey's emerging forms of activism. This aims expressly to work with organic groups rather than social movements or NGOs. Increasingly, what the center refers to as "civil initiatives" choose not to seek formal status as associations in order to maintain their agility and low profile. This is especially true of many ecology and LGBT groups as well as the so-called Vote and Beyond initiative, which sought to build reform coalitions after elections in 2015. The center

(continued)

> *Box 2.1 continued*
>
> seeks to link these increasingly widespread loose networks together and to provide them with a range of strategic advice and mentoring.
>
> In parallel, representatives of Turkey's main civil society umbrella organization, TESEV, talk of a new effort to "reach down" from their longstanding NGO members to the new array of informal networks and "platforms" that have appeared in the last five years. They report that while new government clampdowns have created serious problems for NGOs registered as formal associations, private donations from individuals increasingly focus on volunteer movements—with the share of support coming from domestic sources rising relative to foreign funding.
>
> A separate phenomenon is the unusual and sui generis Gulenist movement: this may not fully fit a standard notion of civic activism, but its network of conservative-religious establishments has become a very distinctively organized, additional form of contention against the AKP government.

structures have struggled to take root in the years since Colonel Qadafi was ousted from power. In Morocco, the February 20 Movement emerged as a non-institutional actor concerned with self-organization and local level agency outside the professional NGO community.[59] A new trend in Tunisia is that of cooperatives taking over and managing land for the "commons." In addition, informal Tunisian youth groups like I Watch and Al Bawsala now monitor corruption and a range of youth issues.[60] "Box 2.1: Turkey" covers developments in that country.

In *India*, two types of activism have grown in recent years. One type is rooted in community movements organized around issues like land rights, the right to food, caste discrimination, resource management, corruption, antirape initiatives, and student activism against discrimination in universities. Many of these new initiatives have a village-level orientation and include areas of high illiteracy, as a conscious reaction against "NGO elites" and their failure to address such sectors of the population.[61] The other strand of activism is the battery of new Hindu conservative movements closely linked to the BJP government of Prime Minister Narendra Modi. Some of these engage in violent attacks against poor Dalit farmers for killing (sacred) cows, against Hindu girls marrying Muslims, against liberal artists and filmmakers, and against university students and professors. The "anti-Romeo" movement has citizen vigilantes patrolling neighborhoods in several Indian towns to separate courting couples.[62]

In *China*, collective action networks have appeared in recent years, focusing especially on health and environmental issues. These initiatives are spreading fast; their informality, caution, and absence of sustained action leave them short of being social movements.[63] Civic organization has also intensified in China around a large number of new participatory budgeting initiatives at the local level.[64]

Russian civil society is not only increasingly restricted but also subject to state-backed moves to promote nationalist-conservative civic movements; here right-wing activism is the result of both top-down and bottom-up dynamics. Some prominent groups, like the Night Wolves gang, are proudly violent. A very different form of activism engages on local issues like housing and transport problems. New groups run neighborhood collective action against road developments, environmental destruction, corruption, and the like. As political opposition has become riskier, increasing numbers of Russians are now involved in this so-called backyard activism. This is relatively fluid but organized through several initiatives like Committee-42 and the Moscow City Coalition. It expressly distinguishes itself from what many Russians describe as "Western-style NGOs" and the notion of civil society being a contentious site pushing for democratization.[65]

More broadly across the Eurasia region, non-NGO civic initiatives have been growing fast in former Soviet states, tackling environmental, consumer, employment, and cultural issues; participants have adopted the term "self-determined" activism to describe these initiatives and distinguish them from what they term "traditional NGO" civil society.[66] In Georgia, conservative groups combining religious and nationalist identities have gained in popularity; while this antiliberal backlash is led by the Georgian Orthodox Church, it is also expressed through local groups set up explicitly to counter the formal rights-oriented NGO sector. These include groups like the Union of Orthodox Parents and the far-right Georgian March that have used violent actions against liberal groups.[67]

In *Ukraine*, new initiatives based on volunteerism have sprung up related to the ongoing conflict with Russia. Self-help volunteerism has funded "citizen soldiers" in the conflict against Russian-backed separatists. "Street committees" have formed to help victims of the war in Donbas and distribute humanitarian aid. Many such grassroots initiatives have strongly nationalistic identities, like the National Militia created in 2017 and the Ukranian Association of Patriots. Indeed, a number of far-right nationalist groups like the Azov Battalion and the C14 youth movement have gained support in recent years. Several political party structures are also rooted in conservative-nationalist civic groups, as with the so-called Right Sector. Alongside this is the rise of more moderate conservative groups linked to the church and campaigning against abortion and same-sex marriage and for more protection of traditional family values. The nationalist groups have grown in response to Russian meddling in the country, while the values-based conservative activism is in part a backlash against Ukraine's convergence with EU "liberal" norms.⁶⁸

Other forms of new activism in Ukraine are more practical and reformist. ProZorro is a volunteer initiative that worked to introduce a transparent and competitive electronic system of public procurement, using innovative commercial platforms to attack corruption. At the local level, initiatives include Warm City, a platform uniting civil society and businessmen around the idea of sustainable development. A chain of restaurants that serve as meeting places for local communities to discuss political and other issues has spread across the country; these were conceived as places where citizens can meet and debate outside the political sphere. Housing associations have also expanded across Ukraine.

Community-based movements were an integral part of *Latin America*'s turn toward leftist populism in the early 2000s. One project counts six hundred new civic initiatives working across Latin America to engage citizens in innovative types of participation.⁶⁹ One part of this trend is rooted in traditional and indigenous rights movements in many countries. Left-wing administrations in Bolivia, Ecuador, and Venezuela grew directly out of these movements and gave the latter a role in monitoring and informing policies through community councils and citizen assemblies. Even as these regimes have drifted into more authoritarian practices, seeking to use citizen forums for instrumental reasons, some local movements are still active.⁷⁰ Bolivian president Evo Morales has derived his support from the social movement he spearheaded.⁷¹ Nearly fifty thousand so-called communal councils now operate in Venezuela; deliberative *encuentros* take place across the continent to discuss neighborhood issues; and self organized community police provide security in countries like Mexico.⁷²

Latinno.net has collected a database of hundreds of new community-level civic initiatives that have sprung up across Latin America in recent years. Examples include the #YoSoy132 campaign in Mexico and the Chilean student movement that has operated since 2011. In Brazil, neighborhood groups have organized to catalog instances of police brutality. In addition, as the *chavista* tide appears to have passed its high-water mark, an emerging wave of civic activism is taking shape with a more conservative identity, focused on issues such as religious education and campaigns against same-sex marriage; examples include the Free Brazil Movement and the Atlas Network that is now influential in several Latin American countries. In Brazil, community groups have tried to close down exhibitions about homosexuality. These kinds of groups played a role in galvanizing public opinion against President Dilma Rousseff in Brazil and paved the way to her impeachment in 2016.⁷³

A first wave of activism in *Africa* was focused on the struggle against colonialism and for independence; a second wave focused on the struggle for democracy; in the last decade a third wave of very different civic activism has gathered

Box 2.2 **Postcrisis civic activism in Europe**

The post-2009 economic crisis in Europe gave rise to a wide range of community-based self-help activism, while dissatisfaction with EU institutional opaqueness has inspired an increasing number of "citizen lobbyists" to engage on specific problems that blight European politics.[74] Activists now organize numerous "participation labs" across Europe to deliberate on policy challenges and the future of democracy.

In Greece, a citizen movement for a "social solidarity economy" organized food parcels, social pharmacies, electricity reconnection, and community self-help centers, under the slogan "No One Alone in the Crisis." In Madrid, activists set up bartering schemes and self-managed social centers within certain neighborhoods to circumvent the impact of austerity, as well as group squats in vacant buildings; one of the highest-profile new movements worked to rehouse people whose properties were repossessed by the banks.[75] In France, since 2012 there has been a dramatic spread of the *zone à défendre* phenomenon that sees civic activists occupying land slated for big development projects.

In Naples, a former prosecutor of the city's most powerful criminal networks swept to power in the 2011 mayoral election on an anticorruption platform and aligned himself closely with the city's social movements—like the progressive and collectivist umbrella organization Massa Critica, working for greater direct democracy and citizen control over municipal governance. The mayor and movement introduced new ways to engage civil service organizations and ordinary citizens with local government around the notion of "commons space."[76] Under a mayor linked to social movement activists, in Reykjavik the Citizens Foundation created Better Reykjavik, a website where residents suggest, edit, and vote on proposals for improving the city, and worked with community organizations to get them involved in a participative Better Neighborhoods scheme.

The Bread Houses Network began in Bulgaria and has now extended to fifteen countries, offering spaces for "collective bread making" as a means of bringing communities together to discuss a range of issues and promote social cohesion through a shared, very practical everyday activity, expressly in contradistinction to the professionalized political activity of formal NGOs.[77] In a similar vein, the Creative Commons initiative aims to make knowledge and innovations more widely available for community objectives; it started as an informal, bottom-up initiative, then gradually grew into a globally connected platform and community.

(*continued*)

Box 2.2 continued

In another example, new neighborhood groups have pressed for affordable housing developments. The so-called Yimby ("Yes, in my backyard") movement started in San Francisco in 2013 and has been copied in many European cities. It is a local-community initiative against anticapitalist and environmental NGOs that try to stop housing projects and thus deprive poor neighborhoods of accessible accommodation. The movement is based on self-organization to facilitate new housing projects in inner-city locations.[78]

In the UK, new civic groups are creating community charters. The 2011 Localism Act has opened the way for neighborhood forums to influence local development plans. In Scotland, civic groups have convened a series of new consultative initiatives called "tings" that involve local community members in discussing solutions to particular problems. In a similar "Act as if you own the place" campaign, a group of civil society organizations have facilitated community initiatives across Scotland to explore ways of gaining more control over local services. To the south, several dozen new civic initiatives combined to oversee the People's Plan for Greater Manchester.[79] Across the country, Citizens UK gathers together hundreds of faith groups, community bodies, social volunteers, and schools to debate political issues and engage local MPs to press for change on very concrete issues like rising rents, wage levels, and job training; this is not a new initiative, but it has grown spectacularly and acquired a significantly higher profile in recent years.[80]

Many other similar initiatives could be mentioned: in Croatia, the Network for Food; in France, the Coop des Communs; in Hungary, a social farming network; in Portugal, Participa, time banks, and Zero Desperdicio.[81] The new Civic Participation Index in Bulgaria has recorded a steady increase in the number and size of informal civic groups in the country.[82] Playing Out is an initiative active across Europe to close off streets and create spaces for children to play. A particularly dense network of initiatives has sprung up in Rotterdam, based around commons-managed reading rooms and health and education facilities. Across the Netherlands, the use of randomly selected assemblies at the local level quadrupled between 2016 and 2017.[83] Citizen assemblies have assumed a notable presence in Gdansk. Nejdřív Střecha (Roof First) is a new Czech community-based homelessness relief group, helping people who have lost their housing find shelter, employment, and documentation.

Alongside this self-help dynamic is a rise in right-wing activism across Europe. The refugee crisis has fueled several nationalist groups opposed to increased immigration; the one known as Generation Identity is a pan-European network of young activists. In Bulgaria, the Committee for National Rescue organized vigilante groups to detain migrants and hand them over to the authorities.[84] Similar groups operate in Slovakia and Hungary; some of the Hungarian groups have ties to the far-right Jobbik party. In addition to antimigrant activity, these groups frequently use anti-Semitic and anti-Roma rhetoric. In Italy, the fascist organization CasaPound organizes patrols to "protect" neighborhoods from migrants and to provide goods and advice to local unemployed Italians. In Finland, the Soldiers of Odin have staged patrols to "protect" local women from migrants following incidents of sexual harassment.[85]

In general, Islamophobia has become a common thread among many far-right civic movements across Europe. In Austria, grassroots citizens initiatives mobilized citizens against the building of mosques. In France, radical civic groups such as Bloc Identitaire and Riposte Laïque mobilized against mosques, women's headscarves, halal shops, and Muslim associations, while the Sens Commun social movement has emerged to press for socially conservative values. The Danish Free Press Society mobilized against legal restrictions on criticism of Islam and immigration. In Norway, similar activist movements include the Norwegian Defence League and the Norwegian Patriots. Far bigger in scale is Germany's PEGIDA (Patriotic Europeans against the Islamization of the West) movement, which began in Dresden in 2014. And perhaps most unsettling, Golden Dawn has brought violent right-wing activism back to Greece, with a military-style hierarchy, assault battalions willing to kill, and supporters embedded in Greece's police and church establishments.[86] Following the 2013 murder of the antifascist rapper Pavlos Fyssas by a Golden Dawn supporter, the movement's leaders were arrested.

More standard, mainstream social conservative causes have also ignited large demonstrations, for example, in France in 2014 and 2016 against gay marriage and in Ireland in 2018 against abortion. In Poland, conservative activism has gained ground under the current Law and Justice government since 2015, and conservative community groups have formed a new coalition to counter the formalized "liberal NGOs" they see as having been too exclusively favored since the transition to democracy. These emergent Polish groups focus mainly on socially conservative values, such as campaigns against abortion; some have also supported a politically illiberal narrowing of constitutional rights, in their determination to counter Poland's

(continued)

Box 2.2 continued

more traditional human rights NGOs.[87] In Slovenia, the right-wing civic group Civil Initiative for the Family and the Rights of Children lobbies for laws restricting the rights of women and against same-sex partnerships.

Rightist activism is often stirring a liberal pushback. In Finland, grassroots groups served as the base for the rise of the populist-nationalist True Finns party; in response, many citizens began organizing campaigns against racism and discrimination—for example, to stop attacks against immigrants on the public transport system. In both cases, this was new activism occurring outside the formal NGO spectrum. Both the liberal and illiberal sides of the political spectrum have generated more dynamic, bottom-up activism. The Initiative in Sweden and the Alternative in Denmark are self-help groups based on coresponsibility, both explicitly attempting to use the new locally grounded activist techniques of the rightist-populists for more progressive agendas. Democracy festivals, which began many years ago in the Nordic countries, have spread to eight countries and grown exponentially in size, now gathering hundreds of thousands of activists and citizens.

---

momentum, focused on more local aims. A new generation of African civic initiatives is animated by a general sense of societal frustration but lacks the big, clear aims of the previous waves of social activism. Much new activism is born of anger that the spoils of Africa's much-celebrated economic takeoff are unevenly distributed.[88] Related more specifically to conflict, women's groups have emerged pressing for peace in several African countries—Liberia being a trendsetter—through a range of innovative campaigns and community actions.

In Sudan, small student-led movements began to appear around 2011, employing a range of campaigns against the government of Omar al-Bashir. They also organized around the provision of humanitarian relief. In Kenya, a People's Parliament has formed in which citizens can discuss issues outside both party and NGO structures, while a Flour Movement focuses on the right to basic foods. In Uganda, the Black Monday initiative sees people dressing in black at work in a protest against corruption. In Zimbabwe, the WOZA movement started as a group of mothers, not engaged in professional activism but concerned about day-to-day economic issues; it has grown to over eighty thousand members and has gradually addressed a broader agenda of political issues too. Some grassroots movements are radical and violent; Boko Haram in Nigeria is one example.

Conclusions

Civic activism is changing shape across the world. It is doing so in quite diverse ways. Some emergent activism is extremely informal, while other activity is still relatively structured. Some networks and movements are openly confrontational, but others have a more collaborative relationship with the state. Some are very modern and professional, while others are more traditional and are community, kin, or faith based. Some new activism is very large-scale, pushing for national-level changes; some is very small-scale and modest in ambition. Some is progressive; some, conservative and nationalistic. In some cases, contemporary activism builds on and updates civic forms that have existed for a long time, while in other cases, it seeks more qualitative innovation. While contemporary campaigns, groups, and movements clearly share many common features, there is in fact no single model of the new activism.

In broad-brush terms, citizens are increasingly looking for solutions in localism and citizen-led initiatives based around the notion of the civic commons. Much new activism is not directly confrontational so much as "prefigurative"—an increasingly used term that refers to groups acting in a way that paves the way toward or prefigures a new type of politics and society. The emergent civic activism is as much about the values of community as it is about issue-oriented advocacy. As lines blur between different parts of political and social systems, civil society today seeps downward into informal community networks more than it did a decade ago. Activists talk of communitarianism as a guiding idea; left and right have different versions of this, but both feel it drives a new momentum behind civic activism in response to the perceived failings of both states and international cooperation.

Some interpret the new activism primarily as a culture of collaborative community activity designed to circumvent the iniquities of neoliberal capitalism and the ravages of economic crises. Those engaged in such mutualism, sharing-economy, and peer-to-peer initiatives are immersed in practical local actions more than they target macrolevel political aims. Yet they are by their practices contributing toward new systems of work, social organization, community relations, and knowledge sharing.[89] This embodies a broader trend toward "networked governance" where the influence of citizens, civic organizations, markets, and governments all intertwine in patterns of shared authority.

To some degree, there has been a transition from the comprehensive, ideological political struggles of the past to a new politics of grassroots movements, with relatively narrow, concrete goals. Activism today is less related to generic "global ethics" than ten years ago. Ten years ago, the emergence of "transnational collective action" was judged to be the most interesting and meaningful trend in civic protest.[90] This has now changed.[91] While global-level civic campaigns of course continue in many areas, today's most vibrant activism is strongly rooted in national or subnational political debate and concerns. The kind of people involved in these local, community campaigns are quite different from the class of professionalized activists that dominated civil society in previous years. The balance between the global and local, the general and the specific, the macro and the micro have shifted.

A key change associated with these trends—to be detailed later in the book—is that civic activists are far less in thrall to the international community today. They make a point of setting their own priorities and reaching down into local communities, while being less ready to mold themselves around external actors' agendas. Much of the rising conservative activism sets itself very openly against the international community and its support for the kind of "liberal elitist NGOs" that the new rightists believe are out of touch with local concerns and values. While many familiar problems of the traditional NGO models persist, change has already advanced to such a degree that global civil society has a very different feel from ten years ago. We will return to this crucial point in chapter 8.

A final caveat: although innovative forms of civic organization have become widespread, it is important not to overstate their reach. Even if it aspires to be more inclusive than traditional NGOs and other civil society organizations, the new activism still involves small percentages of the population. Many movements may displace the leadership role played by a narrow circle of civil society advocacy professionals, only to create their own relatively circumscribed cadre of new activists or community leaders—a problem explored in greater depth in chapter 7. And while the breadth of new activism is indeed highly significant, this should not blind us to the parts of societies where apathy is still prevalent and popular frustrations apparently insufficient to kick-start civic campaigns. Nor does it offset the fact that in many locations conditions are simply too difficult for civic initiatives to put down roots. As we will stress throughout the remainder of the book, the new civic activism is notable for its breadth and dynamism but also struggles to solidify its presence and to attain transformational change.

3

The spread of global protests

In parallel with the emergence of new organizational forms of civic activism, there has been a rise in mass protest. While this form of activism is not new, mass protests have become more frequent and more geographically widespread than before, and those involved in them have deployed innovative tactics. The previous chapter established the main *organizational forms* of the new civic activism; this chapter moves on to look at one type of *event* closely associated with this activism. While not all the organizational forms of civic activism identified in the previous chapter generate mass protest, some of them increasingly do.

Although analysts have previously tracked a general mainstreaming of protest activity over the long stretch of the postwar period,[1] my concern here is to examine what appears to be a particularly notable spike in protests in the shorter space of very recent years. The chapter presents some of the main facts about and features of today's mass protests. And it explores what lies behind the apparently inexorable rise of mass demonstration, searching for both the commonalities that link different protests and the contrasts between them.

Protest surge

Scenes of mass protest dramatically erupting all around the world have repeatedly captured media headlines in recent years. The sheer ubiquity of such events is eye opening. While there have been previous periods in which large-scale social protest has played a prominent role in politics, in these periods protests were clustered in one or two regions or a relatively small number of countries. Today protest has become a global phenomenon. Protests have occurred in every region of the world in the last several years. They have occurred in poor countries and rich societies, in democracies and autocratic states.

This clustering of protests cannot be mere coincidence. It reflects something of broader and more structural significance. The recent concentration of protests suggests that fundamental change is stirring within the underlying nature of global politics. Political flux is deepening, as citizens demand more of their governments. Protests represent one part of the new kind of politics associated with a fundamentally reanimated ethos of civic activism.

Protest intensity has been increasing for around a decade. The 1980s saw the last relatively high level of protest intensity, with mobilizations linked to the last days of the Cold War. Now, a new peak has been reached in very recent years.[2] Several surveys and data collecting initiatives provide an overarching picture of the rise in global protests. In one of the first studies to identify the new surge in popular revolts, the Economist Intelligence Unit listed sixty-nine states experiencing protests between 2009 and 2013.[3] Another dataset reported over three thousand protest incidents in Africa and over nineteen thousand in Asia during 2016.[4] The GDELT (Global Database of Events, Language, and Tone) data collection program records a rise of approximately 5 percent in protest intensity since the early 1990s; the graphs show the scale of this rise by region, based on the GDELT data.[5]

Another database reports that in the last decade the number of protests has been greater than in the three previous decades combined.[6] An extensive survey carried out by the Initiative for Policy Dialogue and Friedrich-Ebert-Stiftung reports a steady increase in the overall number of protests year on year during the last decade. In 2006 there were fifty-nine significant protests across the world; in 2013, more than double that number were recorded. By region, the highest number of protests has taken place in higher-income Western countries, followed by Latin America, then East Asia, then Sub-Saharan Africa; the number of protests in North Arica and the Middle East has fluctuated most, with the most

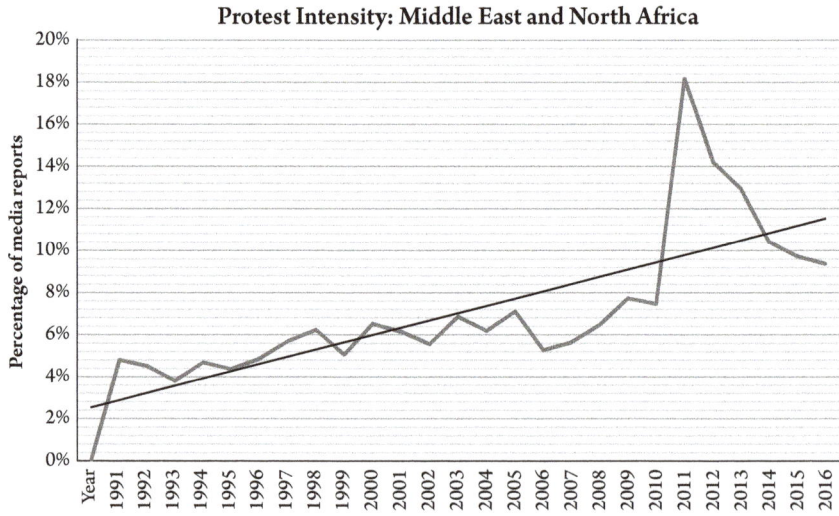

Protest Intensity: Middle East and North Africa

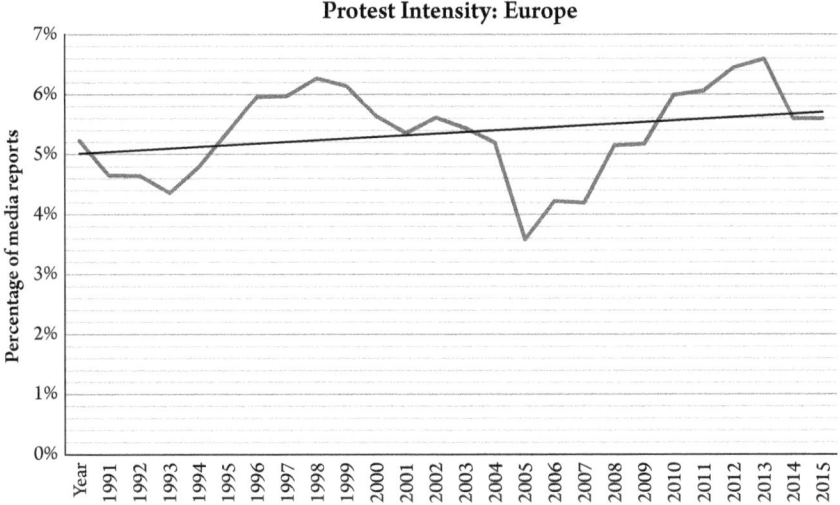

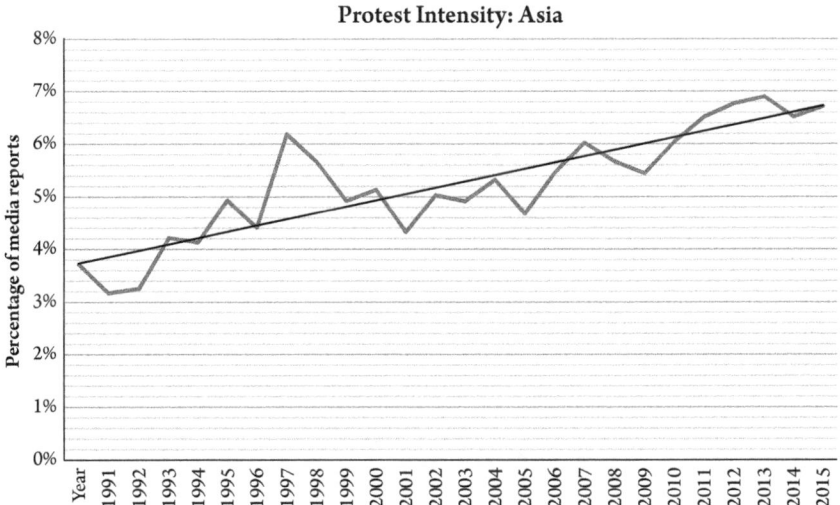

dramatic spike of any region seen in 2011. The average size of protests has also increased.[7]

For a while it seemed that the spike in global protests might have peaked. There was a burst of revolts in 2011 and 2012 associated with the Arab Spring and the Eurozone crisis. As these calmed somewhat, there was an impression that the protest upswing was perhaps ephemeral. But now it is evident that discontent still simmers. Civicus talks of a "second wave of dissent." After a concentration of revolts in 2010–12, there was a lull as protest leaders regrouped and sought to assess successes and failures, and then a new burst of civic energy from

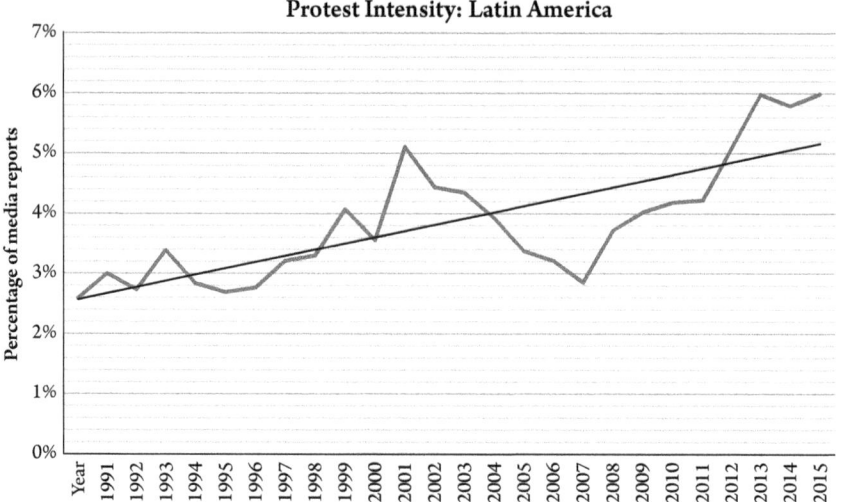

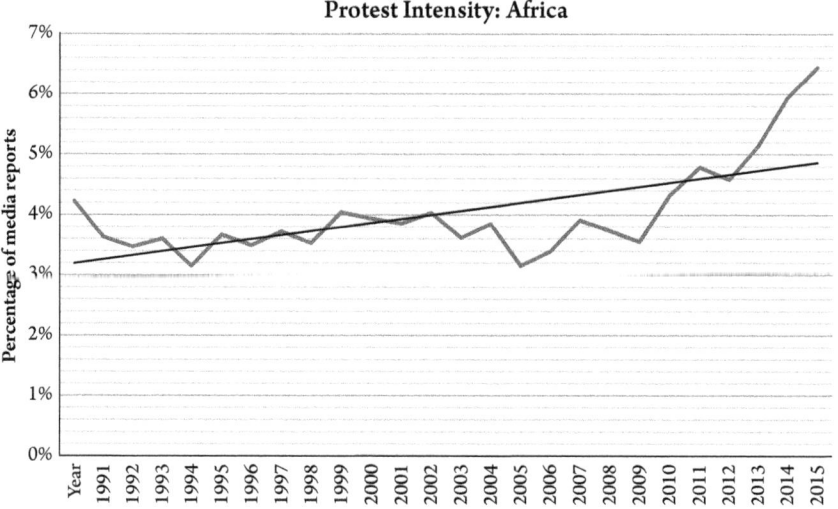

2014.[8] In a sample of European countries, the percentage of individuals that participated in a protest increased from 12.6 percent over the 2005–9 period to 42.1 percent for 2010–14.[9]

While some of the antiausterity protests and Occupy mobilizations might have at least temporarily abated in the West, elsewhere in the world there have been notable cases of more intense civic discontent. The International Labour Organization's Social Unrest Index recorded a sharp increase in global protest activity in 2016—an increase that pushed the index to a record high above its forty-year average levels of protest.[10] In 2016 new protests rocked the Democratic Republic of Congo, Ethiopia, Indonesia, Iraq, Kazakhstan, Moldova, Thailand,

Yemen, and Zimbabwe. In 2017 global protest entered another upswing, with notable revolts in Argentina, Belarus, Gambia, Hungary, Korea, Kyrgyzstan, Mexico, Morocco, Paraguay, Romania, Russia, and Venezuela—to name but a few examples. In 2018 the trend has continued with protests hitting Armenia, Honduras, Iran, Jordan, Nicaragua, Slovakia, Tunisia, and others.

Although the current wave of protest is sometimes likened to the 1848 European uprisings, in geographical terms it is actually far wider than any previous clustering of protest events. This suggests that the trend is broad and structural, not a haphazard collection of random protests. Protests in different countries seem to be feeding off each other. The current wave often appears to be self-sustaining, with each protest making the next one more likely. Each time a critical mass of protesters accumulates, people previously too fearful to protest are more likely to overcome their hesitation. Protests become like chain events. Discontent reaches a tipping point. Feedback loops drive an exponential spread of protest. The result is a global shift that goes beyond the mere temporal clustering of separate, individual protests.

Around the world

The scale and reach of protests can be illustrated through a summary reference to just a few of the recent large-scale revolts from each region of the world. This summary cannot hope to examine exhaustively every major protest event, but by telling the story of at least some of the most important uprisings of recent years it demonstrates just how widespread the trend has become and illustrates some of the core dynamics at work in these mobilizations.

Middle East and North Africa.

Egypt. Hundreds of thousands of protesters flocked to the streets in Cairo and other Egyptian cities on 25 January 2011, in a "day of rage" against poverty, unemployment, government corruption, and political repression. As the government intervened with increasing brutality against the protesters, more people joined the revolt. Eventually, over two million Egyptians mobilized. Tahrir Square in Cairo became the scene of one of the iconic and most emblematic protests in the new wave of civic activism. The protests were powerful enough to bring down the regime of President Hosni Mubarak. The complicated story of what happened next—and how success turned into failure, and an altogether murkier picture for Egyptian civil society—is told in the next chapter.

Iraq. Protests in Iraq started in 2015. Protesters numbered hundreds of thousands and included Sunnis, Shias, and Kurds, in cities across Iraq. The Shia-dominated government was not spared admonishment from Shias fed up with corruption and ineffective governance, as well as the weak response to the rise of Islamic State. Protesters criticized the ethnic-based quotas upon which the power-sharing constitution is based, on the grounds that this had created a self-serving elite. In a second wave of revolts, in April 2016 Shia protesters organized by the cleric Muqtada al-Sadr overran the Green Zone in Baghdad. They called for the sectarian-based government to be replaced by a technocratic administration. There were tensions between Sadrists and the social movements that had kick-started the first protests in 2015. While the protests then abated as the focus switched to an offensive against Islamic State, they returned in summer 2018 after elections failed to move Iraq beyond the paralysis of intersectarian haggling.[11]

Iran. The Iranian Green Movement led "Where is my vote?" protests in 2009, in which hundreds of thousands took to the streets of Tehran demanding civil and political liberties after regime-controlled elections. After several years of relative quiet, in December 2017 and January 2018 a new round of protests took place in around sixty Iranian cities. These protests were more geographically widespread than in 2009, although the total number of protesters was smaller. The protests continued for a week and became more confrontational; riot police killed over twenty protesters.

These revolts began when the government announced cuts to welfare subsidies while increasing funds for religious institutions. Their focus became more political, with many protesters shouting for members of the government to resign; popular unease with Iran's role in propping up the Syrian regime, along with minority Kurdish grievances, also provided impetus. The middle-class and student organizations associated with the Green Movement were not prominent in this revolt. Indeed, the working-class and unemployed youth who were in the protest's lead explicitly rejected any link to Iran's organized "reformist" groups. Clerical hard-liners stirred up these protests in conservative provincial towns in order to undermine President Hassan Rouhani's reformism but then lost control of the revolt; conversely, proreform activists came out on the streets to express their disappointment that change was not happening fast enough.

Morocco. The February 20 Movement organized protests in 2011. While this movement faded from view, further revolts have occurred more recently in Morocco. From late 2016, large-scale protests have flared in the northern region of Rif, lasting into the latter half of 2017 and 2018. The protests began when a fish vendor was crushed to death as he tried to recover his merchandise that officials had thrown into a garbage truck. The so-called Hirak movement coordinated the protests. The Moroccan regime clamped down hard, arresting protest leaders. Each time it did so, bigger protests took to the streets, with marches taking place in Rabat and other cities in solidarity with the Rif protesters. A Rabat march in June 2017 was the biggest since 2011. Hirak leaders said they had learned lessons from the February 20 experience, namely that they should limit themselves to very concrete demands for improvements in local infrastructure, health, and education. One Moroccan writer described these protests in terms of a shift from "human rights advocacy to very concrete actions by non-politicized citizens."[12]

Lebanon. In January 2011 Prime Minister Saad Hariri's government collapsed when Hezbollah and its allies pulled out of the cabinet in a dispute over investigations into the 2005 murder of his predecessor and father, Rafiq Hariri. Supporters of Saad Hariri protested against Hezbollah's nomination of Najib Mikati, a billionaire businessman, for the post of prime minister. Thousands of Sunni Muslim protesters took to the streets in Tripoli, Sidon, Beirut, and other cities, frustrated with the country's sectarian political system. The so-called March 14 Alliance mobilized hundreds of thousands of protesters calling for the disarmament of Hezbollah. Despite these protests, Mikati duly became prime minister and formed a cabinet dominated by Hezbollah.

In July 2015, the so-called You Stink movement began after Beirut's main landfill site was closed and thousands of tons of rotting rubbish piled up in the capital's streets. The government's failure to address the crisis resulted in a broadening of the movement, as a coalition of civic groups emerged with grievances against governmental incompetence and corruption. The movement grew to involve hundreds of thousands of protesters. The demonstrations shifted from merely demanding a resolution to the rubbish problem to calling for political reform. Some demanded changes to the electoral system that would produce a new parliament; others sought to oust key political figures, including the environment minister and even the prime minister.

Tunisia. The self-immolation of a young, unemployed Tunisian graduate selling fruit without a permit sparked a revolution that forced out President Zine el-Abidine Ben Ali. In late 2010 and early 2011 hundreds of thousands of people, including students, teachers, lawyers, journalists, human rights activists, trade unionists, opposition politicians, and even police officers, took to the streets in cities across Tunisia, until the president fled the country. Since then, protests have rumbled on. In 2016 there were around five thousand social protests around the country, and in 2017 this jumped to ten thousand.[13] These protests have been ignited by a whole range of grievances from university conditions, job losses, terrorism and security concerns, uneven regional development, the stalling of democratic reforms and religion. Tunisian activists define them as "nonmovements," more locally focused and spontaneous than even the most informal social movements prominent in the 2011 uprising.

For several months beginning in April 2017, hundreds of protesters barricaded an oil and gas plant in Kamour in the south of the country, complaining that oil companies were leaving the impoverished region without jobs and its fair share of revenues. New protests rocked Tunis in September 2017 after the government passed a law giving impunity to former regime members, brought a raft of former Ben Ali acolytes into the cabinet, and pushed back local elections. In December 2017 the so-called Hassebhom movement orchestrated protests against the government's proposed security law that would hand significant powers to the police. And in January 2018 protests rocked a dozen Tunisian cities in response to price rises and tax hikes. On this occasion, a small informal movement called "What are we waiting for?" undertook sporadic actions in at attempt to ignite protests; more people then came out to demonstrate independently from this group. Economic problems were the main trigger, but people were also frustrated that the consensus-oriented coalition government was increasingly distant from ordinary people.[14]

Turkey. The so-called Gezi Park protests that took place in Turkey in 2013 were organized by environmental groups against government plans to build a shopping mall in Istanbul's central square. The protests expanded because of police brutality and because they tapped into incipient dissent over the government's creeping authoritarianism. When the government ordered in the police, who deployed particularly brutal tactics, a far larger number of people joined the protests. Workers' groups then mobilized, harnessing an undercurrent of frustration among poorer classes. At their peak, the protests involved over two million people.

After a lull, protests flared again after the April 2017 referendum that handed President Erdoğan vastly increased powers. These revolts emerged out of local community "No" campaigns and also involved NGOs and opposition parties. Additionally, in July 2017 opposition parties coordinated a walk from Ankara to Istanbul in opposition to President Erdoğan's tightening authoritarianism. The march took place under a general banner of "Justice" in an effort to gather a wide range of democrats. On reaching Istanbul, the march had swollen to 1.5 million people. As more groups joined, the list of protesters' demands grew to include a whole collection of economic, social, and identity-related issues. Unlike in the Gezi protests, party cadres and NGOs cooperated in running the march.

Yemen. Protests in Sana'a in 2011 pushed President Ali Abdullah Saleh to step down after thirty-three years in power. Popular discontent, fueled by widespread unemployment and government corruption, soared in late 2010 after the ruling party proposed to amend the constitution so that Saleh could stand for reelection when his seventh term expired in 2013. Protesters included students, lower- and middle-income workers, human rights activists, lawyers, judges, diplomats, and opposition supporters. Young protesters formed the Civil Coalition of Youth Revolution, an alliance of more than ten thousand revolutionary youth activists. The alliance was not aligned with any political party so was able to convene important tribal groups in solidarity with protesters. While a unity administration eventually took office, Houthi rebels later pushed it out. New rounds of protests have continued as citizens tire of the lack of political reconciliation in the country. In August 2017 hundreds of thousands took to the streets in Sana'a to protest against the rebel Houthi government.[15]

Post-Soviet space

Armenia. In 2015, what were dubbed the Electric Yerevan protests brought thousands out onto the streets. The motive was a steep rise in electricity prices. With these prices controlled by a Russian supplier, this trigger was linked to a broader discontent with Moscow's influence over Armenian politics. Protests also focused on more generic concerns over corruption. Then, in July 2016, a new wave of protests erupted after the government detained an opposition leader; as gunmen from the opposition group took a number of policemen hostage, large crowds took to the street to demand President Serzh Sargsyan's resignation. This so-called Sasna Dzerer movement was driven by specific concerns over government positions in the conflict over Nagorno-Karabakh and also by general frustration with nepotism. Even bigger protests erupted in April 2018, with several hundred thousand mobilizing against Sargsyan's attempt to perpetuate his rule by moving from the presidency to the prime minister's office. If war veterans had been prominent in the Sasna Dzerer movement, these new protests involved a wider and less organized cross-section of Armenian society. While an opposition politician, Nikol Pashinyan, spurred the revolt, it did not have any formal institutional organizer. The protests intensified until Sargsyan resigned.[16]

Azerbaijan. Inspired by the Tunisian uprising and initially sparked by online antigovernment campaigns, protests erupted in Azerbaijan in early 2011. The protesters were mainly young activists, backed up by opposition politicians and party supporters. They mobilized against the corruption of President Ilham Aliyev's government, the country's high unemployment rate, poor living standards, police violence, the absence of political reform, and citizens' lack of rights and freedoms. Each successive protest over a period of several months was disbanded violently by the authorities, and hundreds of protesters, including opposition leaders and well-known journalists, were arrested, beaten, and detained.

Belarus. After a disputed presidential election in December 2010, a large-scale protest took place in Minsk. Tens of thousands of protesters took to the streets after it was announced that President Alexander Lukashenko had won a clearly inflated 80 percent of the vote. Protesters included opposition supporters, youth, and the general public, led by a fragmented array of unregistered opposition leaders and new civic groups. They used a range of tactics such as occupying main squares and attempting to storm government headquarters. The police beat demonstrators with batons and loaded hundreds into prison buses. Hundreds of protesters and opposition candidates were arrested and detained, many for long periods without charge.

A series of protests continued to press opposition demands after 2011, and young Belarusians began organizing themselves creatively online and offline. In summer 2016 thousands of protesters gathered in Minsk to take part in "clapping protests." In another protest, hundreds gathered with mobile alarms set to go off at 8:00 a.m., symbolizing a need for the country to wake up. In March 2017 several thousand people protested against the government's so-called social parasite law that effectively imposed a fine on people for being unemployed. Protesters included members of traditional NGOs but also many unaffiliated citizens. The government eventually cracked down hard, and police arrested hundreds of protesters.

Kazakhstan. In April and May 2016 a wave of protests took place in several cities across Kazakhstan, a country that had not seen any nationwide revolts since its independence in 1991. The protests were provoked by government plans to lease agricultural land to foreigners and were spurred by anti-Chinese resentment. They also reflected deeper grievances about corruption, declining living standards, and economic uncertainty linked to falling oil prices. The protests were spontaneous and without clear leaders. The authorities detained hundreds of protesters but avoided deadly violence, as they feared further destabilization.[17]

In *Kyrgyzstan*, mass mobilization led to regime change in 2005 and 2010. In March 2013 protests broke out again in Osh, the country's second-largest city, with protesters demanding the release of three opposition leaders. In May 2013 the protests spread to two other towns, and several hundred protesters stormed a gold mine, clashing with riot police. In early 2017 protests erupted twice after the government arrested two opposition politicians; protesters momentarily stormed the parliament building.[18]

Russia. Regime-controlled elections in December 2011 sparked so-called March of Millions protests in several Russian cities. Participants included a mix of well-known opposition figures, political parties, NGOs, anarchists, and individuals without any affiliation. Many joined to protest for specific issue-based grievances, quite different from the concerns of the political opposition.[19] The protests gradually dwindled through 2012.

In the start of a new round of unrest, in March 2017, anticorruption protests were coordinated by the opposition leader Alexei Navalny and brought an estimated twenty thousand people to the streets in sixty cities across Russia. The protests' main target was the corruption of Prime Minister Dimitri Medvedev, but they also manifest a broader hostility to President Vladimir Putin's rule. They involved a broader participation of citizens than the previous round of antiregime rallies in 2011 and 2012 and were flanked by a dramatic surge in local-level protests organized around related grievances in small towns throughout Russia.[20] The focus on corruption seemed to trigger a strong concern among a wide section of the population beyond those politically opposed to Putin. Young people accounted for a larger share of the protests than ever before; this was in part because the trigger was a YouTube film uncovering Medvedev's corruption. Another day of protests in June resulted in more than a thousand arrests across multiple cities; this time the protesters focused their ire more directly against Putin, in addition to the issue of corruption. Similar protests took place in October 2017 and in early 2018 prior to presidential elections in March. After those elections, the day before President Putin's inauguration in May, sixteen hundred protesters were detained across twenty-seven Russian cities; these protests took place under the slogan "He is not our tsar."

Elsewhere in the post-Soviet region, protest activity has also intensified. Huge protests rocked Moldova in 2015 and 2016 against a political elite that stole 10 percent of the country's GDP in a banking scandal; a new revolt broke out in June 2018 when Moldova's courts struck down an activist's victory in Chisinau's mayoral election. Tumult has also extended down into the Balkans. An uprising in Macedonia saw hundreds of thousands on the streets to protest against government wiretapping measures and then again after the ruling party lost elections but initially refused to cede power in 2017. Protesters in Serbia stood their ground for more than two weeks after an April 2017 election was won by incumbent prime minister Alexsandar Vučić thanks to suspected poll manipulation. In Georgia, on the same day in May 2018, liberal groups protested against homophobia, and conservatives demonstrated in favor of the family—giving a very direct snapshot of the country's polarized civic sphere. The dramatic Maidan revolt is covered in "Box 3.1: Focus on Ukraine."

Latin America

Brazil. Protests have flared in Brazil since 2013, for a variety of reasons. In 2013 people took to the streets to complain about the cost of bus fares. Large mobilizations then targeted the huge investments made for the 2014 World Cup and the 2016 Olympic Games, centering on the corruption involved in the preparation for these two events. In over a hundred cities around the country, around two million people protested. Then in 2015 and 2016 Brazilians took to the street against President Dilma Rousseff and her role in a corruption scandal involving the state energy company Petrobras. In March 2016 between four million and six million people protested when corruption allegations were made against former president Luiz Inácio Lula da Silva. Brazil became deeply polarized between those who supported these two leaders of the ruling Workers'

Box 3.1 **Focus on Ukraine**

In November 2013 President Viktor Yanukovych backed out of a trade deal with the European Union, triggering a series of protests in Kiev. Protesters demanded that Yanukovych sign the abandoned EU association agreement. The protests quickly grew to well over a hundred thousand people and were joined by men and women of all ages from Ukraine's middle-class and urban areas. As the regime responded with violence, protesters began to demand that Yanukovych resign.

There was no single organizer in charge of the uprising; rather, a coalition of grassroots groups and activists provided very rough strategy guidelines. Although sparked by Yanukovych's pivot away from the EU, the protests were fueled by long-simmering frustration with the country's kleptocratic leadership, poor democratic standards, cronyism, corruption, political repression, and economic mismanagement. By December, eight hundred thousand protesters occupied Kiev's city hall and Maidan Square. Several thousand protesters lingered in the square into the new year, setting up tents, barricades, and food stations. Rallies of hundreds of thousands of people were held every Sunday.

Some in the Maidan action adhered to a maximalist agenda of removing the regime and deployed radical tactics. Others just wanted the regime to reconsider the EU association agreement. Others pressed a nationalistic anti-Russian agenda. Protesters' demands escalated when the regime killed demonstrators. Maidan was a path-dependent protest, evolving in its aims during the several months during which it ran.[21] When opposition party leaders opened negotiations with Yanukovych, protesters did not support them as legitimate representatives of the revolt and the protests grew, until the president was forced to flee.

These protests were qualitatively different from the so-called Orange Revolution uprising that Ukraine had gone through in 2004—and the change illustrates the broader trend in activism. Local activists stressed that this "Second Maidan" was almost the antithesis of the "First Maidan." In 2004 political leaders had been in the vanguard, and the square had mobilized in support of those figures; in 2014 citizens were against this very type of traditional leadership. In 2014 the protesters were in constant conflict with the political parties and politicians that joined them.

The movements at Maidan's helm did not reach out to the east of the country, where some small-scale protests also occurred in 2014—an oversight that would come back to haunt the Kiev authorities. Some of those involved feared that the revolts did not translate into a mass, popular engagement pressing for democracy but once again ended up with a small group of really committed activists and CSOs keeping pressure on the government.[22] Some of the new activism that did establish roots beyond this circle of familiar CSOs was not especially liberal or democratic, and some involved violent tactics. In March 2017 war veterans and nationalists organized large-scale protests to close the border with the two separatist-held areas in Donbas and push the Kiev government to harden its stance against Russian tactics.

In October 2017 more than five thousand protesters laid siege to the parliament in Kiev, angry at the president's failure to enact anticorruption laws. Further protests followed in December 2017, after the government used questionable legal process to arrest the former Odessa governor Mikheil Saakashvili as he campaigned against government corruption. And in January 2018 the killing of a prominent human rights lawyer once again sparked large-scale mobilizations in several Ukrainian cities.

Party and those who wanted them in prison. The size of protests grew as a result of this highly charged political environment and eventually led to the president's impeachment.

Venezuela. Protests in Venezuela intensified in January 2014 after the murder of a well-known actress. They were concerned more broadly with the alarming increase in crime rates, a trend that had begun well before the death of President Hugo Chávez in 2013. Protests spread in 2016, after the opposition's victory in the 2015 parliamentary elections. Two demonstrations in September and October 2016 gathered more than a million people. A wave of so-called *guarimbas* started, in which protesters closed streets with burning tires and barricades. Overall in 2016, more than five thousand protests were registered in Venezuela, most of them related to the defense of political rights. Venezuela's turmoil worsened even further in 2017, with several months of demonstrations and an increasing use of violence. Into 2018 these protests seemed to be moving toward a political denouement with the increasingly repressive regime—a story covered in the next chapter.

Other Latin America states have also witnessed protests in recent years. Protests brought down Guatemala's government in 2015, and tens of thousands returned to the streets in late 2017 after the new president fired the head of the International Commission against Impunity. Over sixty thousand protested in Honduras in 2015 against government corruption; citizens then returned to the streets in late 2017 and early 2018 accusing President Juan Orlando Hernández of using voting fraud to regain power, effectively perpetuating a right-wing regime that had taken power illegally in a 2009 coup. In July 2015 protests occurred in Bolivia over social and economic conditions. In 2015 nearly a quarter of a million students protested in Chile over the government's failure to reform the education system and over wider issues of corruption. Stricken by endemic violence, Mexico has witnessed periodic popular revolts in recent years, in particular when citizens mobilized against the government of Enrique Peña Nieto after the brutal murder of forty-three students in Iguala in 2014 and when hundreds of thousands protested against a 20 percent rise in gas prices and wider corruption issues in 2017. Also in 2017, protests erupted in Ecuador after delays in election results engendered widespread suspicions that the government was manipulating the counting process.

In March 2017 there were protests in Paraguay against government plans to overturn the ban on presidents running for reelection. In the same month, Argentina saw some of its largest demonstrations ever; curiously, these were to defend the government against the tactics being used by the Peronist opposition to impede democratic governance. In May 2017 almost a quarter of a million protested in Buenos Aires against a Supreme Court decision that restored impunity for those convicted of human rights abuses during the country's various periods of dictatorship. At the end of 2017 thousands took to the streets across Peru angered by President Pedro Pablo Kuczyinski's decision to pardon former president Alberto Fujimori, imprisoned for human rights abuses, in return for Fujimori's supporters in the legislature helping to block a corruption-related censure motion against the government. In April 2018 hundreds of thousands of protesters in Nicaragua sought to scupper the government's plans to reform social security payments; these revolts grew over subsequent months and, as the police killed increasing numbers of protesters, began to coalesce a more general hostility toward President Daniel Ortega's undemocratic regime.

Asia

Hong Kong. In 2014 a million protesters took part in the Umbrella uprising, a strikingly high rate of participation given Hong Kong's population of seven million. The protests were triggered when China's government announced it would prescreen candidates for the Hong Kong chief executive election in 2017. They came on the back of several years of other campaigns against China's influence over education, security, and the like. The Umbrella Movement grew out of an intense range of activities such as Deliberation Days and Hikes for Democracy. A student activist group, Scholarism, coordinated the protests. After the initial, large-scale protests were beaten down, social organizations engaged in modest forms of disobedience and noncooperation into 2016. The protests expanded after China's heavy-handed response, but they did not get business elites fully on board, as these feared upsetting Beijing.[23]

As China clamped down hard, so-called localists hardened their demands for full independence from China. In July 2017 sixty thousand marched on the twentieth anniversary of the territory's handover to China. Some protest leaders sought to get the localists to step back from aggressive campaigning for full independence and to build unity around moderate, achievable reform aims. The focus was increasingly on education, with growing hostility to Beijing's plans to impose a program of "civic education" to bolster Hong Kong's loyalty to Chinese identity. China effectively ejected four prodemocracy MPs from the legislature in July 2017; with their place in mainstream politics closed, the activists moved back toward street-based political expression.

Singapore. Since 2013 Singapore has been rattled by political protests on an unprecedented scale. The protests have challenged the ruling People's Action Party on two main issues: immigration and pensions. Singapore's anti-immigration movement took shape after the government released a white paper calling for further immigration to maintain economic growth. Three thousand people gathered in what was the country's largest political protest since independence. A second wave of protests in 2014 and 2015 centered on unease over increases in state pension contributions. Young blogger-activists launched a series of protests demanding that the government return citizens' pension contributions. A judge imposed fines on the lead protesters.

India. The India against Corruption movement coalesced in late 2010, in the wake of two large-scale government corruption scandals. In early 2011 it staged protests in sixty cities across the country. The campaign was energized by the Gandhian tactic of fasting. Twelve million people registered their support for the movement. Protests were nonpartisan, and protesters blocked attempts made by politicians to join them. In addition, protests against the rape of a student in Delhi in December 2013 sparked mobilizations against a whole range of discrimination and attacks against women. For the first time these protests became mainstream events, beyond the realm of small feminist NGOs, and were not led by any specific, professionalized civic group but emerged in a more spontaneous fashion than previous revolts in India.[24]

Indonesia. Hundreds of thousands of Islamists assembled in Jakarta in late 2016 to demand the resignation and arrest of Jakarta's Chinese Christian governor, Basuki Tjahaja Purnama (or Ahok), for blaspheming against the Qur'an. Protesters were mainly Salafists who insisted that high-level government positions should be reserved for Muslims. The protests were a sign of Indonesia's thriving and diverse civil society, but also of the rising popularity of Islamic organizations that combine xenophobic and religious language to mobilize Muslims against Indonesia's Chinese Christian minority.[25]

South Korea. In 2015 there were protests in Seoul against worsening economic conditions, job insecurity, and planned restrictions on the freedom of expression. In 2016 far larger protests formed over the curious case of Choi Soon-sil, a personal friend of President Park Geun-hye and daughter of a mysterious cult leader, who was exerting influence over government decisions and gaining personal rewards from the president. Hundreds of thousands of Koreans poured into Seoul to demand the president's resignation; at their peak, the protests involved more than a million people. The demonstrations were South Korea's largest since prodemocracy protests in 1987, and they attracted people from all sections of society, including erstwhile government supporters. The protesters' criticisms soon extended beyond the immediate scandal, as they demanded a curtailment of both presidential powers and the political influence of *chaebol* conglomerates. The protests continued until the president was forced to leave office in 2017.

Many other Asian examples could also be elaborated. Mass protests broke out around disputed electoral processes in Cambodia in 2013 and Bangladesh in 2014. In August 2018 protests over road safety took place in Bangladesh after a minibus killed two schoolchildren; these soon widened into large-scale mobilizations against government corruption and impunity more generally. In 2014 and 2015 the protesters of Taiwan's Sunflower Movement occupied the country's parliament chamber, demanding transparency in cross-strait talks with China. In Nepal, a new constitution sparked protests in 2015, as several minority groups believed this undermined the inclusive principles of the country's 2008 peace accord. In China there are now over a hundred thousand "mass incidents" each year; in December 2017 a protest took place in Bejing against forced evictions of low-skilled migrant workers.[26] In 2015 more than a hundred thousand mainly young people protested in Japan against the government's proposals to develop more military capacity. In August 2017 thousands protested across the Philippines after police killed a student as part of a brutal antidrugs campaign that had left over five thousand dead.

Africa

Ethiopia. Protests in Ethiopia have continued intermittently since 2015. They erupted in the Oromia region in response to the government's national development plan that threatened to displace Oromo farmers from their lands. The revolts then spread to other regions and focused on the regime's broader discrimination against tribal land rights. In October 2017 large-scale mobilizations intensified, related to sugar shortages, government proposals to extend the boundaries of Addis Ababa into the Oromia region, and a grassroots push for decentralization. Against a backdrop of complex tribal alliances and rivalries, it appeared that these protests were the work of local activists wanting to ratchet up pressure on the government, against the will of exiled NGOs. The new wave of protests continued into 2018, now led by university students and focused on broader political repression.[27] When Prime Minister Hailemariam Desalegn dramatically resigned in February 2018, protests redoubled in response to the government's decision to reimpose a state of emergency.

Gabon. When Gabon's election commission announced that President Ali Bongo had defeated Jean Ping by fewer than six thousand votes in the August 2016 election, Ping refused to concede and claimed he had evidence of election rigging. In early September, thousands of Ping supporters poured into the streets to contest the election results. The protests quickly turned violent: protesters set fire to the National Assembly and Port Gentil's city hall and tried to burn down other government buildings. Over a thousand protesters were arrested. Protesters sought to end the Bongo-family kleptocracy that had dominated the country's politics for over forty years. There was a partial recount, but Bongo retained power. Protests calmed after the president opened a national dialogue aimed at reconciliation and offered several ministerial positions to the opposition.

Gambia. In advance of Gambia's December 2016 presidential election, the country experienced a wave of protests demanding reforms to its electoral system as well as an end to Yahya Jammeh's repressive twenty-two-year presidency. Between April and November, Gambian security forces arrested over ninety opposition supporters for demonstrating without a permit. Many of those detained were tortured, and a small number, including two senior members of the United Democratic Party, were killed. After protest videos and the hashtag #GambiaRising appeared on Gambian social media, President Jammeh decided to turn off the internet and block international phone calls on election day. Protests grew up to and after the election, until the president was forced to relinquish office.

Nigeria. President Goodluck Jonathan's decision to remove fuel subsidies in 2012 triggered an Occupy Nigeria protest. This focused initially on the subsidies cut but gradually took on a broader critique of the government and corruption. A particular target was the opaque system of intraelite negotiation and power sharing—a system often celebrated as essential to maintaining peace in Nigeria's deeply fractured society. Youth leaders ratcheted up their actions after security forces killed a protester. The protests lasted a number of weeks before petering out.

Uganda. In 2011 opposition parties protested against the heavily manipulated elections that returned President Yoweri Museveni for a fourth term. The main opposition party then launched a "Walk to Work" protest against deteriorating living conditions and rising prices. The idea mobilized many people beyond opposition activists—for the first time, on a cross-ethnic basis. Some participants wanted to see Museveni toppled; others, simply a cut in food prices. After security forces attacked the main opposition leader, who had to be rushed to a hospital outside the country, the protests subsided. Smaller-scale protests have continued at community level in relation to very specific events like job losses or hospital closures.[28] In 2016 the so-called Jobless Brotherhood group smuggled pigs into Uganda's parliament, and a charismatic activist used creative symbolism in a campaign about girls' education and health; these were both low-budget, innovative forms of protest, outside the campaigns planned by the NGO community.[29]

Zimbabwe. Zimbabwe has experienced a persistent wave of protests since October 2014, driven by the Occupy Africa Unity Square movement and Zimbabwe Activists Alliance—both of these being loose groupings of citizen activists campaigning against corruption and repression. The protests started over basic human and civil rights and the dire state of Zimbabwe's economy. They gradually escalated as Robert Mugabe's regime clamped down further against basic rights. The #ThisFlag citizens movement began in April 2016, giving a further impulse to protest activity. Zimbabweans at home and in the diaspora began posting videos of themselves draped in the national flag and calling for government reforms. The new movements combined online campaigns with mobilization around bread-and-butter policy issues instead of only calling for President Mugabe's removal. They gathered momentum up to November 2017, when the army dramatically pushed Mugabe out of office. The protests continued after that as citizens pushed the ruling ZANU-PF government for deeper reforms. Demonstrations spiked again after authorities declared the ZANU-PF candidate, Emmerson Mnangagwa, victor of the July 2018 presidential election despite serious irregularities in the voting procedure.

Space precludes a full account of Africa's many other protests in recent years, but a number are worthy of brief mention. Sudan experienced student-led protests in 2011 and a broader mobilization in 2013 led by poorer sectors of society, angered by the government's failure to provide relief after floods and by the removal of fuel subsidies. South African students protested in 2015 and 2016 over tuition fees, and in 2017 these #FeesMustFall campaigns broadened out into #ZumaMustFall protests that pitted themselves against president Jacob Zuma's corruption, the nepotism of the whole "liberation generation," the 60 percent youth unemployment rate, and the enduring legacies of apartheid.[30] In the Democratic Republic of the Congo, protests have flared periodically since 2014, aimed at driving President Joseph Kabila from office; church-based organizations played a prominent role in these revolts. In Cameroon, thousands from the country's minority Anglophone community held regular protests from 2016 through 2017 and into 2018, seeking better recognition of their linguistic and other rights. Protests rocked Kenya in October 2017 as the opposition candidate withdrew from an election rerun, alleging government manipulation. In the same month, another round of protests erupted in Togo, aimed at ousting President Faure Gnassingbé from power.

European Union states

Greece. Greece's financial crisis unleashed one of the best-known cases of protest in recent years, as the EU imposed draconian spending cuts as a condition for receiving three bailouts and keeping the country inside the euro currency zone. The Greek antiausterity movement and the Aganaktismeni (Indignant Citizens) movement became the main agent of social resistance against EU-imposed austerity. Protesters initially expressed their anger not only at government cuts but also at the generally poor quality of political institutions. Established groups and new movements like the "I Won't Pay" campaign staged multiple protest activities. Protesters used a range of methods, including public assemblies, the occupation of public spaces, and ironic symbolism. Leftists and right-wing nationalists combined uneasily in the protests, and some tactics tipped into violence.

France. In 2016 a wave of so-called Nuit Debout protests swept through French cities in reaction against labor reforms making it easier for companies to lay off workers, cut overtime pay, and reduce severance payments. In March 2016 thousands of people began to gather by night in Paris's Place de la République. Protests grew in numbers and convened hundreds of thousands of citizens. The movement usurped a conventional protest campaign initiated by trade unions. The organizers insisted on keeping the established left and political parties out of these protests. The organizers attempted to internationalize the movement, calling for a Global Debout; it failed to catch on outside France, however, and remained very much linked to domestic French issues. The protests gradually died down over the autumn of 2016, but the movement continues with a vibrant online presence and campaigns. Protests returned to France in March 2018, after President Emmanuel Macron moved ahead with labour reforms; however, now unions led the strikes and protests rather than the newer-style Nuit Debout movement.

Poland. Protests in Poland began in December 2015, organized by the newly formed Committee for the Defence of Democracy (KOD), a nonpartisan civil protest movement. KOD was founded by a self-employed computer specialist who was avowedly not interested in political power. Protests were aimed against decisions taken by the new Law and Justice (PiS) government to invalidate the appointment of five judges to the Polish Constitutional Court and nominate PiS-affiliated judges to replace them. KOD then mobilized a quarter of a million people against further PiS moves to control appointments to the state television broadcaster. KOD embodied bottom-up protest dynamics, outside formal political structures, involving mainly urban, educated, and secular middle-aged citizens. In 2016 the protests shifted and expanded to react also against the government's proposal to ban abortion, in the form of a so-called Women's March that had no formal organizational body behind it; indeed, over 80 percent of the participants in this protest had not previously participated in any civil society activity.[31]

Another round of intense protests took place in April 2017, this time organized by the opposition Civic Platform party, supported by various other opposition parties and civic organizations, including KOD. An even larger mobilization occurred in July 2017 after the government brought forward new laws undermining judicial independence still further. Reflecting a deepening polarization of Polish political debate, in November 2017 sixty thousand nationalists took to the streets in Warsaw as a counter to these antigovernment marches, protesting against immigration and in favor of Christian values.

Romania. In 2015 protests erupted in Romania after a nightclub fire that resulted in many deaths was traced back to government corruption. The blaze unleashed a wider series of anticorruption protests and campaigns that led to the social-democratic PSD government's fall and the introduction of new measures against graft. When the PSD regained power in December 2016 and introduced a law to water down anticorruption measures—in part to protect its own senior cadres—hundreds of thousands protested across the country. After five nights of protests, the government withdrew the bill. Protests continued, now pushing for the government to resign. After many years of Romanian NGOs focusing on corruption, the large-scale 2017 protests erupted spontaneously with little organizational structure, even of a loose movement-like quality. Tens of thousands of people were back on the streets in November and December 2017 and early 2018 to protest against government attempts to reinstate the impunity rules and against proposed laws that would weaken the powers of the National Anticorruption Directorate and undercut the independence of judges—with a view to circumscribing their ability to pursue corruption cases. Throughout summer 2018, large-scale protests took place across Romania both against and in support of the government.

Of many other austerity-related protests in Europe, Iceland's Cutlery Revolution of 2009 was one of the most iconic and influential. Hungarians were regularly on the streets in 2017, protesting against the government's bid to host the Olympics and then against the regime's efforts to close the Central European University; they then mobilized in April 2018 after Viktor Orbán won a third election. Slovakia witnessed ten-thousand-strong anticorruption protests in April 2017 and again in March 2018 after the murder of an investigative journalist. In the autumn of 2017 large-scale protests took place in Catalonia and across Spain, in favor of Catalan independence, against secession, and then on a smaller scale in favor of dialogue between the two sides. In spring 2018 protests rocked both Slovenia and the Czech Republic, aimed at a range of corruption cases and funding cuts.

Types and combined triggers

One notable factor to emerge from this selection of examples is that different issues are responsible for triggering recent protests. While there are clear points of similarity, protests have different aims and concerns. Some are responses to very specific and local grievances. Some have been a response to austerity concerns. Others have aimed to dislodge nondemocratic regimes. Still others have focused on particular policy issues, like corruption or social challenges. Reflecting this variety of causes, these have most commonly been national protests, focusing on national policy issues more than targeting multilateral institutions. (See "Table 3.1: Typology of protests.")

Overall, the evidence shows a balance between these different triggers.[32] Most protests embody a mixture of different causal drivers. Protests generally contain a mix of *system*-related demands and *policy*-specific grievances. Different protests exhibit a different balance between the systemic and policy dimensions. Today's protests are certainly not regime specific: the foregoing examples show how they have hit all kinds of political system from advanced democracies through to the most closed autocratic states.

There are clear overlaps. For example, antiausterity protests have also often sought deeper democracy, in the sense of participants seeking forms of community-based participation. They have used the language of democracy as a form of community building and social justice. Often, this is a discourse explicitly counterpoised against liberal democracy. Protesters frame imposed austerity as an infringement of democracy and of dignity—meaning that certain common key concerns are shared across protests driven by what are otherwise quite different aims.[33] Nationalists and other right-wing activists often jump aboard; their aim is to correct bad governance but also to use the protests as a springboard for agendas that sit uneasily with many of the progressive aims of other protesters. A mix of motives is invariably present behind a protest's main, headline goal.

Recent protests have most commonly not been class based but have contained a mix of relatively unorganized or unaffiliated citizens—a mass of diverse citizens more than a sharp class-specific mobilization. People become involved in a given protest for multiple reasons, with these reasons interweaving in complex ways and motivating different protesters to varying degrees. Many of the most contentious anticapitalist protests have been led not so much by the working class as by middle-class graduates. Many working-class activists have, if anything, been more likely to engage either in alternative community-level forms of

Table 3.1 **Typology of protests**

Category One. Protests seeking democracy in authoritarian settings, protesting at either authoritarian behavior in general, rigged elections, or presidents changing constitutions to stay in power beyond stipulated limits.

Russia (2011, 2017), Ukraine (2013–14), Azerbaijan (2011–13), Belarus (2011), Albania (2011).

Hong Kong (2014), Thailand (2014), Malaysia (2013), Bangladesh (2014), Cambodia (2013–14).

Venezuela (2014–17).

Senegal (2012), Burkina Faso (2011), Democratic Republic of the Congo (2014), Burundi (2015), Madagascar, Malawi, Niger, Togo, Uganda.[34]

North Africa and the Middle East (2011–12, and after): Egypt, Tunisia, Syria, Libya, Iraq, Bahrain, Jordan, Morocco; Iran (2009, 2017).

Category Two. Protests in broadly democratic—or at least semiopen—states triggered by a decline in democratic quality and the general pervasiveness of corruption. This category captures protests with a relatively even mix between systemic and policy questions.

Turkey (2013–14).

Taiwan (2014), Singapore (2013).

Brazil (from 2014), Chile (2012), Panama (2012), Argentina, Mexico, Colombia (all on and off from 2014), Nicaragua (2018).

Moldova (2009, 2013, 2015–16).

Armenia (2015, 2016, 2018).

Bosnia, Serbia, Macedonia, Montenegro (from 2012).

India (from 2015).

Pakistan (2014–15).

Ghana (2014), Nigeria (2012), South Africa (2012), Tanzania (2012).

Category Three. Anticapitalist or antiausterity protests. These protests have combined opposition to particular spending cuts with anticapitalism and antiglobalization agendas. In Europe, they have also been a product of the EU's democratic deficit (economic decisions being imposed from outside the country in question).

Bulgaria, Croatia, Cyprus, Czech Republic, Greece, France, Hungary, Italy, Poland, Portugal, Romania, Slovakia, Slovenia, Spain, United Kingdom, United States.

activism with more prosaic and practical aims or, at least in some countries, in more conservative-nationalist activism.[35]

Curiously, today's protests can be both extremely tightly focused (on issues like bus fares or a particular development project) *and* extremely vague and generic (railed against charges that "All politics is rotten" or "We must change everything"). Some protest goals are extremely prosaic, others bombastically grandiloquent. They have often evolved during the course of a mobilization, moving from specific to more general goals in the face of government reactions. Participants' accounts stress that protesters have often focused on the mechanics and tactics of setting protests up and only then turned their attention to the substantive question of precisely what the aims are to be.[36] Extensive empirical research finds a combination of rational-materialist and "nonrationalist" or identity drivers is needed to explain most recent protests.[37]

Belying this eclectic mix, there is a tendency for observers to view any particular outbreak of protests through one particular lens. Democracy enthusiasts often tend to label protests as prodemocracy protests. Those focused on corruption tend to see the current protest surge as a global struggle against corruption. Social justice activists instead emphasize the idea of protesters demanding social justice. Economically oriented observers focus on economic demands. Conservatives interpret protests as a cry for stronger national values and traditions. The same protest ends up being portrayed in very different ways by different parts of the media or expert community. For some, the new activism is intrinsically part of the crisis facing late capitalism; for others, it is on the rise today because of political factors and especially the assault on democratic rights; still others see the recent protest surge as a more conservative-oriented quest for identity and belonging.[38]

Some analysts argue that there has been a tendency to overstate the differences between protests.[39] Other studies place more stress on variation, showing that even within a particular region and narrow time period, like the Middle East during the early revolts of the Arab Spring, protest methods, organizational bases, and aims can vary significantly.[40] In truth, it is the very mixture of commonality and difference that most notably characterizes today's protests.

While protesters have certainly shared experiences and adopted common slogans across borders, and while antiausterity revolts in the West embraced a spirit of transnational solidarity, the main targets and organizational frames of most recent protests have been national or even subnational.[41] Although a close-knit international group of regular protest-goers has emerged—traveling from one protest to another, and insisting that these many revolts must be seen as different instances of a single phenomenon—most contemporary protests are framed around local rather than high-level global concerns. European antiausterity activists spoke of cross-border solidarity, but they did not in practice coordinate a uniform EU-level strategy.[42] Protest events on the international stage still occasionally hit the headlines; recent examples include the Women's March protests in both 2017 and 2018 and the protests that disrupted the June 2017 G20 summit in Hamburg. In general, however, today's global wave of protests is in large measure animated by national and community-level particularities.

One striking paradox is that protests are driven by both those who have done well out of globalism and those who have suffered from it. These two camps rub shoulders in many a protest, often employing the same kind of language and adopting similar agendas but coming from diametrically opposed perspectives and aspiring to very different long-term political and economic destinations. In some protests citizens pour into the streets because their living standards are declining; in others, because they feel emboldened as their lot improves. In this sense, patterns of activism and protest reflect the well-documented trend of middle classes rising in developing states but being squeezed in rich economies. Both sets of change are unleashing similarly contentious forms of activism, but for diametrically opposed reasons. Moreover, if in Western states many protests are about retaining entitlements in the face of cuts in welfare spending, in developing states they often revolve more around price rises making basic survival more arduous.

Conclusion

The brief summaries of some of the main protests that have occurred in recent years show just how powerful a phenomenon these mass mobilizations have become in global politics. While waves of protests have occurred regularly stretching back a long time in history, the sheer number and geographical spread of today's revolts are striking, as is the quest for new types of protest tactics. The will to protest has markedly increased in every region of the world. In many countries, multiple protests have taken place: once one revolt occurs, it appears more likely that subsequent uprisings will happen in the following months and years. When so many protests attract over a million participants, or at least hundreds of thousands, it is clear that we are witnessing a new popular determination to confront power—and citizens' greater willingness to act outside the regular channels of political pressure and representation.

It is striking that today's protests share many common features. Many erupt in ways that are not widely predicted. Most seek to prevent established political actors, parties, and well-known civil society institutions from playing a dominant role. Many begin with relatively modest concerns but take on more ambitious and radical aims as their momentum grows and where regimes attempt to end a protest with violence. In many protests, the very act of citizens gathering together and self-organizing is as important as the protesters' declared end goals.

While there are notable common features, however, it is clear that there is much diversity and heterogeneity in the factors driving today's protests. Protests may be driven by a common loss of trust in institutions, but the reasons behind that declining legitimacy of established political channels can vary enormously from one case to another. If some protests have adhered to relatively peaceful and well-ordered tactics, others have become part of a society's descent into instability, low-level social violence, or even outright conflict.

Although protest intensity may have increased, its reach must be kept in proper proportion. Most protests occur in capitals and involve a modest percentage of the overall population. Many may be no more inclusive of underprivileged or marginalized sectors of the population than are the much-maligned professional NGOs.[43] And there are places where mass civic mobilization has *not* materialized; examples include Gulf and some Central Asian states, along with Cuba.

In sum, while the wave of global protest represents a major trend in international politics, we must take care not to describe this trend in unduly simplistic or sweeping ways. Many of the assumptions that are commonly made about today's protests require some more critical nuance—nuance on whether we are really witnessing a trend of unprecedented civic empowerment; on what is and what is not new about these protests; and on how far the heightened intensity of protests represents a qualitative change in democratic or anti-authoritarian politics.

4

How effective have protests been?

Protests may be spreading globally, but how effective are they? How much change do they achieve? The supporters and architects of the new civic activism are animated by a conviction that their emerging forms of protest are more effective than old-style civil society advocacy. Critics insist that these protests attract copious media attention but achieve little.[1] Certainly, more effort is needed to assess protests' impact, as most analytical focus has so far been on movements' internal and organizational features.[2]

This chapter draws up a balance sheet of the successes and failures of recent mass protest activity. It distinguishes three categories of impact: 1) protests that have had a dramatic political impact; 2) mixed outcomes, with protests achieving some change but far short of the reforms sought by their participants; and 3) patent failure, where governments have been able to outplay or simply contain protests. In attempting an overall assessment, I draw out the factors that determine whether large-scale protest succeeds or fails and suggest some broader implications that flow from this.

Contrasting outcomes

A selection of examples can be given from each of the impact categories.

a) Governments ousted

A small number of protests have succeeded in pushing governments and leaders out of office in recent years. In Africa, protesters unseated President Abdoulaye Wade in Senegal in 2012, President Blaise Compaoré in Burkina Faso in 2014, President Yahya Jammeh in Gambia in 2017, and Prime Minister Hailemariam Desalegn in Ethiopia in February 2018. In Ethiopia, the government sought to appease protesters by dropping controversial development plans and releasing some political prisoners, but the revolt proved too strong to contain. After the prime minister resigned, the government tightened a state of emergency, as the ruling Tigrayan elite attempted to prevent far-reaching regime change; the new prime minister then brought a team of different ministers into the cabinet in an effort to assuage public frustration.

In Brazil, protests succeeded in setting the impeachment of President Dilma Rousseff in motion after she was involved in a corruption scandal in the national energy company Petrobras. In Guatemala, protests sufficed to push President Otto Pérez Molina from office in September 2015 on corruption issues. In Peru, public demonstrations were one factor among several that forced President Pedro Pablo Kuczynski out of office in March 2018 in relation to corruption charges. In Tunisia, protests not only pushed the long-time authoritarian ruler President Zine el-Abidine Bin Ali out of power in 2011 but have since then mobilized to prevent both the moderate Islamist Ennahda and Nidaa Tounes governments from dramatically backtracking on reforms. In Yemen, protests pushed President Ali Abdullah Saleh out of office.

Ukraine's Maidan protests succeeded in ousting President Viktor Yanukovich, somewhat beyond their initial demands for an association agreement with the EU; the force of civic mobilization was so strong here that it even swept aside a deal brokered by international powers to keep Yanukovich in office. In Kyrgyzstan, protests unseated President Kurmanbek Bakiyev in 2010. In Slovenia in 2012 and 2013, general uprisings mobilized the whole country and contributed to the fall of the right-wing government and a number of corrupt officials. In March 2018 protests in Slovakia led to Prime Minister Robert Fico's resignation. The next month, protests in Armenia pushed out Prime Minister Serzh Sargsyan and ushered in the revolt's leader as his replacement.

Protests in South Korea succeeded in pushing President Park Geun-hye out of power in March 2017, after she was impeached for leaking classified government documents to her personal friend and abetting the latter's extortion efforts. In Thailand, protests forced Prime Minister Yingluck Shinawatra out of power in 2014—although here a powerful strand of conservative-nationalist civic activism backed the military then assuming power.[3]

b) Partial policy change and cosmetic compromise

The largest number of cases has witnessed a mix of success and failure, with new forms of civic activism winning some notable reforms or governmental changes but falling short of their full set of stated objectives. In some of these cases the degree of success has been significant; in others the limits to achievement are arguably more notable than what protests did achieve.

A common occurrence is for governments to respond to protests by introducing anticorruption measures, loosening austerity, or backtracking on moves to raise energy prices, reduce social security payments, or hike education fees, but without ceding to demands for far-reaching political reforms. Examples of such partial responses in recent years include Colombia, India, Malaysia, Mexico, Moldova, Nicaragua, Nigeria, Romania, Spain, South Africa, and Singapore.

Other examples relate to more political trade-offs. Cambodia's 2013–14 protests forced Prime Minister Hun Sen into a deal with opposition leader Sam Rainsy to share leadership posts in the parliament and reform the National Election Committee with a view to reducing future electoral fraud. Many saw these as meaningful concessions, even though the prime minister remains in power after thirty years; indeed, he has recently tightened his control, including by dissolving the main opposition party in November 2017.

In Haiti, protests after the presidential election in October 2015 succeeded in getting the electoral commission to annul the victory of government-backed candidate Jovenel Moïse. However, when the election was repeated in November 2016, Moïse won by an even larger margin than in 2015. Opposition parties protested against alleged fraud, but this time without any impact.

In Iraq, postprotest dynamics were complex. Sectarian leaders took over the issue-based protests of 2016 but struggled to win any reforms to the country's quota-based sharing out of ministerial posts. Prime Minister Haider al-Abadi promised a package of reforms in response to the protests, but party elites blocked these. However, the Shia cleric Moqtada al-Sadr then won elections in May 2018 on a platform of reforming the quota system—his victory attributable in part to the afterwash of the protests.

In Jordan, King Abdullah II has responded several times to protests by dismissing members of his government and promising to speed up reforms. Protests in June 2018 led the king to sack his prime minister and withdraw tax increases that had angered large parts of the population. Yet the king has relinquished none of his own power and has gradually tightened restrictions on civil society and political parties; protesters' success in pushing prime ministers out of power has not resulted in democratization. The mixed success of mass protests in Egypt is the subject of "Box 4.1: Egypt."

In Kenya, protests against incumbent president Uhuru Kenyatta's manipulation of elections in August 2017 succeeded in getting the Supreme Court to order a rerun. Kenyatta won, and protesters challenged this result too, but this time without success. Kenya's bout of civic activism in 2017 put Kenyatta on the defensive and led to promises of policy changes but has not brought about any advance in the country's democratic quality.[4]

In Malaysia, Prime Minister Najib Razak lost power in elections held in May 2018. His ousting was not a direct result of the simmering anticorruption protests against him; rather, it came about through the rather improbable return to power of the erstwhile antidemocracy strongman Mahathir Mohamad, now in the guise of reformer. Yet frequent protests in the years prior to the 2018 election certainly contributed to Najib's loss of support—even if the prodemocracy protesters would probably not have wished for Mahathir's return.

The February 20 Movement in Morocco was instrumental in getting King Mohammed VI to agree to a new constitution that introduced several areas of political reform and improved a number of personal civil rights provisions. However, the reforms fell far short of what protesters demanded, and more recently the king has implemented restrictive measures on political freedoms and civil society.

South African students got the ANC government to hold back a tuition increase and set up a commission on education reform. Eventually, societal pressure against President Jacob Zuma for his involvement in a string of corruption cases was strong enough to persuade ANC leaders to undercut his influence over the party. Yet as Zuma stepped down in 2018, the basic dominant-party model based around the ANC was left intact.

In Turkey, it remains difficult to gauge how successful the Gezi Park protests were. After the protests, Turkey's top administrative court ordered the Gezi redevelopment plan to be dropped. A year later it reversed that decision. In 2016 President Recep Tayyip Erdoğan said he would press ahead with the project, but the plan's status remains uncertain. The Gezi protests failed to cohere around a broader reform platform to push back against the regime's creeping authoritarianism.

In Zimbabwe, President Robert Mugabe's fall from power in November 2017 was the direct result of decisions taken by senior army officers, not of protests. Yet the previous years of protest helped set the conditions for this change. When the army made its move, tens of thousands protested in the street to make doubly sure that Mugabe could not remain. The success was only partial, because Mugabe's departure did not open the way for democratization but has led to the empowerment of a new generation of ZANU-PF leaders; the July 2018 election was a serious setback for Zimbabwe's activist reformers.

c) Failure

In other cases, protests have more clearly failed, as the concessions they have won from governments have been extremely limited or nonexistent.

There have been several failures in Africa, where leaders have got term limits removed and stayed in power despite protests. In Congo (Brazzaville), President Denis Sassou Nguesso resisted 2015 protests to start an unconstitutional further term in office. In Burundi, President Pierre Nkurunziza assumed office for a third term in June 2015 despite months of protests against his doing so; in May 2018 he pushed through a referendum allowing him to prolong his rule further,

Box 4.1 **Egypt**

Egypt is an example of both the power of civic activism and its limitations. The combination of social movement work and protest pushed President Hosni Mubarak out of power. It then pushed his successor, President Mohamed Morsi out of office in June 2013. But, of course, civil society has failed to prevent a dramatic reversion to authoritarian rule since 2013, under President Abdel Fattah el-Sisi.

The 2011 protests succeeded beyond their initial aims. The revolt turned violent as security forces used tear gas, water cannons, batons, and live ammunition to disperse protesters. President Mubarak announced on live television that he would not run for reelection. Thousands more took to the streets throughout Egypt, including in Alexandria and Suez; in Cairo more than one million people were on the streets at the protests' peak. Protesters were by now not satisfied with Mubarak's announcement that he would remain in power until September, waving their shoes in the air and demanding the army join them in revolt. Mubarak then resigned. The nineteen-day protest had left hundreds dead and several thousands injured.

In 2013 another round of revolts took place across Egypt, this time against the elected government of the Muslim Brotherhood, under President Morsi. The military backed these protests, which were one part of a state campaign against the Muslim Brotherhood rather than a completely spontaneous form of uprising.[5] The protests were again successful in the sense that they pushed Morsi out of office in June 2013.

Events since 2013, however, reveal the limited extent of such success. The ousting of President Morsi did not sate Egyptians' new proclivity to protest. Protesters organized marches again in 2016, triggered initially by el-Sisi's decision to cede some small islands to Saudi Arabia. Later in 2016 further protests erupted in Cairo after a church bombing. In November 2016 protests organized by the Movement of the Poor were put down with lethal state force.

Yet these ongoing, small-scale protests have had little impact. President el-Sisi now rules by decree on an increasingly wide range of measures, through an ineffective but brutal and intrusive state. Civil society freedoms have been dramatically curtailed. Many of the organizations that helped coordinate the 2011 and 2013 protests have been closed down or now struggle to operate in any meaningful way. While a degree of civic ethos persists, Egypt is more authoritarian than it was before Mubarak was ejected from power.

triggering another spate of protests. In Togo, regular protests since 2011 have similarly failed to get President Faure Gnassingbé to step down; he has stalled on promised constitutional changes well into his unconstitutional third term in office.

In Uganda, a range of civic campaigns and protests have not dislodged President Yoweri Museveni or obliged him to implement any significant reforms. Indeed, here many years of original and innovative activism have resulted in an even more repressive, dictatorial, and militarized regime. In similar fashion, after the 2013 protests in Sudan left two hundred dead, the regime of President Omar al-Bashir is still in place, refusing to meet citizens' demands on economic and humanitarian relief issues.

In the Democratic Republic of the Congo, President Joseph Kabila clung on to power despite several years of on-off protests. In 2014 protests succeeded in blocking Kabila's preemptive attempt to change the constitution to allow him to remain in office beyond 2016.[6] When Kabila's second term ran out in December 2016, the strength of protests meant that the president felt compelled to negotiate a deal under which he was to step down in 2017. Yet in practice Kabila continued in office and put back elections to December 2018. In August 2018 Kabila suggested he would step down after these elections—indicating that protests might finally be having some impact. However, Kabila was to hand power to the secretary general of his own ruling party, leading many to suspect that he would continue to rule from the shadows. Moreover, at this stage it was far from certain that free and fair—or indeed, any—elections would actually be held.[7]

Most protests in the Middle East and North Africa have had little positive impact. Syria is perhaps the most tragic case of failure. Here, initially peaceful protests for political reforms ushered in a violent conflict without dislodging the Assad regime from power; activism tipped over into civil war and a growth of radical jihadi groups, not peaceful democratic change. Lebanon's You Stink campaign lost traction after 2015, with the government's promise to build new landfills unimplemented and sectarian leaders still firmly in control.[8]

Iran's 2009 protests demanding civil liberties and free and fair elections provoked a government backlash. Authorities closed universities in Tehran and blocked mobile phone transmissions and access to Facebook. Votes were recounted but the results equally manipulated. Over twenty-five hundred protesters were arrested and eight were killed in protest-related clashes until the so-called Green Movement lost momentum after 2010. In Bahrain, the regime sought to assuage protesters by opening a national dialogue but then clamped down even more harshly against civil society, provoking heightened unrest in 2017.

The same sobering limitations are also evident across the former Soviet space. Activism in Belarus has elicited little in the way of concessions from President Alexsandr Lukashenko. In response to a new wave of protests in 2016 and 2017 against a tax on the unemployed, the government announced a moratorium on the proposal but refused to revoke its plans. In Azerbaijan, innovative forms of activism have had no effect on the regime's intensified authoritarianism. Protests in Russia seem to have been almost counterproductive, as they led to a sharp increase in state repression. Russian protesters failed to build a coalition beyond the urban middle class and actually gave President Vladimir Putin the pretext for clamping down harder against civic activism.[9] Despite the stirrings of 2017, in the end protests did not occur around the Russian elections in March 2018; only after Putin comfortably won a fourth term did further revolts take place.

Many protests inside the European Union have proved just as ineffective. Protests in Greece led to a referendum vote against austerity, only to have the government ignore the result. In France, the Nuit Debout movement did not get the government to stop its labor reforms. In Poland, protesters have not got the government to relinquish its hold over the media and judiciary, although separate protests got it to withdraw the proposed ban on abortion. In 2017 internal and external pressure convinced the Polish president to block several of the proposed laws giving the government greater control over the judiciary. One major law giving the government powers over judicial appointments was ratified, however, and the PiS's general assault on liberal values continues.

The Chinese government made no concessions to the Umbrella Movement in Hong Kong, beyond rhetoric about preserving the current "two systems" arrangement, and effectively appointed the territory's new governor in March 2017 with scant democratic input. In late 2016 it removed two notable Umbrella Movement leaders from the legislature. Protest leaders say that young people are now uncertain about whether continuing the movement is worthwhile, especially in a context of harsher crackdowns being carried out at China's behest. Young people feel excluded from Hong Kong's economic success and are concerned mainly about high property prices; many protesters have begun to focus on these issues, frustrated at their failure to secure any loosening of China's authoritarian grip.

For an example from South America, see "Box 4.2: Venezuela."

Effectiveness: an assessment

Overall, outright successes are relatively rare. One extensive study calculates that no more than a third of democracy protests have led to sustained improvements in democratic quality.[10] Another study reaches a similar but broader conclusion, that only about a third of recent protests have achieved any kind of success at all.[11] Yet other research finds that protests have become less effective over time,

Box 4.2 **Venezuela**

In Venezuela, the government of Nicolás Maduro has been challenged regularly since 2014 without being driven from office. Social turbulence has rumbled on, as Hugo Chávez's death in 2013 has left the fate of the Bolivarian revolution uncertain and a sharp decrease in the oil price has left the government short of resources to keep its social programs afloat.

The opposition has grown in strength since 2014 and has been able to take to the streets of Caracas with increasing impunity. Antiregime activists began to demand a recall referendum (*revocatorio*) against Maduro, presenting a petition to the National Electoral Council to begin this process. This was not successful, as the government blocked the petition.

The regime's hard-line inflexibility unleashed larger and more frequent protests in 2017. Large-scale protests took place after the *chavista*-packed Supreme Court took over the parliament's powers. The protests were powerful enough to force the court to reverse its move, keeping the opposition-held parliament in place.

Protests rumbled on and spiked a week later when the government barred opposition leader Henrique Capriles from running for office for fifteen years. April and May 2017 saw Venezuela's biggest protests yet, as Maduro put troops onto the streets and over thirty protesters were shot dead. Protesters were now calling for immediate elections, while Maduro threatened to disband parliament completely.

The impact appeared to be counterproductive. Security forces and paramilitary groups affiliated with the government responded with force, injuring and arresting over a hundred protesters. The government dissolved the opposition-controlled parliament and held elections for a new National Constituent Assembly to rewrite the constitution. Protests decrying Maduro and calling for new presidential elections continued on an almost daily basis. As the government response became more brutal, so the protest movement, in turn, became more violent. Though most Venezuelan protesters continued to engage in nonviolent resistance, a sizable radical element known as La Resistencia fought government tear gas and water cannons with rocks, slingshots, and Molotov cocktails.

Protesters now came from a diverse cross-section of Venezuelan society, from young people to senior citizens, and from white-collar professionals to unemployed workers. Health professionals, families, business owners, and devout Catholics each held separate protests to register their complaints

(*continued*)

> *Box 4.2 continued*
>
> with the Maduro government. This was very different from previous protests dominated by the political opposition.
>
> President Maduro has so far withstood the successive waves of protest and activism against his rule. He offered talks to lure less radical opposition factions but has rejected demands for institutional changes. Amid more protests, Maduro secured reelection in May 2018, through a heavily manipulated election in which the opposition did not participate. However, while the regime has retained power, it has lost effective control: in 2018 protests have morphed into community looting as food shortages worsen.

claiming that nearly 70 percent of civil resistance campaigns succeeded during the 1990s, compared to 30 percent since 2010.[12]

These surveys would appear to substantiate the critical perspectives on recent protests. Sceptics might note that the multicountry Occupy revolt that promised an end to capitalism seems to have left little legacy. Some studies conclude in a downbeat mood, suggesting, for example, that in the Middle East and North Africa a decade of innovative new activism and sporadic revolts has not changed the region's basic equation of strong states ruling over weak and fissiparous civil societies.[13] Even in the cases of "success" listed above, many protesters came to feel disillusioned because systemic problems and imbalances persisted in the period after corrupt and self-serving leaders were pushed from power. While protests may have been powerful enough to defenestrate a president or regime, what comes next can make that success look relative.

Nevertheless, in many countries protests have undoubtedly managed to advance at least part of their objectives. Even in those countries where they have failed to secure anticorruption measures, improve social justice, or dislodge authoritarian regimes from power, protests have often changed the terms of debate and placed sensitive topics firmly on the public policy agenda.[14]

A complicating implication of this is that protests can often have indirect or intangible effects, which are difficult to quantify or even to identify. Protesters often say they are concerned with projecting a certain mode of thinking and resistance. Protests can set off a chain of connecting previously disconnected people and increasing their awareness of and commitment to action.[15] Some academic-activists insist that effectiveness should be measured not by whether protests lead to tangible reform but in terms of their "signaling" power: even where revolts fail to bring about immediate change, they signal widespread discontent with certain issues in a way that undercuts regime power and credibility.[16]

This reflects experts' view that mobilizations need to be seen as expressions of a cultural change rather than measured only in terms of immediate political gains.[17] Leaders from the umbrella civic organization Solidaire explain their aim is to "change the weather," reshaping culture as a precursor to political change. The impact of building networks, new coalitions of actors, and an ethos of solidarity can be more important than whether a protest succeeds or fails in winning one or two immediate policy changes.[18] As protests become a routine way for people to meet up and forge shared identities, this has positive and less positive implications: such indirect impacts can help sustain an ethos of activism over time but can also take urgency away from the quest for tangible change.[19]

Notwithstanding these caveats, it remains important to explain variation in outcomes. Overall, recent experience presents a wide range of outcomes from contentious civic activism. These range from the most dramatic and surprising successes, where long-entrenched regimes have been unceremoniously pushed out of power, through to cases where sustained campaigns and protests involving huge numbers of people have met a brick wall of resistance from governments that refuse to entertain even modest policy changes. A question that arises from this breadth of varied evidence is: What accounts for the difference? Can we identify the factors that determine the difference between success and failure in today's civic activism? Or are such events simply too haphazard for us to extract any clear conclusions?

Several factors are relevant: protest size, context, tactics, demands, and international support. Each of these plays a role in conditioning protests' impact. Yet the evidence suggests that none of these factors offers a completely convincing explanation on its own. Consequently, it is important not to reduce our assessment of the new civic activism to any single factor. Indeed, there is a degree of mystery here: factors that analysts have often talked about as being vitally important and that we might intuitively think would be strongly influential in fact come up short in terms of how much variation in outcomes they can explain.

Size. Perhaps the most obvious question to assess is whether effectiveness is a straightforward function of the size or breadth of a mobilization. Is activism more likely to succeed when it involves large numbers of highly committed people?

Certainly, in cases like Ukraine and Egypt, the sheer scale of social mobilization played a role in making presidents decide to abandon office. In Brazil, the removal of President Rousseff would probably not have taken place if the scale of protests had not been so vast. Conversely, we can identify cases of failure where activism was confined to a relatively narrow section of the population and failed to garner wide support. This would include the likes of Azerbaijan, Russia, and, arguably, Venezuela.

But there are also cases where the correlation between size and impact is weak. There are examples where protests drew large numbers of protesters yet did not succeed. The evidence shows several cases where mobilizations that failed were just as large in scale as those that succeeded. Large numbers of citizens mobilized in Belarus, just as they did in Ukraine. There were large-scale protests in Jordan and Morocco, just as there were in Egypt and Tunisia. Mobilizations equally large in scale took place in Burundi and in Senegal. Both Thailand and Malaysia experienced large-scale protests. And yet in each of these comparisons, outcomes were radically different.

Tactics. A second variable relates to the question of whether some protests succeed because they adopt better tactics and methods than those that fail. Is the crucial difference between success and failure a matter of the types of actions that protesters choose to pursue? One argument is that protests have become more effective as activists have employed an effective mix of long-term movement-type tactics with episodic protest—meaning that a solid bedrock of quiet, day-to-day activism explodes into protest when certain tipping points are reached.[20]

Activists' better tactics have helped mobilizations become larger, more visible, and longer lasting. Some of the more successful cases above show that activists have become much more sophisticated in their actions and planning. The key has often been asymmetrical action—not confronting authorities on their own terms, through aggression, but finding campaigns that embarrass and ridicule them, and to which they find it difficult to respond. Part of what we see today in effective activism is the outcome of several decades of lesson learning. Movements have sometimes gained huge circles of support through very prosaic community activities of the kind most regimes ignore, and these then create stronger foundations for protests to have significant impact.

Successful groups have compiled manuals, mapping out effective strategies based on an understanding of a group's capacities; targeted communication; realistic goals; innovative ways of framing issues; and the careful but flexible sequencing of campaign activities.[21] They have found creative and subtle techniques that often do not cross the line into full-blown protest—ironic clapping in Belarus, the salute from *The Hunger Games* in Thailand, people simply standing motionless in Istanbul's Taksim Square, colored-painting symbols in Macedonia, puppet theater in Syria.[22] Conversely, failure is more likely where ostensibly leaderless groups have collapsed under the weight of in-fighting, paralyzed in their tactical choices by the lack of clear lines of authority and the inability to make difficult strategic trade-offs.[23]

Again, however, overall the evidence is less than fully conclusive on the role of different tactical choices. Some of the more successful activism has been chaotically organized, while some failed campaigns have been meticulously run. It is not clear that radically more innovative or original tactics were used in Ukraine than in Belarus, in Burkina Faso than in Uganda, or in Tunisia than in Morocco; indeed, if anything, the opposite was the case, with the really innovative methods being deployed by the three cases of failure in this list. Even where brilliantly original tactics are deployed, protests are not easy to sustain if authorities hold out for long enough.

Demands. A related explanation might focus on the variation in protesters' demands. We might expect those protests seeking relatively modest policy changes to be more easily and frequently successful than those trying for more ambitious goals—and in particular those seeking to oust a sitting government and change political regime type.

Once again, the evidence offers some corroboration here but does not entirely produce the results one might expect. Some of the most successful activism has pushed for the most ambitious goals. In contrast, some campaigns that have adopted carefully delineated and modest aims have failed. The successful cases have often been instances of civic pressure pushing regimes out of power. Several failures are instances where activists have pushed for relatively modest changes in economic policy or corruption laws.

As noted in the preceding section, often governments divide protesters' broader agendas from some of their more specific demands. In this sense, a protest may be framed in terms of very sweeping systemic aims but succeed (only) in winning very narrowly defined policy adaptation. Whether protests begin with broad or narrow aims, their tangible impact can tend to converge on partial policy change. Participants in Occupy protests stress that after police evicted them, popular assemblies on issues such as debt prospered in many neighborhoods. They insist they may not have changed the system but did push governments to address the worst excesses of the financial sector.[24] "Box 4.3: New civic activism in the United States," at the end of this chapter, examines the Occupy movement and other, radically different forms of emergent activism in the United States.

Critics may feel that protesters set their goals unrealistically high or in a way that lacks clarity. Activists, for instance, sometimes seek a rather improbable combination of better growth and democracy with economic autarchy and traditional values. Yet these concerns are part of a search for answers to unresolved policy challenges, through routes that get new demands onto the agenda, at least to some extent curtail elite power, and leave more democratic space for citizens to start dealing with contemporary uncertainties on their own terms.

Context. It might be argued that protests' effectiveness in recent years is not related to the features of that activism per se but rather varies across different regime types. While context and regime type are of undoubted importance, however, the correlation with civic effectiveness is far from being absolute or overwhelmingly convincing. The evidence shows that protests have achieved considerable impact in some political contexts that one would have thought would be resistant to change. For example, before 2011, few would have predicted that protest in Tunisia would be vastly more successful than in other Arab states. (In fact, much speculation abounds in Tunisia over why President Bin Ali fled so precipitously, when he had put down previous protests with ease.) Conversely, in apparently more receptive contexts, social movements have often failed to elicit a really far-reaching degree of reform—cases such as Bolivia, Morocco, Moldova, or Jordan.

It might be reasonable to expect civic activism to be more successful in democracies than in nondemocracies. Certainly, governments in countries like Brazil, India, and Nigeria have adjusted and responded constructively to some civic activism. Conversely, some very closed regimes have revealed themselves to be highly brittle and succumbed to civic pressure in dramatic and unpredictable fashion. Once again, the democracies-autocracies divide is of some explanatory relevance but leaves much variation in outcomes unaccounted for. Indeed, in some nondemocratic settings, innovative forms of contentious activism have proved more influential and important precisely because regimes resist influence through open and competitive, mainstream political representation. Some evidence suggests that protests have a bigger impact where the quality of democracy is low, as they provide an alternative outlet for civic influence to formal channels of democratic representation.[25]

The cases above show that more open and conciliatory regimes have often calmed tensions by offering partial reforms, in a way that preempts profound changes to a country's political or economic systems. Closed autocratic or semi-authoritarian regimes may resist civic activism more brutally, but when they reach the limits of resistance they can fall more absolutely and suddenly. Related to this, the new civic activism often wields influence where defections and rivalries occur among regime insiders; indeed, these insider dynamics often act as a kind of conduit or transmission belt for civic influences. In this sense, civic activism has impact to the extent that it magnifies and widens divisions that have already taken root within regimes. This fits the cases of Tunisia and Ukraine, where parts of the state and security establishments played a bridging role to protesters and civic movements.

Clearly, context will always be important, and yet there is a degree of circularity to the "context is all" argument. It often comes close to an assertion that governments respond favorably where they are structurally likely to respond favorably—which is almost a tautology. The interesting follow-on question is what precisely creates this receptivity to change. The cases above demonstrate that this is not as simple as dividing strong from weak regimes: there are apparently strong regimes that either crumble or grant concessions to activists, while there are apparently weak regimes that withstand considerable pressure. All this indicates that the interaction of cause and effect runs both ways. Some protests are successful because the context is receptive. But some also help to *make* that context receptive and for that reason succeed.

International support. I will examine international support for the new civic activism later in the book; suffice it to flag here that the external factor is often raised to explain why some revolts succeed and others do not. To some extent, the international dimension does seem to have been at play. Ukrainian activists received support from outside before the Maidan revolt to a greater extent than Russian activists before the 2011 protests in Moscow, for example. One argument is that success occurs when the West entraps regimes into reform commitments on which they are eventually obliged to follow though.[26]

Yet in general, international support would appear to be a secondary rather than determining factor. The Maduro government in Venezuela has been left with few friends and allies internationally; it is largely isolated yet remains in place. The regimes of Presidents Bin Ali and Mubarak were receiving large amounts of international support, and certainly more backing than new-style activists were attracting within these two countries; yet in these cases, the regimes fell. Some protests that gained a high international profile failed, while others that did not benefit from internationally coordinated tactics fared much better: compare the European antiausterity protests with those that pushed presidents from power in several African states. Some protests have made a difference against regimes that were clearly not entrapped by reform promises to Western powers.

International support tends to follow effective civic momentum more than it creates such traction. That is, international support tends to support civic activism where some kind of political breakthrough has already occurred; it plays a role in anchoring and locking in change more than in fomenting the early stages of protest. Chapter 8 returns to and expands upon this point.

In sum, an important implication flows from all this: each possible explanatory variable is helpful but also incomplete in accounting for variation in the impact of new civic activism. A combination of factors needs to be taken into consideration in each country or example of civic protest if we are fully to understand the reasons why such activism succeeds or fails. The crux for explaining the impact of the new civic activism lies in uncovering how tactics, political context, and goals all relate to each other as a particular revolt evolves over time. It also invites consideration of an additional factor, which is the relationship between new and old civic activism—a subject examined in the next chapter.

As indicated, many analysts and activists remain skeptical of attempts to measure impact as they insist that protests are mainly about building relations, constructing support networks, and changing consciousness. While these are certainly core elements of the emerging activism, surely more research is needed into protests' results. This is *not* to say that activism lacks value where it does not produce dramatic political or policy breakthroughs. Rather it is to call for a deeper understanding of how both tangible and intangible impacts can vary so much across different movements, countries, and political contexts. Research is needed to build up a multifactor picture; it is not possible accurately to extract from today's emerging civic activism any universally applicable laws of what makes it successful or ineffective. The balance of success and failure of today's "will to protest" is to be found in how several factors combine with each other in varying ways across different countries.

Conclusion

The wide variation in impact cautions against making any all-encompassing generalizations about today's protests—whether to dismiss these as an ineffectual sideshow or beatify them as a vehicle for effective popular influence over politics. One problem in recent years is that many accounts of social protests are written by analysts involved practically with these mobilizations—meaning objectivity about the movements' strengths and weaknesses has sometimes been in short supply. It is not always easy to quantify just how much of a difference a particular protest makes—certainly in terms of its impact on aspects of political culture that are less tangible than calls for a specific policy change. But it is undeniably the case that recent protests run the whole gamut from major, game-changing impact through to ineffectual disappointment.

While there are cases of resounding success and unmitigated failure, most protests achieve mixed results—some degree of success combined with a failure to secure maximalist objectives. Even as many governments have become more repressive, they have also become more willing to concede on what they see as relatively minor issues as a tactic to prevent protests escalating. Overall, a combination of variables needs to be assessed to account for any single protest's degree of impact: the size of mobilization and the tactics deployed by the protest itself, the political context, the achievability of demands, the degree of international support. It certainly appears that there is no straightforward equation for determining what ingredients produce a successful protest; one set of protest characteristics may work well on one occasion but not in another instance. In this vein, one broader factor to be fed into the equation is the subject of the next chapter: how new-style activism and protest stand in relation to more established forms of civil society activity.

Box 4.3 **New civic activism in the United States**

In the midst of financial crisis, the Occupy movement was the highest-profile symbol of new civic activism in the United States. This originated with the September 2011 Occupy Wall Street protests, which spurred parallel Occupy protests both globally and across the United States. The demonstrations were largely nonhierarchical and nonviolent, although there were clashes with police forces when Occupy camps were cleared in late 2011 and early 2012. Occupy's goals were imprecise, centring on advocacy for the "99 percent" against a corrupt corporate elite in a time of increasing inequality. Although the movement failed to bring about far-reaching changes to economic and social policies, it did have an impact. Many local campaigns to raise minimum wages succeeded on the back of the Occupy movement.[27] Veterans of the movement went on to generate a wide range of other activism in the years after 2012.[28]

The Black Lives Matter movement began organizing online in 2013 when a Florida neighborhood watch coordinator was acquitted of murder after killing a black teenager, Trayvon Martin. The movement gained further attention in 2014 when a police officer killed Michael Brown in Ferguson, Missouri. Subsequent deaths of African Americans, either killed by police or committing suicide while in police custody, sparked further protests. The movement claims a nonhierarchical structure and operates through local chapters, many of which are involved in other political campaigns such as the affordable housing movement. Several cities, such as Chicago, have announced reforms to policing in response to the protests.

The Antifa movement dates itself to militant leftists in 1920s Europe and formed in the United States out of anti-white-supremacist punk fans in the 1980s.[29] Antifa has become much more visible under Donald Trump's presidency. As an anarchist-leaning direct action group, Antifa stages militant demonstrations, regularly clashing with police and white supremacists.

At the other end of the spectrum, far-right activism has grown dramatically in the last few years across the United States—although its adherents are still relatively modest in number. The Patriot Movement includes a disparate group of militias, survivalists, Christian fundamentalists, and radical libertarians. The Oath Keepers militia deployed in response to the Black Lives Matter protests. A Patriot Prayer rally in Portland in August 2018 clashed violently with an Antifa counterdemonstration. Since Trump's

(*continued*)

Box 4.3 continued

election many of these groups' rhetoric has become less antigovernment and more Islamophobic. Some strands of conservative activism have effectively fused with the Trump administration in a mutually sustaining partnership (although other right-wing activists oppose Trump as not representing genuine conservatism on many issues).

Other militia groups have been active in the American West, mobilizing on issues related to federal government land rights. A related group of militias focuses on border security. The Arizona Border Recon is one well-known such group; its members deploy to intercept drug traffickers and migrants on the US-Mexico border.[30] The group insists it is a legitimate civil society organization that cooperates with government agents and (despite being well armed) eschews violence. It joined the Oath Keepers and white nationalists at a Trump Unity Rally in 2018.

Beyond left-right struggles, US civic activism has intensified on more specific issues in recent years. The Crowd Counting Consortium calculates that ten million to fifteen million people participated in marches in Trump's first year in office and that this represents a higher number of protesters than ever before in US history.[31] The Women's March took place in January 2017 in protest at President Trump's inauguration. With an estimated nationwide participation of over three million people, it was the largest protest in American history. In addition to protesting the president's misogynistic comments and boasts of sexual assault during the campaign, the march has been credited with inspiring many first-time female candidates, who won several state offices in the 2017 elections.[32]

While these large-scale protests have stolen the headlines, new civic activism has also emerged in the less dramatic form of local campaigns. One such initiative has formed against rising housing prices and the transformation of established neighborhoods, especially in New York and on the West Coast. This has triggered the so-called Yimby ("Yes, in my backyard") movement. It presses for more housing, in opposition to conservationists and others who are against development.

Another community effort is the Anti-Eviction Mapping Project, which seeks to document gentrification-driven evictions in San Francisco. These movements tend to be aligned with minority and LGBT groups, who are often the most vulnerable to eviction, and have secured the passage of rent control laws or antieviction measures in some local jurisdictions. In New York in 2017, the Brooklyn Anti-Gentrification Network organized a sizable march in opposition to developments supported by local representatives.

The so-called divestment movement has grown on many campuses to demand that American colleges and universities refrain from investing their endowments in certain types of business, most notably the fossil fuel industry. The movement frequently occupies university administration buildings; it is led by students with loose ties to 350.org, an environmental advocacy group also associated with antipipeline protests.[33]

The best known of those antipipeline protests took place in 2016 to oppose the Dakota Access Pipeline, which was scheduled to run through the Standing Rock Indian Reservation in North Dakota. The protests were organized by Native American leaders but also attracted substantial support from liberal environmentalists. One notable group involved in the protests was the International Indigenous Youth Council, a faith-based organization incorporating Native American activists from across the country. Although the protests succeeded in sparking increased online discussion of environmental issues and Native American rights, the pipeline was approved by the Trump administration and is already operational.

The March for Science, staged on Earth Day 2017, also had environmental overtones. Although demonstrations occurred on every continent, the largest march was held in Washington, DC. The movement began with informal online discussions among scientists, motivated by concerns over Trump's public rejection of scientific consensus on issues like climate change and vaccines.[34] While the protest's ostensibly apolitical aim was to defend science and evidence-based polices, it became widely seen as part of a broader pushback against the Trump administration.[35]

Following the February 2018 shooting at Marjory Stoneman Douglas High School in Florida, a substantial movement emerged calling for strengthened gun control. This involved several large-scale protests across the United States and a large demonstration in Washington, entitled March for Our Lives. This demonstrated an emerging trend: protests organized around single issues have increasingly cut across and woven their way into the overarching cleavage between leftist and rightist activism in the United States.

5

New versus old civic activism:

Rivals or allies?

What is the relationship between the emerging civic activism and more established civil society activity? Many of the self-styled new activists see their struggles as being born out of sharp competition with traditional NGOs. These activists can also be strikingly dismissive of the utility of engaging with political parties or other established actors like trade unions or local administrations. As we saw in chapter 2, for many observers and activists the new forms of civic activism are largely defined by their contrast with preexisting patterns of civil society activity. In this view, the new civic activism is largely at odds with old-style politics; to the extent that it grows and spreads, it displaces traditional styles of politics and advocacy and ushers in a fundamental change in the type of organized social activity that stands between the citizen and the state.

This chapter presents evidence that suggests a more mixed picture. There are certainly cases where the old and the new activism have clashed. But there are other cases where they have dovetailed more productively with each other. The new civic activism sometimes acts as a replacement for established types of civil society activity, but not in every context. I probe the broader implications of this mixed picture and draw out the factors that determine whether the old-new relationship is harmonious and constructive or antagonistic.

Competition and displacement

The prevalent view is that the new civic activism is gradually pushing aside more traditional types of civil society organization. Even if new movements and old-style NGOs and parties may say they seek to work together, many feel that in practice they compete ferociously with each other. The very reasons why the new civic activism has emerged push it toward a relatively antagonistic relationship with more established forms of political representation. Many participants and observers describe it as standing fundamentally at odds with an "old activism" represented by the advocacy campaigns of professional NGOs, mass membership organizations, and pressure exerted through the channels of representative party politics.

Indeed, many writers criticize new activist initiatives for functioning in isolation and refusing to reach out to other civil society actors, political party cadres, or state reformers. They express concern that many activists around the world now have no prior involvement in either formal civil society organizations or party politics. New forms of activism and protest are seen as a response to the changing nature of political parties; as these become more professionalized and less rooted in mass membership, so looser civic initiatives and grassroots networks fill the gap. These movements have given birth to a large number of issue campaigns, local petitions, and discussion circles that have an increasingly uneasy relationship to mainstream party politics.[1]

The antipathy runs both ways. Many NGOs in their turn seek to hold the new activism at bay. Civicus paints a sharp divide between the two forms of activism and laments that very little effort has been made to "build bridges between new movements and existing CSOs, to help sustain civic action" and that traditional NGOs still need to show a basic willingness "to reach out to newly active people to offer pathways for participation."[2]

Several examples can be cited. In the context of the economic crisis in Europe, protests and community activism have set themselves explicitly against the NGO initiatives supported and promoted through formal EU initiatives.[3] One of the original convenors of the Occupy movement in the United States reflected self-critically that today's activists fail to make the necessary alliances with other kinds of reformist actors or to make moves toward a "hybrid movement-party ... disciplined enough to govern," concluding rather harshly that protests invariably become little more than "an exercise in infantile futility."[4]

One Russian protester insists the new activism is a "different civilization" from the old activism. Research on anticorruption movements shows that the breach between new and older activist groups has widened in places like Brazil, Guatemala, and Lebanon; only rarely have recent struggles against corruption produced alliances between these NGOs and new informal movements.[5] In Malaysia, satirical video blogging is a popular tool for youth engagement in political debates; here, bloggers distance themselves from the organized opposition and prefer to call themselves "responsible citizens" rather than be identified as "civil society."[6]

A study of the Middle East and North Africa finds that many new civic initiatives in this region resist links with existing NGOs, opposition groups, and Islamist groups.[7] Even in Tunisia, new movement activists say they feel alienated from the "insider" NGOs that have managed to retain a dominant role in the country's lauded consensual transition—complaining that NGOs are part of an elitist process that has allowed former members of the authoritarian regime to return to power, put the brakes on a truth commission, and advance draconian antiterror laws. In Egypt, the new and old activists cooperated in the 2011 revolution but fell out in 2013 over how far they should accept the military's assumption of power; the traditional NGOs were more willing than were the new activists to accept this as a necessary step to displace the Muslim Brotherhood from government. Tensions rose in Gaza as by May 2018 Hamas appeared to be taking over the territory's new-style civic movements, provoking a fatal crackdown from Israeli security forces.

Research in developing countries finds that new civic movements have established a particularly powerful presence in non-Western states and the global south precisely because they have set themselves up in contradistinction to an NGO model that is seen as being very northern and Western in nature. These "global south" movements see themselves as having more radical and far-reaching agendas, rooted in local-level mobilization rather than big campaigns on cross-cutting global issues.[8]

Some writers stress that across Africa there is a fundamental divide between grassroots, popular movements wanting genuinely far-reaching change and NGOs staffed by the middle class aiming simply to keep their own privileges and stall radical reform. Tensions surfaced, for example, in Nigeria when unions and older NGOs joined protests against a hike in fuel prices but resisted the call from new, community-based activist groups to use this as a launching pad for a broader assault against the government. In Uganda, a similar falling-out occurred when the formal NGO sector expressly kept its distance from the new "walking activism." And in Sudan, new student and neighborhood groups in Khartoum fought with larger and more formal NGOs for control over protests.[9]

In Latin America, the "old civil society" has often become associated with a relatively conservative agenda of holding at bay more radical, informal civic movements from marginalized sectors of society, like new groups of antimining or black community activists—with these two types of activism locked in deeply polarized ideological tension.[10] Rural movements remain old-style in most of the developing world and are not part of the new digital world of activism that dominates the international headlines. The new activists have made little effort to build bridges to such communities, leaving a deep divide between urban-cosmopolitan civic mobilization and the work of more traditional, rural activists.

Fusion

The most common view on the new civic activism is the one that stresses this kind of competitive relationship with the old activism and mainstream politics.

But the evidence suggests that this only tells part of the picture. Often the old and new forms of activism are not directly at odds with each other, and in some instances they have even nourished each other in a mutually supportive fashion. Some research points to increasing links and "surreptitious symbiosis" between NGOs and looser activist movements.[11] Moreover, where this positive crossover occurs, civic activism tends to be more successful.

There are several such positive dynamics at work. One is that new and older actors sometimes *form pragmatic alliances*, motivated by a desire to broaden out the constituency of support behind certain reforms. Some observers detect the emergence of a multiactor activism in which loosely structured movements, NGOs, the media, public opinion, trade unions, some international institutions, and even governments often coalesce to challenge the status quo on certain issues. Antiausterity and anticorruption protests often involve a mix of students, old-style union mobilization, and an urban underclass. Indeed, some revolts have become so large and powerful precisely because new and old political forms have all joined forces.

Some writers believe that activists have become better at broadening their alliances as they become more experienced. A key development here is a tighter intersection between protest politics and changes in formal institutional politics.[12] In an effort to build bridges, some NGOs have begun to involve diverse local, community-based movements in some of their operational modes.[13]

Emerging and established civic activists can often coordinate because they realize they fulfil complementary functions. Often, new activists generate protests that galvanize public and media attention around a particular local issue—the destruction of a forest, people being evicted to make way for an infrastructure project—and the more established NGOs then work with them to sustain pressure through legal campaigns and political lobbying to push for wider policy change relevant to that issue. In some cases, after protests die down, new forms of activism feed into or stimulate more traditional political action.

Despite their rivalry, in Tunisia some old and new civic actors did form effective alliances. Antiregime protests in 2011 involved new community-based groups, Salafists, trade unions, political parties, and traditional NGOs. These actors squabbled but retained enough cooperation to advance Tunisia's democratic transition.[14] Since 2015 the anti-impunity grassroots Manish Msameh (I Am Not Forgiving) movement includes new informal actors, NGOs, and supporters from political parties. Many community-level protests related to working conditions cooperate with Tunisia's main trade unions. Small collectives have tried to take control of land and agricultural production; loose networks of protest around this issue often bring in the unions after they begin. In 2107 and 2018 Tunisia's biggest established NGOs tried to mediate between protesters, with very maximalist demands, and the political parties. While newer civic groups often complain that the established civic organizations try to take control and sap grassroots initiatives of their more radical aims, alliances still hold to some extent in Tunisia.

In 2016 new and older Turkish groups campaigned together against the government's proposal to allow men found guilty of rape to escape punishment by marrying their victim. As political conditions have worsened in Turkey, community-based self-help groups and long-established NGOs have increasingly worked together on local development projects. The former often mobilize local people against controversial projects that will have deleterious effects on the community, and then national-level NGOs come into to help these groups sustain pressure through legal action and other forms of more political campaigning.[15] Similarly, in Egypt some of the "new spontaneous actors" have gradually sought out the older, formal NGOs to elicit legal help on how to stem the current deterioration in human rights and civic space.[16]

In Latin America, many movements today use a mix of old and new strategies, a combination of measured participation and more radical contestation. Across the region there is an intertwining of radical and less radical civil society that makes it difficult to say that the new activism is more or less transformative, more conservative or more leftist, or indeed more or less effective than the old. In recent years, new and old groups have often come to work together very consciously to combine "good cop, bad cop" strategies and thus maximize the chance of winning concessions from governments.[17] In Burkina Faso, governmental change came (only) when a new civic movement called Citizens' Broom, launched by musicians and using the innovative symbolism of sweeping away the elite, was joined by unions, the political opposition, and some regime insiders.

A second dynamic is that some actions and protests see the *older civic actors play leading roles*. NGOs sometimes stand aloof from the new contentious activism but on other occasions are the lead organizers of radical protest. Extensive empirical studies reveal that traditional NGOs have sometimes been the key mobilizers of recent protests, far from being irrelevant to innovative revolts.[18] Opposition parties and NGOs played lead triggering roles in Malaysia's 2013 Black 505 election-related protests and Thailand's protests against the red-shirt government of Prime Minister Yingluck Shinawatra; in these cases the older civic actors galvanized the new movements at least as much as vice versa. In Georgia and Azerbaijan, NGOs have led protests and have mobilized informal networks and kinship communities to help them do so.[19]

Contrary to much popular commentary, some of today's protests are not "citizens versus the elite" so much as they are old-style political clashes between different interests, ethnicities, or religions, in which traditional actors remain the focal point. Alongside new forms of civil disobedience and various Occupy-style tactics, many campaigns rely on very familiar forms of activism like petitions, traditional rallies, and marches. Opposition parties still play a role in triggering these kinds of activities, which can then lead into protests.[20] In many places, from Honduras through to Egypt, Pakistan, and Bahrain, traditional trade unions have played a lead role in protests.

A third bridging dynamic is that *personnel often overlap*. Many activists involved in new movements also work for NGOs, even if they reject the idea of formal, institutional cooperation between the two spheres.[21] Sometimes the same individuals now lead the new activism, simply harnessing the internet and social media instruments as tools that amplify their campaigning. Informal and fluid citizen movements can end up feeding new activists into political parties and NGOs.[22] One Zimbabwean civic leader insists that new forms of mobilization have helped get young activists more engaged in mainstream politics.

Several civic groups have set themselves up as "bridging initiatives" to filter today's generation of activists into other forms of political activity. For example, one innovative initiative, Apolitical, aims at linking the worlds of social entrepreneurship and reform-minded public institutions, in pursuit of a new type of "public citizenship"—getting new activists to widen their participation strategies into public bodies.[23]

A fourth and related dynamic is that *new movements sometimes change into formal NGOs or even political parties* as they develop—through a kind of institutionalization that is separate from and extends beyond other types of old-new coordination. This echoes an older observation that many grassroots movements morph into formalized interest groups.[24] Many new activist movements try to retain momentum when protests subside by establishing small-scale permanent organizational structures, partially taking on board formal NGO models, so as to be ready to ride the next wave of protest when larger numbers of people become involved again on a sporadic and informal basis.

Today, many political parties seek to import the new civic activism into party structures and then style themselves as hybrid "party-movements." Many parties are now moving away from the notion of having lifelong, largely passive memberships to consulting wider networks of citizens on a more regular basis to coshape policy agendas.[25] Indeed, this could prove to be one of the new civic activism's most enduring impacts: the way its core ethos is being incorporated into more traditional vehicles of political representation, blurring the division between members and nonmembers, or between insiders and outsiders.

One of the most high-profile cases of at least partial fusion of the old and new politics has taken place in France. Here, President Emmanuel Macron launched La République en Marche, which brands itself as a movement rather than a political party. Although this was Macron's politically motivated creation, it also grew out of a series of bottom-up volunteer circles and open citizen conversations that involved nearly thirty thousand people. The movement was a curious combination of top-down and bottom-up dynamics. It crowdsourced its manifesto and grew to count on nearly half a million adherents, eschewing formal party-style membership fees in order to embrace more informal styles of local activism. While criticism has grown that the movement has gradually become a more top-down vehicle in the service of Macron's presidency, this remains a notable case of party politics molding itself to the new ethos of active citizenship.[26]

Another example is in Ukraine. Many of the new Euromaidan movements have transformed themselves into more structured NGOs or have entered politics. One example is the Reanimation Package of Reforms, which began as a loose grouping of Maidan activists but has become the largest formally organized civil society coalition in Ukraine.[27] The iconic Automaidan movement—which organized citizens to ferry protesters in and out of the Maidan revolt—has morphed into an organization monitoring corruption. The Crimean SOS and Donbas SOS volunteer groups turned into professional NGOs and now partner with United Nations bodies. The founder of the citizen initiative ProZorro became the minister that implemented an e-procurement strategy. Even if concerns remain about how well grassroots volunteerism is connected to other areas of political activity, Ukraine shows that constructive moves "from protest to politics" are possible.[28]

In Morocco, members of the February 20 movement set up their own NGOs as the 2011 protests ran out of steam. These include education initiatives like l'Organisation Marocaine des Jeunes Décideurs; Tafra, which works on plans for a fully constitutional monarchy; new human rights initiatives like the Institut Prometheus pour la Démocratie et les Droits Humains; political art initiatives like the Mediterranean Human Rights Cinema, Racines, and Théâtre de l'Opprimé; OuiShare Maroc, which works on collaborative economy ideas at a local community level; and SimSim–Participation Citoyenne, which works on participative citizenship through digital apps. Conversely, in 2017 some of the mainstream human rights NGOs and opposition parties began to cooperate with protesters in Rif, seeking to raise their demands to the level of national political debate.[29]

In Hong Kong, the Umbrella protests built on several years of burgeoning civic organization in response to tightening political control, and prominent leaders of these groups played a role in the revolt.[30] Part of the Umbrella Movement turned into a formal political project in March 2016 when its leaders formed the Demosistō party. This won a single seat in the September 2016 legislative elections. This meant that Hong Kong's older prodemocracy parties were squeezed out by those with roots in a newer style of local civic activism.[31] In a similar vein, Taiwan's Sunflower Movement spawned several NGOs and in turn the New Power Party that became the third-largest force in the country's parliament in 2016.[32]

Latin America has seen several grassroots leftist-populist movements assume power as political parties—in Bolivia, Ecuador, Nicaragua, and Venezuela. Some writers see in the region's leftist-populist experiments a positive merging of informal community groups with both professional civil society and state bodies. For instance, Bolivia's "intercultural democracy" draws on community councils that feed into formal decision making on a systematic basis, and this has encouraged a reorientation of NGOs, too; a ministerial post is specifically dedicated to coordination with social movements and civil society.[33]

In Lebanon, eleven activist movements coalesced to form the Tahaluf Watani party that competed in elections in May 2018, winning one seat in parliament. The India against Corruption social movement formed itself into the Common Man Party and won seats in the parliament in Delhi. In Myanmar, local community-based groups morphed into a swathe of political parties in the run-up to elections in 2018. In Moldova, the loose grouping of activists that led the 2015 protests through the Civic Platform for Dignity and Truth formed itself into a political party to compete in 2016 elections. Indeed, across the post-Soviet space, so-called self-determined new activists have often ended up forming NGOs or even political parties.[34]

Within the UK Labour Party, the Momentum organization has self-consciously acted as a bridge between the traditional party structures and civic activism, bringing its networks of community-based campaigners and youth activities into the party, helping to increase Labour's membership to a decades-long high.[35] Similarly, in the United States, the Democratic presidential primary candidate Bernie Sanders and his team used local community networks to build a new political platform. At the other end of the spectrum, the Tea Party movement began in 2009 as an antipolitics initiative opposing government bailouts and the Obama administration's stimulus package but has gradually established itself as a more formal, rightist wing of the Republican Party.

Competition and cooperation

The evolution of this relationship between new and old actors is crucial to the future of global civic activism and its role in political and economic reform.[36] A key question is whether the relationship can be positively competitive without being mutually damaging. Often a mix of dynamics exists; "Box 5.1: Spain: fusion, with rivalry" looks at one such example. Cases like those of Tunisia and Ukraine show that coordination between new and old civic activism can work well and has been effective in several countries in recent years. But some degree of competition has often been beneficial, too. To the extent that the new civic activism helps correct at least some shortcomings of more established civil society activity, it has good grounds for not wanting to fuse too closely with the traditional approaches of NGOs. In the best cases, the new and old styles of activism

Box 5.1 Spain: Fusion, With Rivalry

In Spain, the dynamics of fusion and rivalry coexist. The country has often been cited as one of the most notable cases of protest-based activism gaining traction and ending up in parliament in the guise of its own party, Podemos. In many senses, this is one of the most dramatic examples of such activism redrawing the terms of political debate in a remarkably short period of time, as Podemos went from scratch to being one of Spain's biggest and most influential political parties.

Yet this fusing of new and old activism has sparked an ongoing debate about how activists can translate an ethos of a broad-based civic movement into the political sphere without killing off the very philosophy that drove their initial citizens' uprising.

Increasingly Podemos has had to address the challenges involved in trying to operate as a mainstream political party and as a protest movement. After a fierce internal battle, in early 2017 it took a decisive turn back toward being an unambiguously leftist rather than "transversal" organization, styling its representatives in parliament as "institutional activists." While many of the group's members insist that this move effectively takes activism to the heart of formal, institutional politics, many observers conclude that Podemos has sacrificed its chances of winning political power in deference to this traditional identity. It remains unclear who has had the greater impact: those in Podemos who decided to enter mainstream politics or those protest movements in other countries that refused to do so.

Separate from this, a key development lies in how the new civic movements have fed into innovative forms of municipal-level politics across Spain. Eight Spanish cities voted new activist-based organizations into mayoral power between 2015 and 2017. One of these was Barcelona, where the city council crowdsourced a whole collaborative economy plan in 2016.

Madrid has also become a central hub for open, participative urbanism, with hundreds of community groups organizing to take control of public spaces for shared use, raising funds to do so, and collecting ideas through so-called open-source urban planning. These groups are not NGOs but movements that have formed within communities, often through citizen laboratories that now meet regularly to plan daily activities, many related to shared-economy-type activities in the wake of the financial crisis. They have in some senses leapfrogged the formal, structured civil society sphere to be directly involved in the municipal government under the Ahora Madrid collective.

Activists running participative digital platforms acknowledge that it was when the Ahora Madrid coalition took office in the city government that they were able to expand and progress in their work, in partnership with reformers in the political sphere. This group runs monthly citizen meetings specifically on how to improve democratic participation in the city. In 2018 it worked to launch a City Observatory to be made up of citizens chosen by sortition; this will enable a group of around fifty residents to get ideas onto the agenda and possibly make some decisions where reforms are blocked in the city assembly. Again, however, the tensions between radical activism and mainstream politics linger beneath the surface. Ahora Madrid began to splinter in 2018: some of its social movement members resisted policy concessions, while others argued that mainstream politics required pragmatism.

In Catalonia, civic activism has quite dramatically become a matter of high politics. A cluster of grassroots movements morphed into the Catalan National Assembly and then the CUP (Popular Unity Candidacy) party that won seats to the regional parliament—holding the balance of power and pushing forward the controversial independence referendum on 1 October 2017. Protests here ran the full gamut in terms of their relationship to mainstream politics: highly politicized protests were called by political parties in favour of secession; these were met with antiseparatist protests coordinated by civic groups elsewhere in Spain with a conservative-nationalist identity; then protests were run with participants dressed in white to call for dialogue between the two sides, expressly excluding political parties and barring both Catalan and Spanish flags. In a highly charged atmosphere, here civic activism has both infiltrated mainstream politics and set itself against representative processes.

supplement without duplicating each other. Effective civil society action has often resulted from combined doses of new and old civic activism. The old and new styles of activism have sometimes coordinated without adopting the same modes of action or issue campaigns as each other. They each have particular strengths, and their combination seems to be most promising when they feed into each other's activities in complementary fashion.

To a modest degree, opinions on this question are shifting. As many citizen initiatives and protests have at least partially run aground, some activists talk of a need to revisit their rejection of traditional forms of politics and their antipathy toward professional advocacy NGOs. Many movements have begun to evolve and are today far from being purely destructive "rebels without a cause." Many activists are beginning to realize that new-style tactics are not a substitute for building networks with more traditional forms of direct organization and action.[37]

For their part, NGOs are also showing an incipient willingness to rethink. They are beginning to realize that informal networks and movements can add to the effectiveness of traditional NGOs by deepening connections to grassroots communities and a wider net of citizens that are not necessarily politically engaged in a traditional sense. If and when new movements can bring the concerns of these broader pockets of social discontent into an engagement with the issues that drive professional NGOs, they can help strengthen the latter's legitimacy and representativeness.[38]

The new wave of protests has not completely sidelined NGOs but is rather pushing them into a different function: the role of conduits between party politics and new movements. An increasing number of NGO representatives talk of the need to adopt a bridge-building role. They see themselves well placed to offer some kind of transmission belt between a turbulent and still-inchoate world of protests, digital activism, and networked movements, on the one hand, and the atrophied and underperforming channels of representative democracy, on the other hand.

The director of the International Civil Society Centre insists that if traditional CSOs are to find a useful new role, they must adapt: "they will have to turn themselves from closed, branded and defended entities into open platforms serving frontline activists."[39] There is a vital job to be done of harnessing the anger of informal movements and channeling their energy into other civil society and political channels.[40] The pertinent metric here is whether the new activism is pushing established civil society actors to improve and update their activities—more than whether it is eclipsing the old NGOs.

While much hostility has infected relations between new and old activism, on some issues these relations may have been rather too cozy. Some activists see a danger that new civic activists and NGO leaders may end up suffocating each other as they try to overcome their mutual hostility. Some observers detect that this is indeed beginning to happen: new movements have influenced NGOs and in some cases helped breathe life back into such organizations by pushing them toward local networks and grassroots issues, but as this happens the old NGOs in turn influence new civic initiatives and push them toward NGO-ization.[41]

Joined-up activism need not entail new-style movements converting NGOs wholesale to the new activism, any more than it involves the former being dragged into an NGO-type structure and approach. While there are nascent signs on both sides of a greater willingness to cooperate, each set of actors still fears being co-opted by the other. Emerging activists can be strikingly suspicious that the big NGOs and other formal civil society organizations are opportunistically out to ride on the coattails of the new activism's greater legitimacy. They fear the prospect of the large, well-funded NGOs simply swallowing up smaller and less powerful community movements and, under a discourse of partnership, squeezing out their lifeblood. In turn, some NGO personnel worry that issue-focused, professional advocacy could splinter and fragment if it gets too close to the world of disruptive new civic activism; NGOs certainly feel that they are on the defensive, as the new activism has become more fashionable and has seized the initiative in many countries from long-standing civil society organizations.

An increasing number of activists seek a judicious balance of coordination and competition. Some measures of better coordination are about new and old actors maximizing their mutual complementarity, with the new civic activism helping NGOs link downward to fluid grassroots networks, and NGOs helping the new activism link upward to more targeted and structured political processes. While in a small number of cases bottom-up civic movements, NGOs, trade unions, and political parties have dovetailed with some effectiveness, such cooperation is in general still embryonic.

At the same time, alongside such coordination, rivalry can be healthy. The new and old civic activisms offer alternative routes to political and social influence. In some situations, new-style movement activities may be most appropriate, while in others, more formalized NGO campaigns may be able to achieve more. The relative potential of each set of actors will depend on the issue at stake and the political context within which it is being pursued. With such a varied global context of different policy challenges and political situations, citizens can benefit from having different types of civil society at their disposal.

In short, the new civic activism that has emerged across the world is unlikely to displace the so-called old activism, while the old activism cannot improve without incorporating and responding positively to the new civic activism. Arguably, the pertinent division is not between new activists and established NGOs per se but between those in both new and old groups trying innovatively to link different spheres of political engagement and those not willing to explore such bold rethinking.

6

Digital activism:

Game changer or chimera?

The high-profile activism of recent years is in part the story of digital technology and social media. Coverage of any given protest invariably refers to the important role played by social media in the event's organization. Many reports attribute such importance to this dimension that they verge on describing new civic activism as the very creature of social media, driven by and inseparable from the rise of Facebook, Twitter, and a range of other online applications. A commonly held assumption is that spectacular advances in information communication technology (ICT) have facilitated qualitatively different types of civic activism.

The political significance of ICT is a vast topic. There are hundreds of experts analyzing the world of digital democracy, so-called civic tech, hacktivism and cyberactivism. This is an area encompassing many dimensions that fall well outside the scope of this book. My interest here lies in the very specific question of how new ICT tools relate to the sphere of civic activism. ICT has been a mainstream civic activist tool for two decades now. I ask what the current phase of digital technology adds that is new and how this relates to the book's focus on the changing patterns of contemporary civic activism.

It is undeniably the case that digital technology has been essential to the kinds of civic activism outlined so far in this book. New technology has shaped and expanded the tactical options available to today's activists. Of course, while many celebrate ICT advances, an equally common viewpoint is that the importance and value of social media have been hugely overhyped. I suggest that both these perspectives have some validity, before outlining a potential or incipient new phase in digital technology that may fine-tune its impact on civic activism.

Digital democracy on the rise

Digital technology has begun to transform many dimensions of political activity. There are now thousands of intensively used applications and platforms across the globe offering tools for online campaigning, petitioning, and voting. In many countries, these initiatives are sophisticated and far advanced, even mainstreamed into political activity. Crowdsourced ideas have been fed into several processes of constitutional change. Many local administrations offer online platforms for citizen input. Tools for citizens to present new policy ideas are proliferating.

The changes injected by these forms of so-called civic-tech have been exhaustively chronicled. Indeed, the advantages they are assumed to offer are now a relatively staple part of commentary on political events around the world. Bestselling books have been celebrating for several years the potential that ICT offers to "organize without organizations."[1] While ICT is a far broader concept than digital activism as such and does not necessarily entail the latter, ICT-based initiatives have added several layers of impetus to previous forms of activism. Some of these advantages are to do with better organizational capacities, some are about the breadth of citizen participation, and some are about evading governmental control.

Perhaps the most common observations made about social media activism relate to the way these give civil society enhanced organizational capacity. Social media have, of course, become routinely used to mobilize large number of citizens. They enable protests to morph and change shape at short notice in response to government efforts to contain revolts. They facilitate the coordination of protests across different locations. It is in this sense that so many protests in recent years have been labeled "Twitter revolutions" or "Facebook uprisings."

At a deeper level, many online apps are designed to broaden political participation. Digital technology can widen the public sphere quietly and gradually before a peak of protest is attained, an attribute equally as important as the better-known role of social media in calling people out to the streets.[2] Online activity makes individual citizens marketers, promoters, and disseminators of political ideas. This goes far beyond Facebook being used to convene protests and rather betokens a whole new, participative form of political communication and democratic practice.[3]

Online voting and forums allow a wider section of the population to find its voice and exert effective influence. They allow more people to get involved in decision making and in holding elites to account. Civic crowdsourcing makes decisions more participative and inclusive, and also fairer in its outcomes—its supporters claim.[4] So-called tech-optimists feel that the nascent wave of technologies like virtual- and augmented-reality tools will move the political use of ICT to a whole new level of online involvement in voting, town hall debating, and monitoring of decision making.[5]

Some digital experts argue that what gives today's online activism its qualitative difference from previous activism is that technology now conditions the very rationale, structure, and tactics of a movement. Many civic actors simply bolt a few ICT tools onto activities that otherwise remain similar to those of the classic NGO; they harness ICT for very specific purposes. The incipient step beyond this is where activism and digital technologies are coshaped, feeding off each other.[6] If in some cases digital technology simply gives well-established civil society organizations a new set of tools to improve their existing work, in an increasing number of instances it creates a qualitatively new "logic of connective action"—a whole new style of activism that does not require of its participants the same shared ideological frames or formal organizational belonging as traditional collective action.[7]

In this vein, an increasing number of activists do not simply use digital tools for organizing protests and other campaigns but also deploy online tools as part of their activism—using tactics like distributed-denial-of-service attacks, virtual sit-ins (flooding a website with a huge number of simultaneous requests for data), and email bombing (paralyzing an organization's email system by bombarding its in-box with a wave of emails).

Among the many thousands of online apps, some are directly pertinent to the new civic activism examined in this book. Several emblematic activist tools have become highly influential. The Liquid Democracy platform is now used across the world. The Loomio app is also now in widespread use and has been behind a number of influential new civic initiatives; the National Assembly for Wales used it to widen citizen input into local health policies, for example. The Accela Civic Platform offers cloud-based solutions to strengthen communities' collective engagement initiatives and is used in over two thousand communities worldwide.[8] The DemocracyOS app, developed by the Argentine Net Party, enables online deliberation and voting on policy proposals.[9] Civi is a constituent relationship management system that helps civic groups manage relations with their stakeholders.[10]

OuiShare is a collective international community focusing on the collaborative economy; it connects people, ideas, and projects in pursuit of the sharing economy. This involves so-called fablabs, crowdfunding, and help for the peer-to-peer economy and for society in general.[11] Chayn is a global, volunteer-run open source project that produces crowdsourced resources such as informational websites and Snapchat counseling on how to fight online harassment, using technology to empower women experiencing violence and abuse. Crowdpac is a crowdfunding platform for political campaigning in the United Kingdom.

IserveU is an e-democracy platform launched in 2015 that allows organizations to put decisions out to their constituents, interact with them through conversation forums, and collect votes on key issues; the platform also makes top-rated comments on both sides of a debate visible to undecided voters to improve the quality of open deliberation. MobileActive.org facilitates citizen-generated and crowdsourced election monitoring and has been used in countries like Ghana, Kenya, Mexico, India, Lebanon, and Sierra Leone. Phone2Action is a civic engagement software platform that organizations use to acquire and engage supporters and connect with elected officials.

MoveOn has pioneered online organizing and advocacy in the US based on rapid-response political campaigning and grassroots member participation. In Poland, civic-tech experts launched a Personal Democracy Forum to explore how to enhance the democratic impact of digital technology. A common use of digital platforms is for monitoring and mapping, with new apps now tracking instances of sexual harassment in Egypt, police brutality against African Americans in the US and the arrest of protesters in Russia, to name only some of a huge number of such examples.[12]

There are many examples of ICT tools having a tangible impact on the effectiveness of civic activism. The ProZorro platform has transformed anticorruption and public procurement policies in Ukraine. In Kenyan elections, software developed by the local nonprofit organization Ushahidi has given citizens an online platform for public participation in monitoring election-related fraud and violence. In Argentina, while the Net Party has not won any seats in the legislature, its DemocracyOS software has made an impact in enabling citizens to debate proposals put forward by the Buenos Aires municipal government. In Chile, the ChileCompra e-procurement system has given citizens better scrutiny over corruption in government contracts. Such e-procurement systems are becoming increasingly ubiquitous across the world.

In Iran, the opposition Green Movement relied heavily on digital tools. After the regime pushed that movement underground, an innovative range of more subtle civic initiatives emerged. My Stealthy Freedom is an online women's rights movement that began in May 2014. As part of its "stealthy" opposition to the country's hijab law, the exiled journalist Masih Alinejad created a Facebook page where women from inside Iran share photos of themselves not wearing their hijab. In 2018 this took on a new prominence, with increasing numbers of women posting such shots after the protests that took place at the beginning of the year. This was aligned with a White Wednesday initiative that had women wearing only white scarves on that day of the week. The #MyForbiddenSong campaign opposes the ban on woman singing in public, and #IranianWomenLoveCycling defies the fatwa claiming that bike riding threatens a woman's chastity.

ICT tools have been especially important in fueling civic activism at the municipal level. It is being used to help organize online referendums on specific local issues. Civocracy provides an online platform for cities to engage citizens in a myriad of ways. Decide Madrid managed fourteen thousand online proposals from individual citizens in its first year in operation, 2015–16; two issues attracted support from the requisite 1 percent of the population and were voted on in 2017 (one on transport tickets and one on environmental measures). The social movement Barcelona en Comú expanded its online platforms and town hall meetings with a wider range of citizens to draw up its municipal program, under the emblem of widening the "participatory commons." Barcelona's digital city initiative is essentially about designing open source platforms to get citizens involved in decision making but also aims to facilitate sharing mechanisms and self-help dynamics at the community level.

The Paris city government made €500 million of its budget available to be spent in accordance with decisions adopted through an online participatory budgeting process. The Seoul city government's Online Procedures Enhancement (OPEN) system is one of the longest-running e-procurement initiatives and is credited with significantly reducing corruption in the Korean capital. SocialBoost provides for online participatory budgeting across Ukraine. FixMyStreet is a widely used web platform in the UK that enables people to report public service delivery problems—things like streetlamps and potholes that need fixing. Similar initiatives have sprouted in many other countries.[13] This is where civic tech has had its strongest impact.

The positive notion underpinning all of this is that of *sousveillance*, the idea of citizens keeping tabs on authorities—the mirror image of surveillance. Some analysts insist that recent evidence shows that online petitioning gets more people involved in very effective forms of instantaneous, so-called flash activism.[14] All this fits with the notion that enhanced resources can be expected to produce higher levels of and more effective activism, as technologies become available to progressively wider circles of the population.

An additional factor driving the use of ICT is that it gives civic activism an ability to evade state control. One recent report notes that "as physical spaces become increasingly constrained, more activism takes place online."[15] Online activism has been helpful for reviving civil society in politically closed countries. This is because it compensates for civil society's inability to organize in standard forms by creating an alternative forum for activists to express views and disseminate information.[16] Tunisia is a case where online mobilization ignited protest in a highly closed regime where traditional civil society struggled to operate.[17] Some statistical studies suggest that digital activism has increased the overall degree of critical political engagement in authoritarian settings.[18]

Some studies suggest that online activism has gradually refined itself and become more effective. Unlike in its early days, it has begun to involve people not previously politically engaged. The reduced costs of online activism have begun to get around the classical free-rider problems of collective action. Citizens' involvement in microactions online—clicking a "like" or agreeing to a petition—is now capable of scaling up to a change in macrolevel political dynamics. It is driving a reenergized if rather chaotic pluralism.[19]

In this era, most online campaigns fail, but the small numbers that succeed have a very big impact. So the difference between failure and success in political activism becomes wider. And it is difficult to predict which issues will suddenly become the subject of a dramatic cascade effect. There can be long periods of stasis, punctuated by dramatic eruptions of mobilization. Political change becomes nonlinear. Even if online activism is too disparate to function like an ideal-type deliberative forum, it adds impetus over and above the classical concepts of political influence and accountability.[20]

Downsides for civil society

Notwithstanding all these significant advances and benefits that come from digital technology, it is not entirely good news for civic activism. Skeptics argue that its presumed benefits have been oversold. Its impact has been limited to a narrower range of the population than tech-optimists suggest. Today much of the focus is on the way that ICT is helping governments and powerful economic interests against citizen-oriented activism.

ICT simply changes the terrain on which democrats and autocrats do battle as they each strive to master digital technology.[21] The disappointing paradox is that in the same period that has witnessed such a spectacular spread of digital technologies, democracy has plateaued across the world and the problems of injustice and corruption have worsened.[22]

Without denying the undoubtedly galvanizing effect of new technologies, it is necessary to ask more critical questions about the impact of ICT. The principal doubts and risks for civic activism are as follows:

Tensions with the ethos of citizen mobilization

While those involved in cyberactivism insist that the new apps and online tools go hand in glove with the ascendency of new contentious citizen movements, they can in practice sit uneasily with the development of group-based, active political involvement. A standard observation is that online voting risks undercutting the notion of organized civic activities—and almost stands as an alternative to rather than a catalyst of civic activism. Online "slacktivism" can detract from and undercut sustained political activism. An often-repeated concern is that ICT-based activism is hollowing out or circumventing political parties and parliaments.

This is related to wider doubts about the way in which ICT may be contributing to a depoliticization of society. Overall, very little use of the web is political; many people are increasingly drawn into the soporific world of exchanging selfies and video clips. Social media risks drawing people away from the kind of engaged ethos of participatory politics that ignites activist movements. The online blogger may have no tangible link to practical day-to-day issues in his or her community and represents almost the antithesis of the pragmatic self-help ethos that many activists are seeking to develop. One digital activist acknowledges that online campaigns often succeed by creating the impression that they involve large numbers of people when "we are just three people in a room."

One activist who cofounded the Argentine Net Party stepped out of the organization expressing disappointment with the fact that the its flagship DemocracyOS platform—aimed at enabling people to instruct legislators how to vote—had not fostered real "citizen participation" but just allowed a very select group of individuals to express an opinion online.[23] Online activism in Italy's Five Star Movement has been declining for the past two years while the outfit's mobilization of voters through traditional, old-style politics has actually increased.[24] The SimSim initiative in Morocco reports that MPs have so far been reluctant to answer the questions submitted to them through the app.

Civicus fears that online activism shines a spotlight on very catchy campaigns like the Ice Bucket Challenge and others that involve celebrities, and that these often divert attention away from less catchy and longer-term reform challenges. This creates a "disconnect ... between campaigns that capture the public imagination and those that advance real change."[25] Some fear that crowdfunding is losing its activist edge as it is increasingly taken up by the business sector and professional consultants who advise on raising money through a whole host of initiatives like Seedrs, VentureFounders, Kickstarter and SyndicateRoom. An activist from the Electronic Frontier Foundation warns that the internet no longer works as a benign democratic agora but has turned into a commerce-oriented shopping mall.

If some say online activism celebrates hyperindividualism and undermines the collective ethos of traditional activism, others fear it is generating conformist group-think. Often it overamplifies the most strident voices and pressures others into accepting uniform views that now get disseminated so widely they iron out healthy political variation. Some futurologists see technology gradually emasculating the whole centrality of the free-willed individual and undermining this crucial cornerstone of humanism and political liberalism. Only a few key individuals are needed to oversee the technological management of these systems, and the vast majority of citizens are absorbed into a mass dataflow that increasingly determines choices, outlooks, and actions. Critics warn that current trends are not so much about technology giving activists greater power over politics as they are about politics as a whole losing control of events and of individuals.[26]

A step further in such tensions is that many of the right-wing and illiberal civic groups chronicled in previous chapters have risen on the back of ICT tools. Digital technology offers a platform of magnified influence to groups espousing intolerance, violence, illiberal politics, and ethnic separation. Nationalist Buddhist groups used social media to stir up hatred against the Rohingya minority in Myanmar. In many Western states, so-called identitarian movements are now among the most successful users of ICT for their campaigns against immigration. Conversely, ICT is displacing some of the key mainstream liberal media outlets that in previous decades played prominent roles in supporting democratic transitions.

Another widely cited example: ICT tools amplified Islamic State's appeal and have given the organization a disproportionately high global prominence.[27] IS manages several production companies for professional preparation of the audiovisuals it puts onto social media. Managers of Telegram, the messaging app used by IS, are in an uphill battle as they remove dozens of sites linked to the group every day. Some terrorism experts classify today's loose networks of radicalized jihadists as a new type of social movement that relies heavily on a sophisticated deployment of ICT tools, very different from the rigidly structured terror groups of the past and more akin to the fluid forms of protest that have formed around other issues in recent years.[28] The former Google employee Wael Ghonim, who was one of the initiators of Egypt's 2011 revolution, turned against social media, feeling it had ultimately been of greater help to radical Islamists and the military than to centrist democrats.[29]

Engaging the already engaged

Related to this, even those with a generally upbeat view of cyberactivism admit to doubts over how far it has expanded the circle of engaged citizens. The core promise of digital democracy is to widen the number of citizens involved in political decision making. But the number of those who are aware of and use these tools continues to be relatively limited. Indeed, in many cases cybercampaigns still attract even fewer people than are involved in classical NGOs and political parties. Most cyberactivists admit that the number of citizens who take advantage of new tools—like the platforms that local administrations offer to invite proposals from citizens—is often very small. Many new ICT tools are moving ahead with great sophistication but are not yet anywhere near being instruments of mass engagement.

A 2013 Pew Research Center survey in the US found that well-educated and better-off people are more likely to be involved in online activism—as they have generally been more likely to be engaged in offline, party, and NGO campaigns. The results of this survey suggested that online and offline activists were not two separate groups of people; digital activism seems to be adding a new set of tools for those already engaged in activism, as opposed to creating a new pool of civic activists.[30] Recent quantitative studies show that the relatively wealthy, young, and well educated have so far been more likely to use online voting, largely because they are more au fait with the internet and trust it to a greater extent than do other sections of society.[31] In another empirical study, civic-tech experts found that these platforms have not yet widened citizen participation sufficiently to overcome inequalities in political engagement; moreover, ICT platforms tend to succeed where reformers inside government already support reform and are willing to partner with digital activism for their own aims of managerial efficiency in service delivery.[32]

Talk to the organizers of the many "citizens assembly" platforms now in operation and they are likely to admit that those using them are often the "usual suspects" from more established NGOs and traditional forms of political organization. In Paris's 2016 participative budget process, sixty-seven thousand voted on how to spend the allocated €500 million euros—less than 2 percent of the city's total population. A study of the burgeoning civic-tech sphere in France found that in the febrile electoral atmosphere of early 2017 when the National Front was riding high, online apps tended to exclude those sectors fed up with the established political parties even more than traditional offline activism did.[33] Civic-tech participation is often self-selecting, not part of any formalized democratic process.

Ironically, the more ICT spreads beyond its early phase, the more it may lose some of its advantages: the very proliferation of digital voices and sites can fragment messaging and make it harder to mobilize really large numbers.[34] One expert notes that social media have led to segregation rather than a healthy agora, and to a "disintegration of the general will."[35] One civic-tech leader admits "we have learnt that social trust can only be built offline," in parallel with online activism. As algorithms increasingly drive social media in a way that reinforces people's preexisting preferences, this militates further against a widened pool of cross-cutting political engagement. Tim Berners-Lee, the founder of the web, has written about this self-selecting narrowing of political debate representing one of the major challenges ahead for online activism.[36]

Critics fear that digital technologies may be widening economic inequalities and concentrating power in fewer hands. Richer citizens are more likely to be involved in digital activism than poorer citizens. Digital activism presumes a certain degree of acquisitive well-being that offline activism does not require. The phenomenon of "digital exclusion" has become a staple part of debates among technology experts and activists. The United Nations now compiles an E-Participation Index, which measures the use of online tools to promote citizens' access to information and involvement in government decision making. This index demonstrates that digital activism is related strongly to levels of wealth; the top ten states in the list are all rich, the bottom ten all extremely poor. This implies that such tools are widening differences in activism rather than allowing the developing world to catch up.[37]

Stuck at the local level?

There is a widespread feeling among activists that ICT has proved itself most useful and effective in highly localized activities and campaigns. There is greater doubt about how suited digital technologies are to scaling up civic activism from the local to the national or international level. Most impact is felt in relation to local-level issues, not controversial national-level questions. So far, it has helped improve standards of municipal public-sector management far more than it has influenced macrolevel trends in democracy. The use of big data in "smart cities" is crucial but not the same thing as wider democratic participation. One smart-city activist reports that the challenge of democratic accountability has not yet been married to smart-technology solutions for transport policies, antipollution controls, energy efficiency, and the like.

Some optimists suggest that e-participation initiatives are slowly beginning to move from the local to national level and attract larger circles of voters.[38] But such trends are no more than incipient and sporadic. The irony is that in an age of digital technologies that break through spatial limitations in social mobilization, more and more activism is highly localized—perhaps the very opposite of what we might have expected from digital activism's spread.

One example of this relates to participatory budgeting. Digital technologies have been used to expand the scope of the participatory budgeting offered by local administrations. This is generally regarded as a great success and lies at the heart of city-level advances in activism. However, there is a huge step from citizens making online inputs into what kind of local services should be prioritized within municipal budgets to their influencing the broader contours of economic policy. The challenge of economic policy lies not simply in voting how to spend already collected money but in deciding how to raise that money in the first place. Online platforms have not yet got a hold on having citizens decide on the right balance between taxes and spending, or how to distribute both the costs and benefits of public policies. Digital-skeptics complain that the lesson from participatory budgeting is that citizens have limited understanding of what their spending proposals imply for overarching national economic policy.

Instrumental debate?

In many spheres it is not clear whether cyberactivists are really interested in a wider, more pluralistic *process* of policy decision making or in one particular set of *end goals*. Much cyberactivism is so entrenched in one particular set of aims that it can sometimes appear to lack the very pluralism it advocates for the rest of society. It is striking that activists running new online political apps stress these are designed to build consensus, bridge differences, and link issue concerns together—but in practice they then deploy the technology for highly confrontational actions on very specific issues and seek to advance strongly adversarial positions.

One illustration: in many initiatives there is a close association between the use of ICT and anticapitalism activism. One may agree or disagree with activists' aims of challenging capitalistism and neoliberalism—my point here is not to judge this—but it is significant that their focus is on a particular substantive goal more than a qualitatively different kind of democratic debate bringing together contrasting viewpoints for mutual learning and compromise. On the other hand, if the reform or overturn of capitalism is the declared aim, then in some senses cyberactivism is not nearly radical *enough*. It offers little indication of exactly how a modest amount of online voting can be expected to have such far-reaching, systemic effects.

The same is true of rightist civic activism. While many civic-tech tools have been used by progressive groups to allow citizens to vote for new public services options, conservative-illiberal groups use the same tools for less progressive causes that are more about restricting rather than enlarging rights. When such a prospect appears, progressives can become more ambivalent about the value of online tools in deciding local issues. Both rightist and leftist activists celebrate digital activism as and where it abets their own agendas, without being especially positive toward its potential for transversal, bridge-building deliberation. Neither makes much apparent link from digital activism to any underlying theory of structural change in social, economic, or political relations.

Vulnerability and control

As the technologies of digital activism have evolved, their darker flip side has come increasingly to the fore: namely, the fact that they seem to help state surveillance and multinational interests just as much as they empower the individual citizen. The Freedom House *Freedom on the Net* survey reports that internet freedom has been decreasing since 2010. An increasing number of governments use "keyboard armies" or "trolls"—paid online agitators—to manipulate web content, spread fake news and progovernment views, and attack government critics.[39] Scholars call this phenomenon "astroturfing," a government-sponsored counterweight to grassroots civic activism.[40]

China has one of the most restrictive environments for digital activism. Online platforms such as YouTube, Google, Facebook, and WordPress used by civic activists elsewhere are blocked in China, and authorities also heavily censor domestic platforms and even private text messages. The Chinese government blocked the name of Liu Xiaobo, the Nobel Prize–winning human rights defender who was jailed for digital activism in 2009 and died of cancer in prison in July 2017, from searches on Chinese social media platforms. The so-called 50 Cent Party of trained and hired online propaganda producers has existed and grown steadily since 2005.

In Russia, the government orchestrates cyberattacks against independent media and civic activists' online accounts. Russian trolls hit the global headlines after they tried to influence the US presidential elections in 2016, but they were active within Russia long before that, helping to discredit opposition to the Putin government. The government obliges operators to provide them with access to activists' and journalists' private information. The Russian authorities also block online resources that are used for civic mobilization. They put pressure on Russian and foreign internet platforms to store users' data in Russia; LiveJournal, a Russian-owned blogging platform, moved its servers from the US to Russia and banned "political solicitation." The government forced the Yandex.Money platform that was used for crowdfunding by opposition activists to ban money transfers for political purposes. While digital activism has been an important part of the Russian protest movement, it has struggled to scale up from very small islands of online exchanges to a level capable of pushing back against these and other government tactics.[41]

Other governments have increasingly followed Russia and China. In 2017 Freedom House found that thirty countries out of sixty-five that it analyzed attempted to control online discussions in this manner. Techniques have become more advanced, in particular because government trolls are using search algorithms to increase their visibility and penetration into trusted content. In Venezuela, President Maduro created "digital militias" to spread progovernment messages. Twitter has been used extensively in Venezuela to spread disinformation about the opposition, NGOs, and antigovernment protests. In Turkey, the ruling AK party hired six thousand people to manipulate online discussions and attack government critics.[42] Indonesia has a Muslim Cyber Army to protect religious morals through online tactics. The Vietnamese government has put together a ten-thousand-strong cyberwarfare unit to defend the communist regime. The Egyptian regime closed down over five hundred websites over 2017 and 2018.

Along with content manipulation through paid online commentators and automated accounts, many governments are also resorting more frequently to "hard-power" techniques of blocking and removing online content and criminalizing digital activism under the pretext of national security and the fight against terrorism. In Thailand, under the pretext of protecting national security, the authorities have tightened the country's Computer Crime Law, increasing punishment for loosely defined cyberoffenders.[43]

In places like Bahrain and Ethiopia, online activism has left activists vulnerable because government hackers have been able to track down civil society leaders more easily; the digital technology that these activists initially celebrated has been turned cruelly against them. Several internet multinationals have been caught out in countries like China for refusing to protect activists' personal details from highly repressive regimes. One new trend is of governments creating false online campaigns to trick real activists into signing on and thus exposing themselves to government surveillance software. Regimes have also used new technologies to assist antidemocratic coups, often outweighing any gains from the use of online petitions and the like for minor local decisions.[44]

Social media make it easier for governments to locate and track citizens while seducing activists into overplaying their hand—making them think conditions are ripe for revolt when the basic groundwork has not been done and thus leaving activist groups exposed to government repression.[45] Digital surveillance can be especially controlling in this sense at the local level.[46] Experts admit that the use of big data and digital technology in elections, though it has helped get more voters registered and spread information about candidates, has so far struggled to help make sure elections are actually meaningful, or free and fair.

Against this backdrop, a whole new agenda of antisurveillance now animates civic activism—which feels much more defensive than in the early days of digital campaigns. Ironically, much sensitive action is being pushed offline and back to traditional methods, with activists trying to evade internet controls as these become more intrusive. European companies are still among the biggest suppliers of surveillance technology to nondemocratic regimes; in 2018 the European Parliament proposed restrictions on such exports in an attempt to bear down on this problem.

Many debates among activists are now about the control of data and the difficult task of striking a balance between open availability and privacy. Activists' deepening concern is that large IT multinationals are gaining most from the rollout of new technologies for initiatives such as that for smart cities. They fear

Box 6.1 **Combating digital counteractivism**

A fast-developing area of civic work is that of protecting online activism from hacking, government surveillance, and the control of large multinationals. A whole area of activism, now growing exponentially, operates through organizations that focus on protecting "digital users at risk" and offering emergency help for activists suffering malware attacks. A few notable examples from hundreds of such initiatives include the following.

Access Now protects and promotes the digital rights of users at risk around the world. With offices on four continents, it aims to advance laws and global norms in the area of digital rights and online security by developing rights-respecting practices. It runs a 24/7 Digital Security Helpline to support civic activists, journalists, and human rights defenders. It also provides grants to organizations protecting digital rights: in 2017 it supported nearly fiftiy organizations and activists in twenty-six countries.[47]

Founded in 2003, the *Tactical Technology Collective* is a nonprofit organization headquartered in Berlin that aims to advance the skills, tools, and techniques of rights advocates in their work with information and communications. Each year it reaches thousands of activists, human rights defenders, and journalists through training courses and workshops, as well as millions more through its website, toolkits, guides, and awareness-raising videos. Tactical Tech helps civic activists protect their digital privacy and security.

Benetech is a Silicon Valley–based nonprofit company that develops software for social good and works to promote education and human rights, protect the environment, and reduce poverty. Benetech has developed free open source software and provides training for human rights defenders in over fifty countries on how to record and protect sensitive data.

The *Information Safety and Capacity* (ISC) Project assists civil society organizations and independent media to build their defensive capacity in information security. Mentoring and support services provided by the ISC Project include assistance with attacks or forced closure of websites, the monitoring of email traffic and computer infection by malware and viruses, and the recording of text messaging and mobile telephone conversations.

International human rights NGOs such as *Front Line Defenders*, *Article 19*, and *Protection International* now include digital protection in their capacity-building programs and tools for human rights activists worldwide and in their global advocacy agendas. Front Line Defenders organizes

(*continued*)

Box 6.1 continued

training for human rights activists and provides one-to-one assistance through a network of digital consultants based in different regions of the world; it also gives digital protection grants to fund protective equipment and software. Similarly, media NGOs such as the Committee to Protect Journalists and the Centre for Investigative Journalism run courses on information and technology security for journalists and media workers at risk.

Founded in 2012 by the Freedom Online Coalition, the *Digital Defenders Partnership* (DDP) aims to keep the internet free from emerging threats. The DDP provides funding and services to bloggers, cyberactivists, and journalists, including emergency grants to activists under attack as well as long-term funding for organizations' capacity building. It also runs the Hivos Digital Integrity Fellowship, which deploys digital security consultants for six to eight months to civil society organizations that need assistance. The DDP has developed a Digital First Aid Kit, an online guide to deal with the most common types of digital threats.

The Engine Room supports civic activists enhance their digital security. It has been involved in upgrading *LevelUp*, a global community of digital security trainers, educators, and practitioners that aims to "help the helpers." Its mission is to improve the quality of training provided to journalists, human rights defenders, and other individuals by generating shared cyberstandards, collaborative regional networks, and educational resources to counter online threats.

The *Virtual Road* is a project of Qurium—the Media Foundation, based in Sweden, which provides secure hosting to major independent news media in Azerbaijan, Sri Lanka, Burma, Rwanda, and Nigeria. *Bellingcat* is a digital forensics initiative that carries out crowd-sourced fact-checking. *First Draft News* undertakes fact-checking of digital media and on social networks. *Civicus* runs a project trying to get online data generation back into the hands of citizens and away from large companies.

The *Electronic Frontier Alliance* is an information-sharing network comprised of grassroots groups promoting digital rights, with a shared commitment to the principles of free expression, security, privacy, creativity, and access to knowledge. The initiative defends civil liberties in the digital sphere by linking grassroots activism to technology development. *Digital Rights Watch* was founded in 2016 to uphold citizens' digital rights in Australia. Many civic-tech activists have developed companies providing digital security services, with examples including Security-in-a-Box, Signal, the Guardian Project, and Me and My Shadow.

> Recognizing a broader strategic dimension to these challenges, the *Coalition against Unlawful Surveillance Exports* (CAUSE) campaigns against Western sales of digital platforms that help regimes control activism. Reflecting the gravity of these challenges, governments and digital activists have in some instances moved closer. French and Dutch security agencies developed relatively successful counteroperations to neutralize Russian attempts to influence the countries' respective elections in 2017—with governments and civic actors working together through a combination of defensive IT measures, efforts to counter fake news, and raising awareness.[48]

that hegemonic providers are better able to determine social choices. Five US corporations—Amazon, Apple, Facebook, Google, and Microsoft—now exercise an astonishing degree of control over opinion formation. Activists are split over whether these corporations can be persuaded to change their rules or whether it is now more productive to start circumventing social media. The latter, pessimistic view gained currency after the controversy in 2018 involving the mercurial consultancy Cambridge Analytica and its mass harvesting of data from Facebook clients. Experts worry about the "privatization of digital governance" menacing open democratic debate and about the growing power of algorithms to evade political accountability.[49]

As the dominant narrative is increasingly one of fake news, misinformation, and hacking, social media and the web seem to have morphed into something that endangers rather than improves civic activism. Such is the scale of this problem that dozens of new civic initiatives have emerged to defend the integrity of online activism and debate. A whole branch of new digital activism is now simply about limiting the negative effects of digital technologies. In this sense, much new civic activism is a form of damage-limitation counteractivism rather than a new avenue of positive empowerment. "Box 6.1: Combating digital counteractivism" outlines some examples of this.

The next phase of digital activism

As digital activism moves out of its first flush of youth, its next, more mature phase of development will center on addressing these shortcomings. Digital activism is going through a process of adjustment; cyberutopianism has evaporated, but it is important to resist going too far the other way in underestimating online activism's benefits. Many technology experts see digital activism to be on the threshold of a new stage, in which more finely tuned strategies will be needed to safeguard the benefits of online civic and political activity.

This new phase will entail a number of challenges. An overriding imperative will be to connect online activism with other forms of civil society activity in a more mutually reinforcing way. Cyberactivism is likely to be more effective the more it feeds into rather than displacing offline protest and activism. Experts concur that detailed analytical work is now most needed on this online-offline connection—how to make it work and how to measure the resulting impact.[50]

Change is beginning to take shape along these lines. A new generation of online apps is moving beyond stand-alone cyberactivism. It is rather about using apps to get people engaged in practical political engagement. This kind of technology is now not simply about providing for the e-voting of isolated citizens within individual, standalone initiatives. Instead of this, the emerging talk among activists is of hybrid models that combine direct and representative democracy. Experts argue this next phase must be about governments and citizens using digital technology to solve problems together—a decisive step up from the current pattern of often ineffectual and sporadic online petitions.[51] Increasingly, activists aim to ensure that online activity leads into the formation of thick bonds of activism offline, rather than being a diversion from such relationships.[52] Arab activists talk about the need to "return to relational activism" alongside digital strategies.[53]

Some platforms are moving in this direction. The Your Priorities application has been used in Estonia, Iceland, and Romania, including by parties and governments, to discover voters' policy priorities; this enables citizens to debate online with other civic and political actors, and then to link such debates to current opportunities in mainstream political processes. MySociety has been used by local authorities in the UK in a similar fashion and aims to be a "booster shot" for those who are active in politics or local affairs, connecting online activity with communal or collective forms of action.[54] Other platforms that move in this direction include Challenge.gov, which enlists citizens to help solve key policy challenges in the US, and vTaiwan, which was developed in the wake of the Sunflower Movement protests to use digital platforms to bring activists and state officials together for offline deliberation.

In Madrid, digital activists say their aim now is to combine their highly successful online platform with offline deliberation, using the data generated through the website Decide Madrid to gather together groups of citizens who share similar concerns. Another aim is to push down the threshold for citizen proposals to trigger some kind of response through mainstream political processes; the current threshold is so high that twenty thousand proposals have resulted in only two policy changes. The Madrid activists working on this have become more measured about the potential of their work: they see digital activism and small-format deliberation involving ordinary citizens as a means of getting onto the agenda possible policy change and ideas, which will then need other means of democratic legitimation.

A growing number of initiatives allow citizens to have direct contact online with politicians and give the latter a space to explain their policies. Brazil has an e-Democracia platform that connects citizens to elected politicians. In France, a Parlement et Citoyens platform allows citizens to contribute ideas to parliamentarians in response to particular issues being debated in the National Assembly; SmartGov synthesizes the results and then hosts a public debate between citizens and legislators in an online discussion, with the latter proposing new bills based on the outcome. In Estonia, Rahvakogu is an online platform for crowdsourcing ideas and proposals for improving Estonian democracy, created by the state in partnership with civil society. After two thousand proposals were submitted online in 2013, these were fed into a public meeting on so-called Deliberation Day, at which three hundred citizens selected sixteen of the best ideas to be formally presented to the assembly by the president. Similar platforms exist in other countries.[55]

A related challenge is to scale up the highly localized use of ICT. Civic activists are exploring how to move beyond campaigns that focus on cleaning the local park, saving the neighborhood school, or organizing community watch schemes against crime. The local focus is a comparative advantage in terms of what digital technology has contributed to politics in the last decade. But it is also an Achilles' heel, to the extent that extremely repressive regimes can be quite content to let activism blossom and succeed in developing local services, well away from really controversial and sensitive national-level political questions. After all, these local achievements can take some of the weight off central authorities and give civic actors scope to let off their critical steam without threatening regimes' power bases.

Some initiatives are moving in the direction of combining local and national tactics. More groups are trying to draw on the model of MoveOn in the US and GetUp! in Australia that are mobilizing citizens at multiple levels for social change through a mix of online and offline activism. In 2016, GetUp! mobilized thousands of people in Australia through online and offline campaigns to protest the deportation of asylum-seekers. In the UK, the membership-based 38 Degrees group campaigns through a mix of highly local and nationwide efforts on national issues ranging from healthcare reform to saving public forests. Members are asked to use one tactic: sign a petition, send a message to their elected representative, or raise awareness via social media. The organization has a network of local groups that meet up locally to feed ideas into national campaigns.[56]

In Poland, Akcja Demokracja was set up in 2015 to organize nationwide advocacy campaigns. It mobilizes thousands of people by combining online petitioning and social media awareness with mass protests across the country on issues like environmental protection and judicial independence.[57] In Romania, DeClic has become the country's first platform for online campaigning; it is multi-issue, nimble, and reactive and makes a virtue of combining online and offline activism.[58] The emerging twin approach of many such initiatives is to mobilize communities in traditional ways around local issues while using digital activism to broaden campaigns at a national level.

In these crucial ways, digital activism shows incipient signs of adapting and moving into a new phase of its development. As it moves in new directions, it is responding to new threats and restrictions but also correcting many of ICT's shortcomings and vulnerabilities that have become evident in recent years. These shortcomings are serious but should not be blamed for all democracy's difficulties. It is perhaps becoming convenient for governments to complain about social media amplifying nondemocratic, illiberal, or extremist opinion when the roots of these views lie in governments' own failures. The key will be more fully to integrate debates about digital technology and digital activism into other areas of democratic reform, rather than treating these as an area apart from "normal" politics. Further progress and rethinking will be required if digital forms are to foster an activism that is fully inclusive; dovetails better with other civil society and political activity, is capable of long-term strategic deliberation, and can resist a full array of nondemocratic influences.

7

Boon or bane for global democracy?

An overarching conceptual question is what the emerging forms of civic activism mean for democracy. Do they improve upon traditional forms of democratic practice and usher in better forms of political accountability? Or do they undercut some of the necessary features of successful democracy building? Do they ensure that a wider range of citizens engages in politics, or do they simply bring turmoil to political debate at the hands of a few destructive opportunists? Is the new civic activism an antidote to the rise of illiberal populism or part of what drives this?

This chapter lays out the diametrically opposed views that exist on these questions. Many analysts see new fluid civic movements as democracy's potential savior and as pioneers of a participative politics that moves beyond a failing template of traditional representative democracy. Conversely, critics believe these movements and protesters are making healthy democratic deliberation increasingly difficult. I argue for a nuanced interpretation, suggesting that the new civic activism is neither democracy's lifeline nor its gravedigger. Its effect depends on a number of other variables; its impact on democracy can be either good or bad, depending on how it combines with these other factors.

Reinvigorated democracy

Champions of the new civic activism are driven by a conviction that it represents a benign change for democracy. They attribute to it several democratic advantages.

Mobilization. Supporters of informal types of activism insist that these are more effective in bringing down authoritarian regimes than traditional advocacy NGOs. They suggest that many recent democratic breakthroughs have primarily been the result of mass mobilization and driven by locally rooted movements, with foreign-funded NGOs playing very little role.[1] Some analysts believe this calls for a paradigm shift in how democratization is theorized.[2] Statistical studies link recent revolts to economic collapse and suggest that the new age of activism tilts the analytical balance back toward understanding democratic breakthroughs as the result of diffuse mobilization rather than smooth modernization.[3] The implication is that the new activism acts as a decisive and necessary conduit for democratic demands and is part of the reason why advances in political reforms have been witnessed in all regions in the last decade—the success stories shown in chapter 4.

Participation. A related argument is that the new activism widens democratic participation. For many of those involved, the emerging activism is about advancing a preference for participative democracy over existing indirect channels of accountability.[4] This is a democracy that is about not simply protecting individual rights but also according citizens the capacity and effective independence to hold decision makers accountable.[5] Protests do not function as a substitute for other forms of participation but increasingly feed into additional democratic innovations. The emergent activism is tied to the spread of citizens' assembles and other participative forums.[6] The prominent theorist John Keane argues that this expansive participation denotes a new and promising form of "monitory democracy."[7]

Representational claims. Many analysts argue that today's new citizen activism ensures more faithful reflection of citizen interests. They celebrate it as an integral part of an incipient shift toward "postrepresentative" democracy. Direct action and self-help organizations reflect people's search for a "nonmediated" form of political accountability. Loose organizational structures today better capture citizens' interests, even though they do not "represent" them in the same way as political parties have long aspired to do; rather, they embody "antirepresentational representation." The new activism involves a whole new type of "representational claim." It is so important because it flows from deep-rooted social shifts such as the loss of traditional authority and the disappearance of fixed, inherited identities.[8]

Deliberation. The emergent civic activism heralds not only heightened citizen participation but also the gradual formation of more deeply rooted democratic identities.[9] Many new civic groups are self-consciously based on consensual deliberation. Some analysts insist a new wave of effective deliberative democracy is spreading through activists' more open and inclusive styles of debating. While experts originally tended to see social movements as somewhat inimical to noncontentious deliberation, newer forms of community activism have increasingly built themselves around better-quality deliberative dynamics.[10] Countering the view that contentious participation and deliberative democracy sit uneasily together, supporters of the new civic activism insist it has facilitated both deeper deliberation and wider participation in a way that is mutually reinforcing.[11]

Direct democracy. New citizen initiatives have been instrumental in getting a huge number of new direct or semidirect democracy instruments enshrined into law: one database records that there are now over 1,500 mechanisms of direct democracy operating in more than a hundred countries.[12] Within the long-running debate about the virtues and drawbacks of direct democracy, a key distinction is between direct democracy mechanisms generated by citizens and those deployed for self-serving purposes by elites. The emerging civic activism is generating more of the former, with encouraging repercussions for contemporary democracy. Today's positive examples of direct democracy entail citizen engagement and debate that extend beyond instrumentalized yes-no referendums.[13]

Practical civility. The kind of practical self-help activism that the book has observed also contributes to improved democracy. It has been suggested that this kind of activism points the way toward "circular democracy"—something different from both the "vertical" politics pursued through single political parties and the purely "horizontal" confrontation of archetype social movements. This is circular in the sense of expanding an everyday, problem-solving praxis of democracy and seeing more democratic social relations as an end in themselves.[14] Activists involved in municipal government insist that participation in relation to very local issues is a form of "citizenship training" that leads to people thinking in wider terms about the health of democracy and broader societal interests beyond their own narrow preferences. Notwithstanding its radical discourse, the new activism is often aimed not at overturning "the system" but at getting the system to work more fairly in relation to undramatic day-to-day concerns.

Democratic variation. Non-NGO forms of civic activism are widely associated with demands for different models of democracy. There is a growing interest among activists in varieties of democracy that are tailored to local conditions or regional values. The move beyond professional, Western-style advocacy NGOs is often associated with this agenda. Many civic leaders believe that the new civic activism not only offers wider participation and deliberation but also opens the way toward alternative templates of democratic practice that go beyond Western, liberal forms. While this is a complex area of analysis, and it is not always clear that locally specific democratic models are well defined in practice, the search for such variation is an important dimension of the new activism.[15]

In sum, enthusiasts for today's civic activism allege that it adds in many different ways to the health and vibrancy of democratic politics. They argue that it is helping to relegitimize democracy on the basis of loose forms of deliberation and localism, the kind of smaller units better able to defend against centralized institutional power, and an ability to move beyond the traditional, limiting political processes of the nation-state.[16]

Significantly, these assertions find some resonance among both leftists and rightists. New debates have taken shape among radical-progressive theorists, with some insisting that the new activism represents a qualitative renewal of democracy that transcends class divisions and the need for hierarchical political control, and that it points toward a democracy of egalitarian self-activity—against skeptics who say that familiar political power is still required to advance a leftist project.[17]

On the right, many conservatives question the view that nativist-populism is intrinsically undemocratic and point out that in many of its varieties it is rooted in local, citizen movements. While scholars have traditionally conceptualized populism as a top-down phenomenon controlled from above by charismatic political leadership, at least some recent populist movements have grown out of bottom-up civic activism—in fact, on both the right and left.[18] This is so in cases as diverse as the Balkans, Greece, Italy, Israel, and India.[19] One may disagree with the policies adopted by populist parties, but their roots in thick networks of local democratic engagement may add some complicating nuance to the assumption that these trends are purely and irredeemably authoritarian. While hierarchical and conservative cultural values have tended to correlate with less participative models of democracy, some recent studies conclude that new citizen initiatives may have begun to unravel this linkage, to some degree at least.[20]

Distorting democracy

Such are the arguments that assert the new activism's democratic credentials. The passionate conviction that animates this activism is matched, however, by the skepticism of its critics. On the critical side of the equation, a first, very basic point is that some of the new activism is at best ambivalent toward democratic norms. Previous chapters have detailed the rise in all regions of right-wing activism that clearly does menace core liberal democratic values. While many of today's ascendant conservative groups have agendas that are perfectly compatible with democracy, some explicitly question core liberal and/or democratic norms. These include the especially notable examples of rightist activism we have outlined in Poland, Thailand, and Turkey—and probably the United States, too.[21] These kinds of groups seek purist national identities against democratic equality and inclusiveness.

Even if some forms of populism emerge from healthy grassroots activism, many observers fear that these inevitably turn against liberal democracy and betray their participative roots. Some experts insist that, even where they grow out of grassroots civic activism, populists ultimately have an understanding of politics that is inimical to pluralism. This is because they claim to represent "the true people" as a homogenous block and thus can brook no dissenting opinions; it is the populist leader and party that decide what the "will of the people" really is, not grassroots civic movements. This perspective dismisses talk of populist movements representing a benign civic empowerment.[22] Populism promises to take on board the concerns of a wider citizenry, but it does not envisage a governance style infused with vibrant activism—it promises to govern for, but not with or through, ordinary citizens. Such movements worryingly dismiss the need for intermediation mechanisms to link society with democratic institutions.[23]

Democratic ambivalence exists on the left, too. Anarchists behind the Occupy movement expressly refused to engage with a democratic system that they believe loads the dice against parts of the population. Some activists also shun deliberative democracy forums as unduly co-opted and individualized, insisting that the new activism has to be about overturning an entire system rather than fine-tuning liberal democracy.[24] From a radical perspective, the new civic activism needs to be more radical than it has been in challenging established democratic norms. Some critical writers insist that new movements have erred in simply celebrating their own internal nonhierarchical decision-making.[25] Perhaps most colorfully, Slavoj Žižek sums up the disillusionment of those who had held such high hopes for the new activism: "I am fed up of these demonstrations of one million people—they are bullshit. A short period of enthusiasm, where we are all together crying and bonding—and then? Ordinary people see no change."[26]

Overall, some academic volumes argue that once a more expansive notion of civil society is used, broadening out from a sole focus on professional advocacy organizations to include the type of informal initiatives that have become more present in recent years, so the positive link between civic activism and democratization begins to break down: a wider range of civic forms reveals a wider range of stances toward democracy.[27]

In an extended essay on the spread of global protests, the Nobel Prize winner (and political conservative) Mario Vargas Llosa writes of a danger: often in history, protesters have had entirely benign and measured aims, but undemocratic leaders have skillfully taken advantage of them and to move a country away from democracy.[28] If this is a familiar conservative fear of protests, some leftist thinkers similarly fear that new civic pressures have once again raised the Platonic specter of mob rule; they argue that democracy needs to move back toward classical notions of limiting the majority and curtailing the ascendant influence of the wayward masses. In this view, representative democracy urgently needs stronger "filters" against the rise of popular civic movements, as the latter have pushed politics toward unreasoned illiberal excess.[29]

A second concern is that the new civic activism embodies almost the antithesis of the democracy-enhancing qualities that civil society organizations have traditionally been assumed to possess. Fears have long been raised that loose civic movements and mobilizations override the healthy performance of democratic institutions.[30] Today's skepticism is especially strong in relation to activists' apparently growing inclination to protest. Skeptics argue that the explosion of protests denotes a malfunctioning or misfiring of the long-supposed connection between civil society and democratic quality. Today's protests are about atomized and disgruntled individuals and reflect individual demands rather than coherently thought-through group interests. Today's protesters oppose and seek to undermine governmental power, but they invariably have no comprehensive governing manifestos of their own. Critics allege that they oppose austerity or elite corruption but have no systemic alternative worked out.

Detractors say disruption has become an end in itself. They lament that civic movements are today reflexively anti-institutional; they do not seek actively to strengthen the institutional checks and balances of liberal democracy but rather grope toward unfocused direct action as a means of circumventing the channels of representative democracy. Some say that one reason why democratization has slowed or plateaued in recent years is that civic activism today is less organized and less structured, and therefore less effective, than it was in the second and third waves of democratization. A common view is that today's more disruptive forms of civic engagement are inimical to the long and incremental process required for building good-quality and stable democracy.[31] They have been described as "an end run around democracy."[32] Some noted theorists detect the emergence of "negative democracy," resting on collective action that is curiously individualized.[33]

A third worry is that the new activism is profoundly unequal and skewed. One of the most talked-about and apparently important schisms in global politics has opened up between the (supposedly) illiberal-leaning rightism of the industrial working classes and the culturally liberal leftism of the democratic, internationalist middle classes. The new forms of civic participation may be good news for countries' overall democratic-quality scores, but their use is even more unequally distributed than traditional forms of political engagement—that is, the wealthier and better educated use them to become more engaged, while others are left even more isolated from democratic influence.[34]

In Ukraine, for example, some fear that the "reliance on spontaneous and unpredictable protest" in the Maidan uprising has magnified regional divisions within civil society.[35] A more general concern related to this is that new urban movements have little contact with the vast majority of the population that lives in rural communities and is not mobilized in the same overtly political sense. The attention focused on urban protests deflects from the far larger pool of disaffected citizenry living in these more traditional communities—meaning that little consideration has been given to the need to enhance democratic civic capacity at this level.

A fourth doubt exists in relation to how internally democratic the new activism really is. Critics of deliberative democracy insist decision making within community civic groups is just as lopsided and unequal as it is within the formal institutions of representative democracy, and that such efforts to displace the latter have not opened up a healthy deliberative form of participation.[36] Some new-style activists have become disillusioned as they feel that the discourse of leaderless horizontality is often a smoke screen for a small handful of particularly outspoken and forceful activists imposing their agenda and tactical preferences.[37]

While a rich set of participatory and self-help processes has spread in recent years—and is often dubbed "the participative turn"—it has had fairly small-scale or micro impacts rather than contributing to more responsive democracy at a macro level. Skeptics lament that participatory citizen initiatives have gradually become diluted from the originally radical and emancipatory concept of participative democracy. To the extent that citizens get input but without much guarantee of having an effect on decision outputs, there are increasing risks of co-option.

Experts carrying out detailed empirical work argue that participatory budgeting has become a more limited, less inclusive, and less radical practice than activists originally intended.[38] In a sense, the limited effectiveness of formal participatory forums has further undermined the reach of traditional civil society strategies and drives activists even more toward very informal types of organization and action disconnected from channels of democratic representation.[39] Similarly, some new activism unwittingly works against democracy: prodded by new civic groups, authoritarian regimes make concessions that defuse critical activism without threatening the essentially nondemocratic nature of the regime.

Moreover, skeptics say that the new civic activism still struggles to define workable linkages to the institutional processes of representative democracy. Much analytical work on deliberative democracy argues that this must be a complement to, not a substitute for, representative bodies.[40] While most activists might agree with this in principle, they can in practice often neglect operational links to the channels of representative democracy. Critics insist that rather than providing a transmission belt between deliberative citizen forums and the political sphere of parties and government, much of the new activism still embodies a spirit of pure rejectionism. In several countries the new activism has made forming new political parties harder.[41]

Conditional impact

Both the positive and skeptical interpretations have merit; indeed, they are not entirely mutually exclusive. It is necessary not to paint an overly uniform picture of the new civic activism—which may have highly beneficial ramifications for democratic quality in one setting but more problematic consequences in another. Rather than reiterating either very broad-brush praise for new civic initiatives or a generic condemnation of such activism, it is perhaps more fruitful to conceptualize the more specific ways in which this phenomenon is altering democratic practice.

A key consideration is if there is somehow an optimal level of the new activism: that it thickens participatory politics up to a certain point but tips over into pathological chaos if it extends in size, reach, and frequency beyond a certain level. This familiar way of posing the activism dilemma is useful but not sufficient. The evidence presented in previous chapters suggests that it would be unduly simplistic to conclude that innovative civic activism is benign in contained and measured amounts but otherwise dangerous for democracy. Rather, the more useful debates relate to the *qualitative* aspects of this activism. In this spirit, a number of qualitative implications of the new activism are worthy of mention.

Erratic democraticness. The new civic activism makes democracy more unpredictable. It makes the unfolding of certain policy debates less smoothly unilinear. It generates higher peaks of intense civic activity and pressure, but invariably combined with deeper troughs of relative inactivity. It is too bleak to dismiss the new civic activism as pure noise and ineffectual posturing; we have shown a mix of success and failure and many combinations thereof. The new activism enshrines a situation where citizens fix limits to what they find acceptable; it increases the likelihood that large-scale discontent expresses itself when policy outcomes and elite actions fall beyond these red lines. But this situation does not seem to make civic influence or policy changes more preemptive. If anything, problems and frustration are more likely to fester until this activism generates dramatic breakthroughs.

Divergence of political dynamics across policies. The new activism leads to a democracy in which relatively large numbers of citizens engage with and mobilize for some issues but not for others. It widens the contrasts between different policy issues. Some issues lend themselves very much to the new kinds of civic activism: anticapitalist campaigns that want to change the whole system, at one extreme, and relatively mundane, apolitical local issues, at the other extreme. But other issues seem to fall outside the scope of the new activism.

New activist initiatives are tightly focused today on issues of local corruption and the kind of nepotism that distorts and impedes the fair and efficient delivery of community-level services. On this issue, democratic decision making has become more participative and more subject to accountability. Contrast this with the relative absence of new activism in relation to, say, major international crises—the atrocities carried out in Syria, the conflict in the east of Ukraine, or many others. On such external issues, democratic decision making remains relatively opaque and free from the critical gaze of new activism. These are simply illustrative examples, but they suffice to show that an answer to the question of whether the new activism is making democracy more responsive and open will vary enormously depending on the issue at stake.

The new activism is conditioning a formal politics that in turn is also more selective and issue based. The new activists may create new political parties, but these tend to be parties that focus on a certain set of issues rather than offering a comprehensive vision for society. That is, activist-generated political parties are appearing, but these resemble that activism to some extent in an effort to move away from the standard party template. They are parties concerned with galvanizing interest and pressure around certain issues rather than with representing a given class of society in all political matters.[42] An even more acute version of this is when prominent activists today make a move into government without passing through traditional party structure at all: this might be construed both as a more direct form of representation and as a form of politics delinked from holistic party programs.

Variation in democratic forms. The new activism exhibits a wider variation of locally specific forms of democratic practice. This observation may seem counterintuitive. After all, one of the themes running through this book is that there is some degree of similarity in the protests and social campaigns that have occurred in every corner of the world in recent years. Activists in Brazil, Greece, Thailand, Belarus, and Tunisia have used the same kinds of apps and social media tools. Yet because this activism is less dependent on standard templates of professional NGOs or political parties, it opens the door to—and is indeed more reliant upon—locally distinctive models of civic practice.

While some protests in authoritarian states militate for the very basic features of democracy, many of the self-styled new activists agitate for radical alternatives to existing Western liberal democracy. The new civic activism is one element of a wider debate about different models of democracy. This new activism is one factor that has given new life to such debates; in turn, a growing concern among civil society actors with democratic variation is one of the motives behind the formation of new types of civic practice. Many examples could be cited. Civic movements in Bosnia and Herzegovina created community-based plenums as an alternative to party-based representative democracy.[43] In Bolivia and Ecuador, new leftist groups saw their activism as part of a search for an alternative to Western liberal democracy. The same concern has animated many forms of Islamist-based activism around the world.

Shifting local-center relations. The new activism exhibits a combination of the micro and the macro. At a very local level, it has reenergized civic vibrancy; at another level, some civic campaigns have focused on the most macro of political questions, especially leaders' fitness to hold or continue in office. It is clearly the case that a wider variety of civic actors is active today. Some focus on the local level and seek to engage the state in providing effective services and policy changes. Others are clearly more fundamentally against state governmental power, even of a formally democratic kind. Even if it is possible to detect a general shift toward more locally based civil society activity, there is a wide variety in the relationship between localism and national debates across different countries.

The balance of these kinds of activism determines the impact on democracy. In some instances, quite new, innovative, and exciting forms of activism at a local level combine with stasis and institutional conservatism at a national level. Russia might be cited as an example. In some senses, the trend toward hyperlocalism may even be extending too far; if there was insufficient localism some years ago, today the risk might be that expectations are too high for what localism can achieve on its own. The pendulum may sometimes be swinging too far toward a focus on very local types of activism at the expense of national and systemic goals.

In other instances, dramatic breakthroughs are made at the national level, only for reformers to find that old practices continue at the local level and militate against far-reaching democratic change. An example would be Egypt after 2011. Overall, the new activism is pushing toward making democracy a slightly more bottom-up and community-rooted set of practices. In some cases, however, it has channeled attention toward a small number of high-stakes national changes, making democratic reform more of an institution-centered process than previously. Again, the impact varies across different settings.

Democracy of intensely organized informality. While it is often pointed out that civic movements are today about informality rather than formal institutional structures, the evidence suggests that they do not create a purely spontaneous form of democracy. Indeed, the number and layers of civic organizations have multiplied exponentially in recent years; we seem headed not so much toward non-organized activism as toward an intensely organized informal, civic sphere. There is a paradoxical combination of chaotic pluralism, on the one hand, with a proliferation of new civic organizational structures, on the other hand. This multiplicity of forms includes new assemblies, committees, forums, decision circles, dialogues, online votes, chat rooms, and the like. The pool of citizen participation may have widened, but it has also splintered among a much larger number of channels that struggles to agglomerate different views into workable policies. The implication may be an intensely vibrant but fractured democracy.

Regime-neutral pluralism. A broader question, beyond its implications for democracy, is what the new civic activism means for the distinction between democracies and nondemocracies. To some extent, citizen movements and protests now seem to reduce the significance—for civil society activity—of differences between formal regime types. As we have seen, the outcomes and impact of this activism do not divide neatly along a democracies-versus-autocracies dichotomy. The long-standing analysis of regime types—the standard examination of what causes and maintains a democratic regime versus the factors that sustain an authoritarian system—needs to be complemented by a study of dividing lines in types of civic activism. Countries with similar types of political regime may experience different patterns of civic activism; conversely, countries with radically different political regimes may see similar kinds of new civic activism. Egyptian activism had more in common with Spain's Indignados than with the form of civil society activity in other North African states, for example.

Conclusion

It is generally agreed that analytical work has paid insufficient attention to the impact of new activism on the general quality of democracy or the prospects for democratization in authoritarian settings.[44] Work on democratization and democracy support, on the one hand, and the analysis of social movements, grassroots organizations, and digital technology, on the other hand, have developed largely in separation from each other. This is despite their dealing with clearly overlapping subject matter and the new civic activism being one among many factors currently changing the face of modern democracy.

This activism offers new opportunities for democratic renewal but also presents risks to and dilemmas for established channels of democratic representation. While the new activism has its hard-core fans and its inveterate detractors, its effect on democracy is in truth far from predetermined. If the new civic activism has become a phenomenon common to many parts of the world, we need a careful understanding and assessment of its highly differentiated impacts on democracy across these contrasting locations and political settings.

The equation is more complex than pronouncing whether the new civic activism is in some absolute sense good or bad for democracy. The analytical challenge is more subtly to work out how emerging civic activism alters the *type* of democracy that is possible and likely to flourish. The new civic activism will make politics less incremental and gradualist, introduce contrasting political dynamics in different policy domains, cultivate a wider range of local practices, change the relationship between national and local politics, and lead to a multiplication of active civic sites.

The new civic activism is not axiomatically good or bad for democracy but will increasingly change the way democracy functions. It will alter the way we need to measure and understand high-quality, fair, inclusive, and effective political process. Its democratic outcome will depend on its own trajectory but also on the way that other civic and political actors react to the changes the new activism brings in its wake. In this vein, the transformed civic activism raises complex questions about the relationship between participation and direct democracy. In recent years there have been instances of direct democracy without deeper participatory movements and, conversely, of new participatory forums not leading to more direct democratic input. The new activism faces a challenge in resolving these disconnects if it is to be part of a more holistic agenda of democratic betterment.

There is much impatience and disappointment that the new activism seems to have failed in its quest to reinvent democracy. It has often pushed governments to revisit certain policies but has not unlocked far-reaching democratic renewal. Pessimists fear the moment for radical change has passed; civic movements continue to thrive, and protests rumble on, but the intense crescendo of new activism around 2011 and 2012 has not served as a stepping-stone to a whole new paradigm of participative politics. Many activists have turned to localism precisely because they feel frustrated at the lack of such a breakthrough at the systemic level.

However, such despair is not fully warranted. More recent trends tell us that the new activism has not run its course and is beginning surreptitiously to weave its way into the shifting sands of democratic practice around the world. Many of the expectations that it could in short order entirely reconstitute democratic politics may have been overblown. But this does not mean that the search for alternative forms of civic engagement has been ineffective or that these forms do not add important ingredients to democracy's future evolution.

8

International support for civic activism

Moving the analysis from the conceptual terrain to policy-oriented questions, this chapter explores what the new civic activism means for international support to civil society. Donor governments and international organizations have been questioning their heavy reliance on traditional NGOs for a number of years, yet they have struggled to come to grips with the emergence of new forms of civic activism. The chapter explains why this is the case, uncovering donor concerns about the new activism's more contentious agendas, the practical difficulties of channeling support to such diffuse civic actors, and many activists' own ambivalence about accepting outside funding. I argue that if donors are to keep pace with the new civic activism, they will need to revise some fundamental tenets of their civil society support.

The need for adjustment

A well-established criticism is that aid donors unduly favor the kind of formal NGOs that pursue aims driven by international powers rather than domestic civil society. Indeed, so close is the association of international donors with this kind of NGO sector that aid agencies are widely seen as an integral part of what has gone wrong with the old civic activism. There is widespread agreement that international assistance has been too focused on a narrow, sometimes exclusive conception of what civil society is, based on Western-style nongovernmental organizations, and that this produces an unhelpful "NGO-ization" of civic activism.

Concerns about donors' inadequate attention to wider conceptions and forms of civic activism have dogged the civil society assistance field for years. Aid agencies retort that these standard criticisms, replayed in hundreds of articles and evaluations, are a caricature. Donors have been aware for many years of NGOs' shortcomings. The United Nations Civil Society and Social Movements research program notes that donors have cooled toward standard, well-known

NGOs at least since the early 2000s as they have realized that big, formal organizations are not well suited to deliver aid effectively to local communities.[1]

Despite recognizing a need for change, however, in practice aid agencies have not shifted their funding from professional NGOs to back emergent civic activism in any significant measure. Overall, donors have made only limited changes to their civil society support. Notwithstanding the growing doubts over old-style activism, most civil society aid still goes to traditional NGOs. In private, most aid agency representatives admit that they are still not set up to support informal activism. Officials from large international organizations like the various UN bodies involved in civil society support can, in conversation, still be highly skeptical about the significance of the new civic activism.

Indeed, Civicus reports that donors seem increasingly conservative and unwilling to take risks with new civic groups. The organization reports that only 1 percent of total development aid goes directly to civil society organizations in the Global South, even after many years of donors committing to "local ownership" and grassroots support. This low figure militates against engagement with the new activism.[2] Major international NGOs admit that in their development projects they are at an early stage in "linking with others—social movements, trade unions, digital communities and faith-based organizations—the transient and the established."[3]

People within aid agencies reflecting on how and whether to support new forms of civic activism admit there has been little overarching policy guidance on this question. It is even unclear if the development community has a solid conception of the distinction between NGOs and social movements, or between social movements and looser forms of civic activism.[4] As one EU diplomat puts it, "We still think in terms of funding 'civil society' and not citizens' engagement."

Donors still have only a small number of programs for "active citizenship," to train citizens in how to use the new tools of modern activism in a democratic way. Some donors insist they now support individuals mainly on a sporadic basis, and this is more effective than searching for new "movements" as such. Very little overseas development assistance goes directly to the city level where a lot of the new civic activism is based. Donors also admit that they are still struggling to build links between new activists and other actors like parties and parliaments—and are generally reluctant to push hard for such links.

A Danish government study acknowledged in 2012 that a "challenge is posed by civil society action worldwide changing from organization-based to nonformal and spontaneous [activity], with evidence that people increasingly want to engage *on their own terms* rather than through conventional CSOs." The agency recognized that this has huge implications for aid funding, implying a need to look beyond traditional support of individual NGOs to "facilitate citizen and community empowerment activism." The study found that donors are gradually "adopting a more pluralistic approach to CSOs, by increasing recognition and support beyond the traditional CSOs to include, for example, activist forums, faith-based groups and professional associations." But it also concluded that donors still limit this shift by preferring formally registered civic organizations, looking for very concrete and quantifiable results, not basing funding decisions on a detailed mapping of informal groups, and being reluctant to support confrontational rather than collaborative activities.[5]

A selection of overarching trends reveals this caution. In particular, donor support for protests has been tepid, at best. The movements that gave rise to the so-called Colored Revolutions in Central and Eastern Europe received some Western support to build their core capacity and infrastructure. In Serbia, the revolutionary student movement Otpor received technical and strategic support from US-based organizations.[6] In Ukraine, North American and European donors supported protest organizations in the lead-up to the 2004 Orange Revolution and again in 2014.[7] Yet in all these cases, international support was relatively limited and reactive, and it did not follow any broadly defined strategy of identifying and backing new forms of civic activism. In recent protests from Armenia to Venezuela, and from Iran to Russia, the default EU line has been simply to call for "dialogue" between the government and protesters and to steer clear of actively supporting the activists.

Some donors have offered modest support for loosely organized indigenous rights movements in Latin America. A number of Western governments have funded organizations working on indigenous issues, most notably Germany, Denmark, Norway, the Netherlands, and Canada. In Bolivia, several donors supported indigenous social movements that morphed into Evo Morales's Movimiento al Socialismo political party.[8] Yet beyond showing concern with indigenous rights in the region, donors have done relatively little to help remodel activism per se.

Trends in the Middle East are even more revealing. In Syria, donors still shun the local bodies that are better able than the large international relief organizations to reach out to small communities. Nor has the international community pushed governments in Jordan, Lebanon, and Turkey to provide more secure status and space for these informal civic bodies. Concerns over the supposed infiltration of radical elements into new movements have led the international community increasingly to disengage from this most dynamic strand of bottom-up civic activism across the Mashriq. Similar patterns can be seen in Libya and Yemen. Palestinian activists complain that a new generation of community-based civic movements is failing to gain international backing because donors remain wedded to backing NGOs supportive of the Palestinian Authority's commitment to peace talks with Israel. Across the Middle East, Western countries' counterterrorism legislation is leading them to cut support for many new activists, fearing any link radicals might have with such groups.

The spirit of the Arab revolts has lived on in civic initiatives consciously prioritizing domestic constituencies and stakeholders and distancing themselves from international funders. The most vibrant parts of Arab civil society today do not rush to international meetings or seek partners abroad; rather, they adhere expressly to a more locally based agenda that stresses their autonomy from such global factors. Western donors have engaged with many state-sponsored "moderate" Islamist organizations but have generally declined to run initiatives for the newer, more autonomous Islamist community groups that have emerged across the Middle East and North Africa in recent years.[9]

In a very generic sense, international organizations and Western powers have also failed to incorporate new kinds of activism into their peace-building strategies. For all the rhetoric about locally oriented peace work, international actors still underplay grassroots civic actors and their organic efforts at reconciliation. External actors like the United Nations Development Programme have for some years invested in so-called infrastructures for peace—inclusive peace committees and the like, involving local elders, tribal leaders, clan structures, and indigenous forums. But they do so only very cautiously, often standing back from local organizations that espouse different concepts of rights and political legitimacy. Moreover, they continue to back elites and the kind of economic and overarching political models that perpetuate the causes of much conflict. All this constrains local movements from pursuing their own concepts of reconciliation and political reform.[10]

Donor profiles

It is instructive to lay out in greater detail the policies of some of the principal aid donors active in the field of civil society support. Their aid profiles show both an incipient attempt to engage with the new activism and the limits to such a shift. "Box 8.2: Private funders" reports on how some private foundations are also working with the new activists.

United States

The US Agency for International Development (USAID) has promised since adopting its 2013 Strategy on Democracy, Human Rights, and Governance to do more to link grassroots activism to NGOs and government.[11] USAID is experimenting more than previously with small grants. It does so in particular through its SWIFT (Support Which Implements Fast Transitions) program. In 2015 the agency also inaugurated a $45 million Small Grants Program intended to foster "locally-owned development" by awarding small grants to organizations that may not be traditional USAID partners and that have not received more than $5 million in support over the last five years.[12] The USAID Forward initiative works to train local grassroots groups in financial management and reporting in order to attract core aid support. Its Local Works program pursues a similar aim of getting funds to very small, local groups. Direct funding to local organizations rose from 9.7 percent of total US aid in 2010 to 27 percent in 2015.[13]

USAID has also developed programs to increase the level of communication between nontraditional civic activists and governments. Up to the end of 2017 Making All Voices Count provided grants to nonprofits and social enterprises using ICT platforms to garner citizens' feedback on policy initiatives and allow citizens to report corruption. Examples included online platforms for participatory budgeting in the Philippines and Indonesia, a web service that allows Kenyans to report complaints about public project implementation and international aid distribution, a polling site that relays the priorities of Ghanaian citizens to the country's district assemblies, and a social network that helps South African community groups link up with formal civil society groups.[14] Despite these examples, in general USAID is still focused mainly on traditional NGOs and remains wary about direct support to nontraditional social movements.

US civil society support is also provided through the National Endowment for Democracy (NED). As the US's quasi-independent democracy foundation, NED has vowed to respond to the new civic activism by providing small, flexible grants tailored to "the needs of grassroots activists in recipient countries." Around a quarter of NED's global grants go to various kinds of new civic activism.[15] Examples of such programs include supporting Movements.org, the online forum that connects human rights activists in authoritarian countries with experts from around the world; getting members of the informal sector involved in Burma's democratic transition; funding the Organizing for Zimbabwe Trust, a local organization working to boost the political participation of Zimbabwean youth through social media; bringing together Haitian civic activists, political party members, election candidates, and private-sector companies to campaign against electoral violence; and helping very informal Venezuelan organizations pushing for decentralization and localized governance.[16]

United Kingdom

Around a quarter of British aid is now spent through civil society.[17] The UK's Magna Carta Fund for Human Rights and Democracy increased from £5.5

million in 2014–15 to £10.6 million in 2016–17. The Foreign Office's recent annual reports and strategy documents relating to democracy and governance work reflect an awareness of new forms of civic activism around the world.[18] The British Department for International Development (DFID) commits to engaging grassroots activists that are beyond the reach of traditional civil society aid. DFID documents talk of partnering with a wide range of civic actors, "including faith and diaspora groups, community-based organizations and social movements."

Programs targeting grassroots activists and smaller organizations include UK Aid Direct, a five-year effort to distribute £150 million to small and medium-sized civic initiatives; the Common Ground Initiative, which awards £12 million in aid to "small and diaspora organizations" focused on Africa; the now-finished Governance and Transparency Fund, which included many new forms of civic activism in its £130 million spending; and support for the aforementioned Making All Voices Count initiative to bolster vertical accountability through ICT platforms.[19]

However, most organizations receiving DFID funding are medium-sized CSOs. All UK aid recipients must meet International Aid Transparency Initiative (IATI) reporting standards, effectively excluding many informal initiatives. Projects supported by the UK's Arab Partnership Fund show no outward signs of engagement with new forms of activism. The £1 billion Conflict, Security and Stability Fund is shifting priorities to the nexus between civil society and conflict, again without any apparent focus on newer forms of civic activism. The comprehensive list of British initiatives in support of democracy and human rights does not indicate any priority effort to back new forms of civic activism.[20]

Sweden

Sweden's development agency, Sida, is arguably the donor most explicitly locked onto the new civic activism. It alludes to the need to support not only CSOs but also groups and individuals and for aid to be more responsive to the erratic flux of civic activism.[21] Sida is building up its own capacity to identify new actors, funding platforms and networks to get old and new civic actors working together, supporting intermediaries and encouraging these to engage with new civic movements, devising a guarantee mechanism to cover the financial risk that other donors are reluctant to incur in backing new groups, and expanding its Civil Society Innovation Initiative. Sida has helped form "strategic partnerships" between Bolivian indigenous organizations and the government.[22] It supports the Poverty Eradication Network, which strengthens Kenyan grassroots actors engaged in local participatory democracy and lacking access to traditional funding sources.[23]

However, Swedish officials acknowledge that the country's compliance with IATI reporting standards may inhibit Sida from partnering with informal and grassroots players that lack the capacity to adhere to such standards.[24] Moreover, as one of its funding modes Sida operates framework agreements with Swedish intermediary NGOs that sometimes limit flexible financing for civic actors.[25] An evaluation of Swedish, Danish, and Austrian civil society programs found that the primary target of funding by all three countries remains traditional service-delivery NGOs.[26]

Germany

German aid priorities stress that new forms of civic activism are emerging and need to be encouraged.[27] The German development agency, BMZ, commits to investing in "weaker and less well-organized groups" that may not fall into the standard formal model of civil society.[28] Some German programs have begun to engage nontraditional civic actors. A civil society support project in Kyrgyzstan provided funding to informal "social groups" distinct from "registered nongovernmental organizations" to push local governments to improve transparency.[29] An "environmental empowerment" project in Thailand involved both informal meetings and formal conferences putting grassroots communities in touch with established NGOs and government officials to improve natural resource management.[30] A partnership between the Konrad Adenauer Foundation and Ghana's National House of Chiefs helped institutionalize local chieftaincies while seeking their commitment to democracy and the rule of law.[31] One German initiative in Ukraine has sought to foster "active citizens," expressly as an alternative to previous projects supporting NGO capacities.[32]

Overall, however, Germany's aid strategy is relatively top down, with the main focus being on supporting state institutions. BMZ acknowledges it is circumspect in engaging with confrontational civic actors.[33] Those German projects that do support civil society only very rarely diverge from traditional capacity-building and civic education activities.[34]

Denmark

Danida, the Danish development agency, has formally homed in on the changing character of civic activism and need for effective grassroots support.[35] It has moved to long-term strategic funding for informal organizations, giving them greater flexibility to absorb funds outside the scope of traditional CSO projects.[36] Danida has shifted more of its funds toward informal and community-based organizations.[37] Danish support to nontraditional movements includes funding to the Baytna Syria civil society center, which helps Syrian CSOs and

Box 8.1 **European Endowment for Democracy**

The European Endowment for Democracy (EED) was created expressly to broaden out democracy funding to innovative kinds of activism not supported by other donors. Its leitmotif is "Supporting the unsupported." The EED has awarded 20 percent of its grants to actors that have not previously received funding—this being the closest proxy measure the organization has for measuring how much of its support is going to newer forms of civic activism. The EED's largest category of support goes to "political risk." The endowment is set to give increasing priority to what it refers to as fledgling informal bodies, individuals, and community forums working on local rights within urban spaces.[38] The EED has an ambitious aim to reach out to new actors, but it requires greater capacity to identify and accompany the innovative approaches it desires. Lacking this capacity, in practice it often falls back on more familiar kinds of civil society funding.

Several examples show how the organization has reached out to new kinds of activism. Some of its most innovative work is in the Middle East and North Africa. EED has supported the new movement SimSim–Participation Citoyenne to create the Nouabook and YourParliament platforms to get Moroccan citizens and their elected representatives exchanging ideas. It has funded the Arabic Federation for Democracy in Palestine that works to increase women's participation in student elections. In Palestine, the EED worked with a student movement, Youth House—outside the standard recipients of international aid—to train graduates to run their own public hearings and put questions to politicians. In Kafranbel, a small Syrian town liberated from the regime in 2012, EED supported centers to train journalists and lawyers.

In several Tunisian provinces and villages, the EED has worked with ordinary, nonpolitically active women to create a community-level advocacy association for social and development issues. It also funds communities and young residents of poor Tunis suburbs to engage in civic issues through art. The EED-funded Arab Puppet Theatre Foundation tackles the political and social issues prevalent among Syrians, Palestinians, and Lebanese through interactive puppet performances. Support was given to Moroccan pop and rap stars to compose, record, and film a song about the importance of voting; the video went viral and became part of a nationwide citizen campaign that included public debates, street actions, and student outreach encouraging democratic participation. In Jordan, journalists are using satire and cartoons to extend limits to the freedom of expression, with EED help.

> The endowment's other priority is the post-Soviet space. The EED was an early supporter of the citizens Automaidan movement, which it also helped become an anticorruption campaign group. In Gagauzia, the autonomous region of Moldova, EED helped an independent journalist launch her own media outlet after she was fired from local TV for not being sufficiently favorable to the demands of politicians. In Crimea, EED is one of the very few donors to provide support to informal groups inside the peninsula in the wake of the Russian annexation. In Donbas, a branch of citizens' television Hromadske TV was set up with EED assistance to provide another view of the conflict on the ground. In Belarus, EED support has enabled activists to engage more with citizens in the regions outside Minsk, to address their everyday concerns. In Transnistria, EED support has enabled a network of informal youth groups to engage in their societies through theater and other creative means.

community-based organizations; a newly tailored civil society support program in Belarus; and Tunisian youth organizations.[39] Yet Danish aid suffers the same limitations as that of other donors. By demanding its civil society partners demonstrate quantitative outputs and comply with IATI standards, Danida struggles to fund informal civic groups on a systematic basic.[40]

Netherlands

The Netherlands is one of the world's largest donors to civil society and promises to support "nontraditional actors" like incipient social movements, unregistered groups, and technology innovators.[41] To help in this it has made grants available on more flexible terms, set up an Innovation Fund for new organizations, extended an Accountability Fund through local embassies, and broadened a Human Rights Fund to focus on small CSOs and human rights defenders. Examples of Dutch funding for new types of activism include support for a Pakistani group promoting interreligious understanding through unorthodox social mobilization techniques, for loosely organized "regular citizens" in Georgia working to reduce hostile attitudes toward minorities, for an alternative citizens news agency working to employ Turkish journalists who have lost their jobs during President Erdoğan's media crackdown, and for Muslim female preachers in Egypt seeking to champion women's rights.[42]

On a less positive note, the Netherlands cut aid by €1 billion between 2014 and 2017, with one of the biggest cuts (€230 million) being to civil society support.[43] Dutch development cooperation has been reoriented toward countries where the Netherlands has concrete national interests. And in practice a large part of Dutch civil society support is channeled through Dutch CSOs that act as intermediaries vis-à-vis Global South CSOs—an arrangement that the government acknowledges militates against a direct targeting of new forms of activism.

European Union

The European Commission's main civil society strategy says support will be directed at both "formal and informal organizations" and that EU policy must respond to the emergence of "new and more fluid forms of citizens and youth actions."[44] The EU's 2014 Action Plan on Democracy and Human Rights commits expressly to increasing European support for new civic actors; as updated in December 2015, the plan commits to prioritizing support for "citizen movements."[45] The European Commission has drawn up over one hundred "Roadmaps" for engaging with civil society in third world countries, with these promising to support "volunteer movements" and community-level networks.

The European Commission is now funding several big contracts to establish hubs for advice and input on new civic actors. It has proposed a single unit to coordinate efforts to get funding more quickly to grassroots movements. In Pakistan, it is running a project expressly designed to reach out to new actors in observing the domestic electoral cycle and political process. It ran similar initiatives in Morocco, Tunisia, and Tanzania to obtain new actors' input into the Action Plan on Democracy and Human Rights. With EU involvement, the Council of Europe has set up an incubator for participatory democracy in cities, grouping together democracy innovators from cities across Europe. In 2017 the EU launched a program to give grassroots bodies a voice in drawing up EU cooperation plans, and in 2018 opened a CivicTech4Democracy scheme to fund innovative digital democracy initiatives.[46] "Box 8.1: The European Endowment for Democracy" details another strand of European support for emerging activists.

Despite all these new initiatives, most EU governance aid still goes to state institutions, not civil society.[47] EU officials admit that relatively little has been done to fund new civic actors, compared to such institutional support. The European Commission published an extensive report on its global civil society support in April 2017; this report makes no mention of any EU strategy for reacting to changes in the nature of civic activism itself.[48] The largest portion of EU civil society funds goes to NGOs working to align their countries with EU rules, despite many newer civic activists arguing that such a focus deviates from and undercuts local priorities. In this sense, these programs suffer from a selection bias: they mainly involve pro-EU groups because these are the ones concerned with convergence on EU norms. Civil Society Europe, an umbrella

> ### Box 8.2 **Private funders**
>
> Some private foundations have advanced further than governments in reaching new forms of civic activism. One notable development is the rise of so-called fund-amediaries to channel money to informal networks—a new type of partner that responds to governments' failure to reach out to new activists.
>
> *Solidaire* is a group of private funders that aims to support new movements and activists, with a particular focus on the US, for "translating movement power into governing power." It has a number of initiatives tailored to the specific features of new activism. One fund, Rapid Response for Movement Moments, helps new groups that emerge very suddenly. Another, the Emergent Fund, helps activists from sections of the population threatened, in particular, by policies implemented by the Trump administration. And another, Movement R&D, is designed to support new actions and tactics that might easily fail and would not meet standard donor criteria.[49]
>
> Another initiative is the civic organization *Rhize*, which set up a Movement Innovation Lab specifically to provide support to link informal civic organizations with the formal NGO sector, with the aim to "create a common infrastructure that closes the formal-informal gap." This has produced a Collective Civic Participation Framework that provides NGOs with a blueprint for supporting informal grassroots movements.[50] In a similar vein, the *Sigrid Rausing Trust* has pioneered engagement with informal community activism, especially in Eastern Europe and the Balkans.

organization for European CSOs, complains of the EU resisting changes that would make the new wave of volunteerism-based movements eligible for funding.[51] Grassroots groups tend to dismiss the EU's various civil society platforms as elitist.

The EU lacks adequate mechanisms to fund fluid, informal groups. Some officials express skepticism that such groups need support, as they tend to flourish so spontaneously. They also fear that the EU would lose its neutral and mediating role between factions and between society and the state if it were to fund confrontational new movements. The EU has kept its distance from the new activists emerging in Russia. In Serbia, it has supported Prime Minister Aleksandar Vučić explicitly *against* protesters—keen to help a nominally pro-EU stabilizing leader, despite his increasingly tight control over state, civil society, and media. Representatives of the Polish Defence of Democracy movement complain at having been rebuffed in their requests for EU support.

Challenges of supporting new civic activism

In summary, most aid agencies and foundations say they realize the shortcomings of too heavy a reliance on NGO support and know that civil society support needs to be broadened out to include the new civic activism, and yet in practice have taken no more than a few very timid steps in this direction. Why is this the case?

Donors are still held back by the fact that some new activism is more explicitly political than the vast majority of NGO activity. This means that outside funding is more likely to get drawn into supporting one side over others in internal disputes.[52] Funders sometimes have doubts over how far new civic groups are representative of citizenries as a whole. The Organisation for Economic Cooperation and Development (OECD) has noted that donor support for new civic movements "entails a certain degree of politicization" that lies outside what many funders have traditionally been willing to contemplate.[53]

As one activist puts it, in their tentative engagement with the new activism "donors want to swim without getting wet." Aid officials report that despite donors' desire to engage with new local organizations, these often do not offer them easy "deliverables." In this sense, there is a common concern that working with new civic activism is highly risky—even though the risk of projects failing to have impact is clearly already high with support to traditional NGOs. Other diplomats fear that today the notion of "civic participation" calls forth the specter of "illiberal activism"—from which donor agencies are keen to keep their distance.

Both donors and civic activists also seem wary about undermining the very features that have given the new activism its vitality and comparative advantage over the old activism. There is a danger of outside support sapping the new activism of its strengths relative to NGOs. Informal civic movements might seek to fit into NGOs' institutional molds simply to win access to funds. Outside support might risk pulling such movements away from their grassroots constituencies.[54] Even if donors do not explicitly or categorically exclude new-type activists, their funding rules are often such that these movements are de facto unable to compete for aid.

Some new activist groups want little to do with aid donors. Many of them have expressed ambivalence and even hostility toward the prospect of outside funding and a preference for maintaining their independence from foreign influence. Some judge that to receive significant amounts of money they would be pushed to adopt agendas more amenable to donors' interests. Some new movements challenge the very concept of Western democracy promotion, not because they reject democracy but because they seek different pathways into and concepts of participative politics. Indeed, this is part of what has put international democracy support increasingly on the back foot.[55]

The practical challenge of *how* to provide aid to new civic activism is also a vexing one. Though donors may rhetorically welcome the idea of grassroots groups being an alternative to advocacy NGOs, they often doubt the feasibility of getting funds to them. New movements' accounting, reporting, and management procedures are less developed than those of traditional NGOs, which presents difficulties to donor organizations worried about skeptical domestic constituencies looking closely at where aid is going. Some human rights activists say they are reluctant to innovate with noninstitutional activism in part because they fear they will lose donor support if they do.[56] Outside support has found it easier to target activists on an individual basis than new types of organization as such.[57]

Finally, many powerful NGOs often seek to limit donors' adjustment away from the old to the new activism. One study finds that donors' decentralization of funding decisions to Global South–based funding mechanisms has actually led to big, classic, capital-based NGOs taking a larger share of funds, as these are able to use their local weight to increase their financial inflows. In this sense, "local ownership" does not always sit easily with donors' express aim of supporting a wider variety of civic activism forms.[58] The more established NGOs fear that donors are actually becoming rather too seduced by the fashionable appeal of new forms of civic activism. They worry that this is drawing donors either into highly political internal issues or, conversely, into very apolitical forms of community self-help support that take the critical spotlight off nondemocratic regimes. Several NGO leaders complain that donors are actually pushing them too hard to include new activists in their projects and that this is becoming the international community's faddish new panacea.

Future changes

A widespread view is that donors should facilitate the "enabling environment" for the new civic activism and relatively apolitical network building, rather than provide direct support.[59] Many donors are keen to limit themselves mainly to indirect support for new civic activism through intermediaries, trust funds, or other mechanisms independent of donors.[60] This is a sensible focus, and much donor activity will rightly take place with such caution—at one or more removes from direct engagement with the emerging activism. But the question is whether donors can do more than this to draw out the new activism's full, positive potential.

In order to facilitate the new civic activism, donors face the challenge of drawing a clearer line between being politically engaged and being politically one-sided. The OECD points out that while donors need to be careful to retain their formal political neutrality, by not engaging positively with the new activists they are in fact adopting a political position by omission—one that loads the dice against the emerging civic activism and its new types of substantive agendas. Civicus argues that donors still need to "recalibrate attitudes to risk, and be brave enough to invest in new organizations and ideas... [and] accept that investing in potential can be as worthwhile as investing in an organization that is guaranteed to produce quantifiable results."[61]

This requires donors to draw up a new menu of support options that goes beyond the traditional path of financial support. This support will need to strengthen new activists' links with other actors—moving both upward into the political sphere and downward to individual citizens. At one level this means helping to bring the issues advocated by the new civic activism into the national and international public space. For this, donors must be willing to back activism on a wider range of substantive issues. The question remains whether donors are open to the challenges that new civic movements pose to dominant paradigms, particularly market liberalization and the various components of globalism.[62]

At another level, more help could be forthcoming to ensure that new movements' authentic base within grassroots constituencies is maintained. While the grassroots focus is generally seen as civic movements' strong point, there are cases where, as they gain a higher political profile, these movements gradually neglect the bases from which their legitimacy first grew.[63] Donors could offer programs to prevent this from happening. Some are just beginning to push for fiscal incentives that would encourage funds to be raised from local sources.

International powers, funders, and multilateral organizations could help mentor new civic leaders and other capacity-building initiatives to strengthen the quality of leadership among the new groups.[64] This kind of initiative might include facilitating regional connectivity between movement leaders in different countries. International actors could help build networks and strengthen intermediaries through convening meetings and joint planning sessions to strengthen overall movement alliances.[65] They might partner with established NGOs to have these act as a kind of holding point for funds that new activists can dip into for very specific purposes without having to apply directly for project financing from donors, with all the heavy administration that requires.

International support could also aim to even out the spikes of turbulence associated with the new civic activism. Engagement could help anticipate where tipping points are likely to be reached in successive waves of activism. Better predictive indictors might prevent revolts catching reformers so profoundly by surprise that they fail to capitalize on political breakthroughs. We have seen in the examples presented throughout the book that the new civic activism often makes dramatic advances but then fails to hold the ground won—and because of this often then suffers a political and economic backlash that leaves its aims even further from being realized. Support is needed especially in the phase immediately after a protest when movements need help to retain some institutional momentum in the face of activists' disenchantment that the revolt has not fully met its aims.[66] International agencies and foundations could do better in seeking to guide the new activists toward the constructive use of mobilizations. Donors could help the new civic activism create a politics that is fully participative without being self-destructively and chaotically turbulent.

To put all this into place, donors would require new funding mechanisms, more flexible reporting and evaluation systems, and whole new modes of operation.[67] Since many grassroots movements do not function along the lines of Western models, funding accountability would need to be defined in a looser way. Donors could also support large NGOs to help new activist groups meet reporting requirements. They might need to obsess less about loosely based movements or those behind unorganized protests moving to "professionalize." There is a thin line between helping activists' organizational capacity—legitimate and necessary when movements' members feel their effectiveness suffers from incoherence and internal squabbles—and forcing them into bureaucratic models they dislike.

Donors will need to develop new metrics for assessing the impact of mass civic action and to be better at capturing and sharing the lessons from success stories. Nonfinancial modes of support will become more germane, as traditional grant-making timelines and evaluation methods are at odds with the nature of most authentic popular movements.[68] International funders will need to be more open to working through pooled financial mechanisms over which they have less control. Many loose civic initiatives simply do not have the institutional capacity to receive funding from outside sources unless donors lighten their support modes.[69] More broadly, activists will eventually need to generate more of their own revenues for local services they provide, based around the notion of social enterprise.[70]

Conclusion

It would be unfair to conclude that donors have not reacted at all to the emergence of new forms of civic activism. Writers still ritually admonish international organizations and funders for blindly adhering to a hopelessly narrow, self-serving, and dated concept of civil society. Many donors, however, have been at the forefront of new analysis about the changing shape of civil society in different regions around the world. Most funders have introduced new initiatives aimed at updating their support programs. The standard critique that donors cultivate a false and arbitrary NGO-ization of the civic sphere in developing societies fails to capture the ways in which aid agencies have begun to rethink their approaches to civic activism.

Nevertheless, in practical terms the updating of civil society support is proving to be an extremely partial and labored process. There is a hesitancy to change on the part of both donors and new civic activists. The latter have been ambivalent over what kind of support they wish to receive from external actors. There is no single, common position: some of the new activists want more international backing; others want the aid community to take a step back and not interfere. Donors will have to walk a thin line, as they are criticized for both ignoring new movements and smothering them with naïve good intentions.

Some of the caution is genuine and well founded. Aid agencies can certainly do a lot of harm to the legitimacy of new activism if they are not careful to apprize themselves in detail of how external support is perceived in different political settings. However, some of the prevailing hesitancy is less easy to justify. Donors should certainly resist the temptation to see the new activism as a panacea or to treat it as a convenient fad—a ready-made alternative vehicle for the funds that have run into problems when channeled through more established NGOs. Rather, the challenge is more qualitatively to rethink the way that civil support is designed and delivered, and to make sure this support is tightly dovetailed in a bespoke manner to the specific opportunities and problems that the new activism presents. This process of adjustment will be difficult, will involve much trial-and-error experimentation, and is likely to last for many years.

9

Activists at risk

A final trend invites a sobering close to our account of the new civic activism. As new forms of mobilization have gained momentum, so many governments around the world have devised means to restrict civic activism. If one part of today's global script is about the empowerment of citizens and social organizations, another part is the story of governments' heightened determination to stifle civic activism. This more clearly negative development is reflected in the tactics that many nondemocratic regimes and even some democratic ones today employ to neuter civic groups and also international civil society support. These tactics go from overt repression to more subtle means of frustrating civic activists. In many cases governments' response to the new civic activism has been ferociously combative.

This chapter outlines the creeping phenomenon of what has come to be termed "the closing space" for civil society. It examines the range of techniques that regimes now use to constrict civic activism and highlights the increasingly large number of governments adopting such measures. The chapter attempts to disaggregate the closing-space phenomenon so as to clarify exactly what kinds of threats it entails. In the context of this book's aims, I am particularly concerned to understand the relationship between closing space and new activism. On this issue, there are signs of an iterative and symbiotic process. The global assault against civil society is both a cause and an effect of the new civic activism. As governments design new ways to restrict civil society, so civil society is driven further toward more fluid, agile, individualized, and even covert forms of activism. However, it is not yet clear that this new activism can succeed in circumventing governments' new restrictions on civil society.

The international community has recognized that the closing-space problem requires serious and systematic attention. The chapter outlines how key donors and international organizations are trying to protect activists at risk from regimes' increasingly draconian tactics. Their efforts to do so represent perhaps the principal change in civil society support in recent years. Yet much firmer, more preemptive, and more coordinated support will be needed if the new civic activism is not to be hounded into submission by governmental onslaught.

Clampdowns and restrictions

The trend of governments bearing down on civil society actors began a decade ago but has accelerated in very recent times. Restrictive NGO laws are becoming more common, but even these are only one part of governments' arsenal. In addition to these laws, there are increasing numbers of arrests, detentions, travel bans, and even assassinations of civil society activists. Particularly worrying cases in the last two years include Angola, Azerbaijan, Burundi, Egypt, Kazakhstan, and Turkey.

Civicus reports that in 2014 there were serious threats to civic freedoms in at least 96 countries around the world.[1] In 2015 freedoms for civil society declined even further, with serious violations in 109 countries.[2] The International Center for Not-for-Profit Law records that 120 restrictive laws were adopted in 60 countries between 2012 and 2015. One-third of the restrictions were on international funding, half applied to the general legal framework for CSO operations, and 20 percent were directed specifically against freedom of assembly.[3]

Regimes are deploying an increasingly wide range of measures, including legal restrictions, political campaigns besmirching CSOs' credibility, unfavorable tax measures, onerous administrative regulations, travel bans, asset freezes, and online attacks. They are also attaching the "foreign agent" stigma to civic activists, placing limits or caps on the amount of money that CSOs can receive from donors, and requiring funding to be channeled through government-controlled intermediaries. Many activists feel more and more isolated; they are stigmatized, meaning other parts of society are reluctant to work with them. Several governments now channel funds into their own acquiescent shadow "civil society" organizations; this tactic has existed for a long time but has become more widespread in recent years.

Just in the last two years yet more countries have adopted restrictive NGOs laws. These include Angola, China, Hungary, India, Israel, Jordan, Kazakhstan, Kenya, Laos, Mexico, Nigeria, Russia, Sierra Leone, South Sudan, Tajikistan, and Uganda. "Box 9.1: Russia" examines that country's particularly emblematic case. China now obliges foreign foundations to register within China itself if they seek to support Chinese NGOs. Even in the one success story of the Arab Spring, Tunisia, the government introduced restrictive NGO laws in June 2017 and is now moving against several village-level movements and councils that have challenged powerful business interests and landowners. The Tunisian

Box 9.1 **Russia**

Russia is probably the best-known case of regime attacks against civil society. The Russian government first introduced restrictive laws on civil society organizations in 2006 and has been intensifying its actions ever since. In 2012 the government introduced a law obliging NGOs that receive foreign funding and engage in vaguely defined "political activity" to register as "foreign agents." In 2014 the Ministry of Justice was empowered to register CSOs as "foreign agents" without their agreeing to this. In 2015 a ban on a new category of "undesirable" civil society organizations was introduced, and the Prosecutor's Office was given the power to close down organizations judged to threaten Russia's "constitutional order, defence capacity or state security."

Dozens of international NGOs and donors to civil society have been forced to leave the country. Russia extended the scope of its legislation even further in 2016, tightening the definition of "political activity" and beginning the process of prosecuting organizations that have not registered as "foreign agents"; reports vary on how many organizations have been closed.

In parallel, the Russian government has started offering active support and funding to "NGOs" that support the state. The government has molded a new type of civil society that works with and is sponsored by the state on social issues. An online campaign got public support for the foreign agents law and sufficed to circumvent parliamentary opposition to this measure.

It is estimated that the number of Russian CSOs has dropped to a third of what it was in 2012, from six hundred thousand to around two hundred thousand. Numerous organizations have faced difficulties in reaching out to the public or continuing their cooperation with state officials due to their "foreign agent" status. The state's stigmatizing of watchdog groups has also divided the civil society sector, as apolitical NGOs are now more wary of cooperating with human rights organizations.

As CSOs refuse to register voluntarily as "foreign agents," the government has begun to use more widely its powers to do this forcibly. It has done so in accordance with an extremely broad definition of "political activities"—to include any advocacy, policy monitoring and reporting, public outreach, engagement with state officials, or research activity. This sweep has affected even groups working on environmental or migrant issues. The authorities have imposed fines on these CSOs for multiple reasons, while also moving against a select group of international NGOs, banning them outright from operating inside Russia.

(*continued*)

> *Box 9.1 continued*
>
> Russian authorities have also restricted internet activism. Legislative changes have enabled authorities to block almost any website and require bloggers to register as mass media outlets. The government now uses anti-extremism and antiterrorism legislation to silence dissenting voices. It has sentenced activists for criticizing Russia's military intervention in Ukraine on social media.
>
> Public assemblies have been severely restricted. Following the wave of protests against the rigged parliamentary and presidential elections in 2011 and 2012, the authorities raised the fines for participation in and organization of unauthorized protest over a hundredfold. After protests against Russia's intervention in Ukraine, the regime further tightened restrictions in 2014. In March 2016 further amendments were made to extend the definition of public assembly, and in August the new provisions were used to prosecute a group of farmers traveling in tractors and private cars from southern Russia to Moscow to protest against land grabbing by agricultural holding companies. Dozens of other activists attempting even modest, stand-alone protests have been arrested and fined.[4]

government arrested over a thousand activists in the protests of late 2017 and 2018 and introduced tight financial restrictions on CSOs.

A 2017 Ukrainian law obliges NGOs to reveal financial details, apparently in an attempt to exert influence over activists critical of government corruption. In one of the most sweeping moves, at the end of 2017 the Pakistani government ordered well-known international NGOs to leave the country; this followed numerous cases of civic activists being "disappeared."[5] In Azerbaijan, all grants from foreign sources to Azerbaijani NGOs and individuals now need to be registered twice: once by the donor and once by the NGO or individual recipient. Grants are subject to approval by the government. No foreign donor has so far been authorized to disburse a grant under these guidelines. In this case, the closing off of civil society appears almost absolute.

Egypt has been an innovator in the shrinking-space phenomenon. Its authorities have frozen the assets of a rising number of Egyptian human rights defenders and NGOs. Under changes to the penal code introduced in 2014, activists risk lifelong prison sentences for accepting foreign funds. The post-2013 military government banned Muslim Brotherhood activities and then used the same legislation to close a large number of civic organizations that it claimed—often tenuously—were linked to the Brotherhood, meaning that hundreds of religious community-based charities delivering basic services have been shut down. While the regime launches legal cases against CSOs, the military is "disappearing" an increasing number of activists. In November 2016 the Egyptian parliament approved the most restrictive NGO law so far. Under this law, if a group accepts foreign funding without permission, it will be immediately closed down. Foreign CSOs are no longer allowed to operate in the country without prior approval from a "National NGO Apparatus." President el-Sisi signed this law in May 2017.

A sobering concern is that the trend is extending into apparently well-consolidated democracies. The Indian government canceled nearly ten thousand civil society organization registrations in 2015; it has tightened authorization requirements for NGOs receiving funding and now forbids them from activities that would damage India's security. In 2016 Israel introduced proposals for "foreign agent" funding rules modeled on those in Russia. In late 2016 the Polish government moved to create a new department to control NGO funding and placed new restrictions on public gatherings and protests. In summer 2017 the Hungarian government introduced legislation restricting CSO autonomy even more dramatically. Elsewhere in Europe, governments in Bulgaria, Croatia, Ireland, Italy, Romania, Slovakia, and Spain have also introduced particularly significant new restrictions of one type or another.[6] In fact, in late 2017 the EU's Fundamental Rights Agency found that *all* EU member states have suffered some kind of restriction to civil society.[7] Governments in the UK and Germany have tried to constrain CSOs from engaging in "political activities"; in both countries CSOs have pushed courts to resist these vague and potentially open-ended restrictions.

The monitoring and advocacy group Front Line Defenders reports that in 2016, 281 human rights defenders were killed in twenty-five countries.[8] Activists who assert land, environmental, and indigenous peoples' rights in the face of large-scale development schemes have been especially vulnerable.[9] According to Global Witness, a record number of environmental activists were killed in 2017.[10]

Threats also come from nonstate actors. In Latin America, criminal gangs and armed groups regularly menace civic activists.[11] Some attacks come not from governments but from right-wing fundamentalist groups. Such groups have targeted atheist bloggers in Bangladesh, Rohingyas in Burma, moderate activists in Pakistan, and Ukrainian community leaders critical of the Kiev government and accused of being traitors by far-right social movements. Some rightist activism is now in direct confrontation with other forms of new activism, riding the coattails of governments' restrictive assaults.

Dissecting the trend

Repression against civic activists is, of course, not new but rather the historical norm. However, elements of the current assault are different: regimes are deploying a wider range of tactics, including very subtle ones, on a more systematic basis, across a wider range of countries, and often targeting not only hard-core, confrontational regime opponents but a comprehensive swathe of civil society groups. In this sense, there are several analytical features of the trend that merit deeper reflection. These features point to a set of broader implications that arise from the battery of civil society restrictions described above.

Drivers. The closing space is part of a general authoritarian pushback against democracy, but it is not only that. Neither is it simply a crusade against human rights defenders. The phenomenon counts many causal drivers, reflecting in part the world's authoritarian turn, in part an emboldened anti-Western social agenda. In some countries, regimes attack civil society for very specific reasons related to their attempts to restrict democratic checks and balances. In addition, sitting atop these country-specific political strategies, the shrinking-space problem is related to the shift of international power away from the West. As non-Western countries have gained power, they have felt emboldened to attack the whole civil society narrative, which they often dismiss as a Western agenda. Some rising powers are advertising growth models that quash civic society as part of their development plans, with some apparent success. Moreover, governments are learning from each other's tactics for containing civic activism; interdependence is a causal driver of civil society weakness just as much as of civil society strength.

Security. The security and terrorism dynamic behind the closing space has become more prominent; concerns over radical groups are now perhaps the most potent driver of government control over civic activism. Governments increasingly use antiterror laws as a tool for disciplining and controlling civil society. This is the case in many Western countries, including France, Spain, the UK, and the US. Over 2016 and 2017 French authorities banned more than 150 public assemblies and protests, and the police have used new counterterror laws to disband peaceful demonstrations with some force. This is also a preeminent trend in the Middle East and North Africa, where Saudi Arabia provides a particularly notable example of a regime using new antiterror laws to define civil society actors as a security threat. Similar measures have been introduced across a spate of developing states such as Bangladesh, Brazil, Chad, Ethiopia, Kenya, Sudan, and Uganda.[12]

Variability. While the closing space has become a global trend, it exhibits varied characteristics across different countries. In some states, governments feel threatened by the new activism, and this is the cause of their imposing civil society restrictions. In other cases, regimes clamp down because they feel emboldened by increased political, economic, and strategic control. Most often, the closing space is the result of a combination of defensiveness and proactive assertiveness on the part of regimes—a curious mix of strength and weakness, of confidence and paranoia.

In some cases, the onslaught is mainly against foreign funding; in other cases, this is a by-product. In some cases, governments ban CSOs from receiving funds from external sources completely. In other cases, they impose a limit to how much CSOs can receive or require funds to pass through state intermediaries, often with the state taking a percentage of the receipts. In some places, regimes use outright violence; in others, requiring CSOs to register themselves as "foreign agents" has been enough to dissuade them from taking international support. Regimes sometimes feel they have a legitimate concern that CSOs should meet international standards regarding financial fraud and tax evasion; in the past some CSOs have been less than perfect on such matters.

Motivations behind the restrictions differ. Some governments are intent simply on making life more difficult for CSOs, increasing their oversight of what the civic sector does, and, in some instances, merely finding a way to siphon off a portion of the money they receive from international sources. For others the closing space is more radically about delinking from the international community in an overtly confrontational manner. Some governments' main target is foreign funding per se, while others seek to weaken civil society actors whether or not they get help from outside the country.

Some governments aim to decimate those parts of civil society focused on controversial political and rights issues, while leaving other parts of the civic sphere relatively free. In these cases, few apolitical service-delivery NGOs have so far been willing to risk their own safety by showing solidarity with human-rights NGOs being squeezed out of existence by a repressive regime. In contrast, for the most hard-line regimes, the use of restrictive measures is part of a wholesale attack on the very concept of civil society—it is an attempt to refashion a direct social contract between citizens and the state that is bereft of any intermediary role of an independent civil society.

Civil society legitimacy. In the latest phase of the phenomenon, regimes feel less need to contrive defensive justifications for their measures. Even a few years ago, most governments tried to dress their attacks on the civic sphere in all kinds of explanations to deflect the international community. Fewer regimes now make such efforts. The burden of argumentation has now switched around to fall on civil society's shoulders; it seems to be up to civic groups to explain why they should have the right to exist unhindered and receive support from outside. This is a major inversion of the whole civic climate that goes well beyond the individual NGO laws that have been introduced. Even where new laws are eventually diluted, NGOs' reputation has often taken a beating by the time this happens. A significant concern is that in many countries the general population does not see the clampdowns on CSOs as particularly problematic.

Impact on the new activism

Government restrictions on formal civil society organizations constitute one reason why activists increasingly search for more fluid and off-the-radar forms of activism. The link also applies in the reverse direction: as informal civic initiatives and networks gather more momentum, governments become even more determined to control the civic space. In a sense, new civic activism is both cause and effect of the global trend toward closing civic space.

The wave of new civic restrictions is pushing some activists into more confrontational tactics, others into more subtle and low-key approaches. One activist summarizes the current context: "Crackdowns lead to either violent civic uprising or caution. It is not clear which will prevail yet." Many activists are increasingly finding ways to meet covertly and keep their activities very simple and sporadic, rather than aiming for permanent organizational structures or ongoing campaigns. They are investing more in increasingly sophisticated encryption technology, but some are also moving back toward more offline activism in an effort to evade state surveillance. They say they have moved from organizing as NGOs to functioning as looser social movements to now existing as even more ad hoc and structure-lite clusters. One notable global trend is toward artistic-based activism—the use of theater, satire, music, and the like being more difficult for regimes to classify as illegal.

In some places, like Azerbaijan, for instance, activists tried looser social-movement-type initiatives, but as the state caught up with these and managed to break them apart, many simply left the country to operate as bloggers and the like on an individual basis. One Russian civic leader explains that protesters have "taken a step back from the front line" as they look to rebuild core support and organizational capacity for the long term. In a highly fractious environment, some activists stress the value of "deinstitutionalization." Civic groups like OVD-Info, which monitors arrests of protesters, have replaced their external support with crowdsourced funds.[13] Searching for less sensitive-sounding terminology, many activists now talk in terms of "social entrepreneurship" rather than "civil society."

The trend toward an activism concerned with directly representing local communities and adopting lower-profile, less confrontational functions is related to civil society organizations' need to rebuild their basic legitimacy with ordinary citizens.[14] Governments often leave new, small community-based groups unmolested—in part as a means to divide them from the larger capital-based professional NGOs that suffer the main consequences of restrictive laws. In the harshest environments, many NGOs have decided to relinquish formal, registered status and seek to work on an unregistered basis. In Ethiopia, increasing numbers of people have become engaged in grassroots development initiatives and charities expressly as a response to clampdowns on NGOs.[15] Activists in Turkey's social incubation center report that fewer activist initiatives now seek to register as formal associations and that many of the formal associations formed after the Gezi protests have reverted back to more informal modes of operation.

In Egypt, the military regime's fierce clampdown on NGOs has begun to give rise to very loosely organized civic organizations, active in almost underground fashion. Today, most activist initiatives are self-consciously local and secretive, keeping their exchanges deliberately ad hoc so as to evade regime repression and focus on practical local issues in a highly charged political environment. Even if a repeat of the mass protests of 2011 now seems unlikely, other forms of activism have intensified in Egypt, like petitions, strikes, assemblies, sit-ins, campus protests, vigils, competition around student elections, and some momentary eruptions of citizen anger in response to killings perpetrated by the security services.[16] The Muslim Brotherhood is now focused on helping Brotherhood prisoners. The organization has splintered; local, community-level circles linked to the Brotherhood run very practical service-related activities, with limited connection to any overarching political organization.[17]

Many regimes are catching up with these kinds of informal approaches to civic organization and mobilization. Many of the regimes introducing harsh NGO laws have also restricted the right to protest, meaning street mobilization is not necessarily an easy alternative to formal NGO activism. Moreover, regimes are wising up to activists' crowdsourcing efforts, as they attempt to replace foreign funds, and have begun impeding these, too. It has become apparent that the closing-space problem is a challenge for individual activists, loose civic networks, and social movements, not only NGOs. The fact that movements are generally more strongly rooted in a grassroots constituency does not make them impervious to persecution and accusations of foreign infiltration.

Restrictions have found their way into even the least political kinds of new self-help activism outlined in earlier chapters. In response to the first phase of the shrinking-space assault, many CSOs sought to adopt a lower profile, move into less sensitive areas of work, and approach political questions from a more oblique angle. Now they are finding that space for even apparently anodyne or apolitical campaigns is increasingly curtailed. The worldwide restriction of civil society space has increasingly affected not only the largest and most prominent international NGOs but also smaller community-based, self-help civic activism.

The international response

Western powers and aid funders have slowly woken up to the closing-space threat. They have begun to develop multiple responses that have far-reaching ramifications for the new civic activism. Donors have begun to adjust to the uncomfortable new reality of the closing space. Crucially for the themes explored in this book, the closing-space challenge is pushing aid donors to redirect their civil society support to new forms of activism.

The area that is changing most dramatically in international civil society support is donors' increasing focus on protecting individual human rights defenders from state repression. Increasingly, aid funding is going to initiatives designed to offer basic protection to individual civic activists. The motif of "defending the defenders" has become increasingly preeminent, as international agencies grapple with the need to protect human rights defenders from regimes' often-brutal crackdowns. It is through this policy lens that most support now goes to new civic actors—in contradistinction to the more traditional forms of institutional support to large, professional NGOs.

UN special procedures and Universal Periodic Reviews are being increasingly used as tools targeted specifically at closing-space challenges. The UN has drawn up extensive lists of legal guarantees for activists. It has also drawn up rules for managing demonstrations, in an effort to get states to agree on basic standards for the policing of large-scale protests.[18] Searching for a new narrative to legitimize civil society support, the then UN special rapporteur on freedom of assembly and association, Annalisa Ciampi, developed an approach of "imagining what the world would be like without civil society organizations" and going back to basics in explaining the benefits of civic activism.[19]

The EU, Canada, Finland, Norway, Switzerland, and the US have drawn up publicly available guidelines for protecting human rights defenders. In 2011 a consortium of eighteen governments created the Lifeline Embattled CSO Assistance Fund, which provides short-term grants to civil society organizations hampered by a tightening of political space and emergency assistance to activists facing significant threats to their security. The initiative is managed by the US Department of State and implemented by a consortium of seven transnational NGOs that work directly with civic activists; it operates with an annual budget of between $2 million and $3 million and has made over a thousand emergency grants.[20]

The Community of Democracies runs a Working Group on Enabling and Protecting Civil Society that comprises thirteen governments (Botswana, Canada, Chile, Czech Republic, Denmark, Mongolia, the Netherlands, Poland, Slovakia, Spain, Sweden, Tanzania, and the US) and the European Union, along with five civil society organizations. This initiative has gathered some momentum, benefiting from the Community of Democracies' large and diverse membership of over a hundred states. The working group holds events, promotes the sharing of experience, and oversees some technical assistance. In particular, its early warning "Calls for Action" have attempted to coordinate international responses to the shrinking space.

In his second term in office, President Barack Obama focused a number of his speeches on the shrinking space, promising diplomatic pressure and intensified civil society support to counteract regimes' harsh repression of CSOs. Obama's resulting Stand with Civil Society initiative is currently in doubt, however, as President Trump has not focused on this issue. The US's National Endowment for Democracy has funded a number of initiatives, including a Scholars at Risk collaboration with New York University to assist activists from various countries in bringing attention to attacks on academic freedom, a project for developing strategies with Chinese internet activists to bypass China's online restrictions, and cooperation with Egyptian activists and human rights lawyers to demand a repeal of Egypt's restrictive NGO law.[21]

The EU has developed a particularly comprehensive set of instruments aimed at the closing-space problem. The EU addresses the issue explicitly in its main security policy document, *A Global Strategy for the European Union's Foreign and Security Policy*, which says the EU will "speak out against the shrinking space for civil society" because this is central to creating resilient states.[22] The EU's Human Rights Defenders (HRD) Guidelines include apparently unequivocal commitments to high-level and public meetings with HRDs, including those in custody or put on trial, regardless of regime reactions.[23] Within its embassies around the world the EU has set up Human Rights Focal Points charged with helping to protect vulnerable groups and individuals. In pursuit of all these political commitments, the EU has developed a range of very specific funding instruments, which are detailed in "Box 9.2: EU efforts to defend civic activism."

Sitting outside the formal EU institutions as an autonomous body, the European Endowment for Democracy (EED) has pursued a number of ambitious approaches to limiting the closing space. In Azerbaijan, EED is supporting individuals targeted by the regime and has increasingly sought to offer protection to local activists not well known in Europe. In Belarus, EED has provided emergency support to media outlets persecuted by authorities, helping them either to avoid prosecution or set up safe operations abroad. In Egypt, as other donors have left the scene, EED has maintained its efforts to liaise with independent reformist activists and youth-based groups. It provided logistical and political support to a leading and internationally prominent prodemocracy activist to continue operations in exile. It helped one Jordanian organization that was denied registration to keep functioning in 2016. And in Libya, it provided support to the Centre for Human Rights Defenders that had to flee to Tunis.

Several European governments have developed their own national responses in addition to these common European endeavors. Swedish projects include a strong focus on navigating hostile internet environments and building wider alliances against the closing space.[24] The UK and Sweden have supported the Digital Defenders Partnership fund to protect internet dissidents from government

Box 9.2 **EU efforts to defend civic activism**

Through its European Instrument for Democracy and Human Rights (EIDHR) the EU has set up an emergency fund that is able to channel funds quickly and directly to human rights defenders facing a moment of acute risk. It has awarded around four hundred grants totaling over €3 million in nearly fifty countries. The emergency fund provides various types of support, up to €10,000: fees for HRDs' legal representation, medical expenses, supporting families of imprisoned activists, security material for offices or homes, and HRDs' evacuation to another country.

The EIDHR also funds a "human rights defenders protection mechanism," known as ProtectDefenders.eu. Under this mechanism, a consortium of twelve international NGOs channels emergency support to HRDs at high risk.[25] With a €15 million budget, it has provided over three hundred emergency grants. A program of temporary relocation grants has supported relocation initiatives benefiting over 150 individuals; one-third of these have been kept inside their immediate region. ProtectDefenders.eu has also delivered training and capacity-building initiatives for over a thousand defenders.

In addition, 25 percent of EIDHR's standard projects target "human rights defenders at risk." These projects have covered human rights defenders' digital security and the particular challenges faced by women human rights defenders. The EU's new Civil Society Roadmaps include some measures specifically related to the shrinking-space challenge. Among them are pressure for easier CSO registration rules, advocacy for tax incentives for NGOs to focus on increasing domestic revenue sources, EU support in the form of mentoring and other tactics that might evade new restrictions on direct funding from external actors, and support for alliances between CSOs and the private sector.

More generally across its main funding instruments, the EU has expanded eligibility criteria for nonregistered organizations and organizations registered in another country in situations where registration in the targeted country becomes impossible. The EU has agreed to be more flexible in order to protect partners' confidentiality when requested to do so, and also to allow financial transfers between project partners to evade controls. Policy makers say that changes to the EU's external funding are now driven in large measure by an aim of focusing more support on those countries where civil society is most threatened. As part of its European Neighbourhood Policy the EU has moved toward fostering "civil society hubs" at a regional level to help civic organizations delink themselves from difficult national contexts and gain solidarity across borders—one challenge being to do this without taking the focus further away from the grassroots level.

Two concrete examples of new EU approaches and responses. In Ethiopia, the EU was able to convince the Ethiopian government to label its Civil Society Fund as a "domestic source," so that it falls outside the government's newly imposed limits on foreign funding. In Turkey, the EU's Sivil Düşün (Think Civil) program is open to all types of civil society, whether legal entities or not, and has increasingly been oriented toward support for individual activists and loosely organized platforms. Many of the funded projects have an innovative feel: cycle activism, citizen journalism, an open source platform that monitors politicians' use of social media, the use of art in participative peace forums, and a campaign exploring new ideas of "what activism means."[26]

repression. Denmark's Danida agency has made flexible emergency funds available to organizations under siege in Africa, Eastern Europe, and Turkey.[27] The Dutch government has created a Human Rights Fund aimed at supporting individual human rights defenders.[28] Private foundations have also adjusted their funding to reflect the closing-space challenge. An initiative of the Fund for Global Human Rights, the Oak Foundation, the Open Society Foundations, and the Sigrid Rausing Trust brings together more than forty foundations concerned about the closing-space issue. In 2017 the European Civic Forum set up a new project to warn of restrictions to activism within the EU itself as part of a wider Civic Space Monitor, in cooperation with Civicus.[29]

Undervaluing new activism?

In a small number of cases CSOs and the international community have gotten governments to either water down restrictions or introduce new legislation committing to protect human rights activists; examples include Burkina Faso, Jordan, Kenya, Kyrgyzstan, Mali, Mexico, Nepal, and Ivory Coast. Campaigns in several African states have succeeded in getting governments to backtrack on proposals to restrict online freedoms, Nigeria and Cameroon being notable examples. Overall, however, the assault on civic activism continues to worsen in all regions of the world. While the international community has developed a series of policy responses, upgraded support for qualitatively new forms of civic activism is not prominent among these.

In general, Western governments are not cutting aid, trade, or strategic relations specifically because of regimes' moves to restrict civil space. Western governments are often still reluctant to raise the issue of closing space in deference to commercial and geostrategic interests.[30] In recent years they have offered new trade, aid, and security agreements to many of the governments imposing the harshest restrictions against civil society. Prominent activists complain that Western governments engage in a lot of generic dialogue about the shrinking space but then decline to respond concretely in particular cases of repression.

Civil society organizations have been particularly critical of the weak response to the Egyptian government's highly restrictive NGO law and its moves to freeze the assets of a number of human rights defenders. In signing the NGO law in 2017, President el-Sisi was apparently emboldened by President Trump heaping lavish praise on him and saying the US would not "lecture" Egypt on internal political matters. In Ukraine, several recipients of European funding were beaten in 2017 for criticizing political corruption, yet the same government continued to receive increased levels of EU aid. In Kenya, an activist working on an EU-funded conservation project was killed in 2018; civic movements criticized donors for leaving them more exposed and failing to confront the government after it had made repeated threats against the activists on this project.[31]

Although most of the policy focus has been on protecting human rights defenders in the most basic sense, such emergency measures do not get to the structural heart of the shrinking-space problem. Among civil society organizations there is a growing concern over human rights defenders relocating to Western countries. While often this is clearly necessary, it arguably evades the real imperative of keeping civil society alive in situ. Some NGO representatives fear that too much focus on evacuating activists inadvertently helps regimes "get rid" of troublesome opponents—at least, if such emergency measures are not accompanied with equally committed positive measures to build stronger civil society resilience.[32]

Donors have certainly begun to explore usefully innovative tactics, like funding activists operating outside their home country or alternative types of recipient organizations such as social enterprises. However, assessments suggest donors have not yet incorporated support for new social movements into their strategies for dealing with the closing-space challenge in any major way.[33] Many activists working outside the human rights domain are suffering repression, and these are being left highly vulnerable by the international community's overwhelming focus on a select number of individual human rights activists. In most of the affected states, donors' overall funding of civil society has decreased dramatically.[34] Donors often fail to help activists well before they are put on trial or targeted with specific restrictive measures. At present, they often recoil from supporting the kind of new activist groups that regimes are already discrediting, prior to their needing emergency assistance.

Donors have done relatively little to help CSOs widen their domestic networks of supporters so that they are better protected when restrictive measures hit. They have largely withdrawn from supporting civic activism in the Middle East and North Africa region, for example, because they failed to build partnerships with local, informal, and traditional networks that might have allowed for a way around the closing-space challenge. Many campaigners are critical of donors for simply "running away" from backing civic activism as restrictions tighten and leaving them highly vulnerable. The international response still needs to move from a focus on protecting a small selection of individual activists to tackling the broader parameters of the shrinking space for civil society as a whole.[35]

In some development agencies the temptation has been to respond to other governments' civil society restrictions by stepping back from overtly political funding and concentrating instead on apolitical, developmental activism. It is often argued now that, in such a heated and toxic political climate, donors need to switch focus completely to support apolitical cultural exchanges and support international networks of writers, artists, journalists, lawyers, and the like that can defend their members in repressive states.[36]

Many emerging civic activists are highly critical of this shift in emphasis. In practice the space for even apparently nonpolitical campaigns is increasingly curtailed. The apolitical approach of avoiding contentious new civic activism is not working well because regimes have increasingly made development NGOs as well as democracy and human rights campaigners the targets of restrictive measures. The deepening of the shrinking-space problem means that it is increasingly difficult for donors simply to circumvent the issue by supporting "nonpolitical" organizations. This may have worked to a modest degree in some places, but the evidence suggests that it has not served uniformly as a means of successfully keeping rights-based issues on the agenda.

A related tactic and concern has been for donors to try to reassure governments that supporting civil society is not synonymous with opposing a regime. Some funders now acknowledge they need to work with those parts of civil society close to or supportive of governments. They have tried to clarify that supporting civil society is not the same thing as supporting the opposition. Populations often now support new restrictions against NGOs because the latter are seen as donor creations. In general, donors are making more effort to reach out to the society as a whole and to explain that their aid is about helping local aims and not implanting a Western system or advancing Western aims. In most cases, however, international funders could still do more to define clear red lines to ensure that their support for the new civic activism is indeed politically impartial.

It is important to note there is a major tension at play: in some instances donors are trying to be more open and explain their funding activities more completely, but this runs against the grain of other changes they are introducing, which are designed to increase secrecy—as some funders are searching for more covert ways of getting support to activists in order to protect the latter from unwelcome attention from government officials. It might be that a good response requires this mix of openness and secrecy. But there is a risk that donors are reacting in ad hoc ways and getting stranded between the two stools; efforts to be transparent and new covert support mechanisms could end up cutting across one another and almost canceling each other out. In this sense, governments can see a focus on the newer forms of civic activism as potentially beneficial but also in some instances as problematic; as yet they lack a clear, consistent policy line on how the new activism relates to the closing-civic-space challenge.

Conclusion

The new civic activism has emerged partly in response to government attacks on formal NGOs. But the new activism is itself increasingly faced with the same challenge of the closing space. To counteract this, a tighter link needs to be fostered between the new forms of activism explored throughout this book, on the one hand, and the closing-space phenomenon, on the other hand. Civic activism has sought to become even more fluid and adaptive than it has been, as it reshapes itself into innovative kinds of organizational forms that are less susceptible to restrictions. Yet the international community is lagging behind in its support for these new kinds of civic activism.

So far the international community has been relatively cautious in taking on this challenge. Crucially, while donors and international organizations have adopted a wide range of measures, they have not yet systemically incorporated a focus on new forms of civic activism as part of their response to the closing space. If they are to defend the new civic activism effectively, they need to map out a clearer strategic approach to the shrinking space, as it is now clear that merely ad hoc and defensive responses will not be adequate. The fate of the new civic activism may rely on a more assertive international diplomacy to protect the right to assembly and the freedom to protest. Donors need to move from reactive to proactive mode in fostering innovative types of activism and getting ahead of the curve to head off regime attacks on activists. This will require more political forms of solidarity if the new activism is to survive the current onslaught from governments.[37] An effective fight against the shrinking space will require much stronger and wider coalitions among civil society actors and international organizations[38] The current situation cries out for a major multilateral initiative in this direction, as well as much more commitment among activists themselves to form effective partnerships with reformers across borders.

10

Conclusion

Ongoing changes to civic activism around the world are profound, accelerating, and in many senses systemic in their reach. This book has chronicled and highlighted just how important and widespread the changes are. Yet it has also cautioned that overly sweeping generalizations need to be avoided in describing these shifts. The contours of an emerging and fast-evolving civic activism are indeed evident. What is new about this activism tends to be more subtle and nuanced than sometimes assumed, however. Both the distension and the boundaries of the new activism require careful assessment. Much media and analytical commentary leaves the impression that the world is pulsating with anger as vast numbers of citizens connect in extensive, leaderless networks. If this is in part indeed the case, the more measured picture is of a varied and multidimensional form of modern civic activism. In this vein, the book offers a number of significant findings about the current state of global civil society.

New forms of activism

A significant degree of change is occurring within civil society as the intensity and range of civic activism mount. While much of this has roots going back some time, activism's evolving shapes and thematic priorities invite a reconceptualization of civil society. Civic activism has become more sporadic, footloose, tactically innovative, daring, effervescent, and intent on carving out local autonomy and ownership; it has become more fluid, spontaneous, fluctuating in its intensity, and in some guises more tightly focused on community aims.

Throughout the book, I have described and summarized an extensive range of new activist initiatives and protests from all regions of the world. I have done so very deliberately to reflect and demonstrate the global reach of the new activism. A select number of revolts have received extensive analytical attention in recent years; the Occupy and antiausterity protests in the West, Egypt's revolts, and Turkey's Gezi protests have been especially well covered. Yet other examples from the strikingly wide and deep pool of emerging activism remain underanalyzed. There is a risk that analytical conclusions are being drawn from what is in truth only a small subset of the emerging civic activism.

As new civic movements have spread, the evidence shows that these emerging forms of civic organization have extended through all continents. Many of these kinds of civic activism have existed for some time but are currently enjoying a new resurgence and qualitative reorientation. They function in different ways than long-established NGOs, although there is often an overlap in some of the features that characterize the older and newer types of civic activism.

The kinds of civic activism that have spread most dramatically can be strikingly fluid and informal, but there is no single model, to the extent that some new activism rests on more solid and traditional organizational infrastructure than others. And the new activism is not just about loose, informal social movements. While many examples of new civic organization resonate with the field of social movement analysis, other strands of emergent activism do not fit this template. Today's civic activism includes much activity that cannot be likened to any kind of "movement." It often takes the form of discrete initiatives rather than movements as such and is often about highly dispersed sets of relations between activists.[1]

Behind this broad, structural trend, it is important to recognize and better understand some of the more nuanced details. Modern activism embraces different forms of activity and very different substantive agendas. Some new initiatives are practical, some political. Some are leftist, some are conservative, while others reject both these traditional labels. Some are peaceful; others espouse a radicalism that can shade into violence. Some are populist, others antipopulist. Some activism has emerged in the confines of closed politics; some has been catalyzed by open politics. Many Western activists have homed in on issues related to economic austerity and often aspire to sweeping change of the entire economic system, while non-Western activists are often grounded in less grandiose goals.

Analytically, such disaggregation is necessary to move debates beyond a simple counterpoising of old against new activism—a division that habitually treats the latter as a monolithic uniform phenomenon. It might be said that the emerging civic activism is partly liberal, partly radical, partly conservative, and partly nonideologically pragmatic—with all these different types of civic identity gaining ground simultaneously.[2]

Civic activists today often focus on very local issues, and activism has to some degree pivoted away from overarching issues of global justice.[3] The high-profile set-piece events at summit meetings that became standard in the 1990s and early 2000s are no longer activism's core—even though episodes like the July 2017 G20 protests and 2018 global Women's Marches still attract much media attention.

National or community rootedness is one of the defining features of the new activism—and one that has gained prominence over internationally oriented NGOs.[4] Activism is today often expressed in a kind of microlevel civic vernacular specific to particular localities. These new forms of activism based around community-level mutualism are so potent and important because they reflect deeper changes in economic production and also social structures. The irony is that incipient hyperlocalism is itself becoming something of a global trend.

Academic assessments commonly assert that in the 1990s and early 2000s many NGOs came to indulge neoliberalism and provide services to replace a shrinking state, whereas the new activism is about creating economic alternatives; a general feeling is that the new activism is more radical than the old activism. The notion of civil society being in the service of neoliberalism is certainly being challenged more ferociously by some new civic activism. The emergent strain of unrestrained activism and protest shows that civil society activity today extends beyond the relatively genteel world of NGOs lobbying on issues that largely fall within the scope of already acceptable policy parameters.

However, this picture does not apply to all types of emergent activism. The common suggestion that old NGO-based activism is conservatively acquiescent in neoliberalism while the new activism is radically progressive risks becoming a caricature. It fails to capture the variation in both old and new activism—and the different, not always antithetical ways in which they relate to each other. On the one hand, many emergent forms of civic activism have become less restrained and more willing to question existing assumptions about democracy, participation, and fairness in a way that most formalized, donor-sponsored NGOs were reluctant to do in the 1990s and early 2000s. On the other hand, much of the new activism is far removed from the pursuit of cogent, well-worked alternatives to capitalism or neoliberalism.

In much of the new activism, a spirit of civic volunteerism and community-level practical organization seeks not so much overt confrontation as indirect workarounds—a middle route between taking on the system and meekly serving it. While it is true that many civic movements seek a more contentious politics, the new activism is often contentious in an *indirect* form. It can often cut across the supposed dichotomy between two sharply opposed conceptions of civil society—that of activism checking but ultimately accepting state power, on the one hand, and that of emancipatory, counterhegemonic activism, on the other hand. This long-standing frame for debating the rightful role of civil society no longer fully captures civic activism's hybrid eclecticism.

Many new civic initiatives are not the kind of overtly antiregime ventures that can be captured through a standard society-versus-regime prism. Rather, much emerging civic activism works more subtly and often covertly. It has adapted to regimes' red lines, and in turn regimes incorporate some activism in a way that helps them survive. In many autocratic settings, today's activism is less a spontaneous project in favor of democracy and more part of an implicit understanding between social actors and the state.[5] The new activism is not always about seeking radical improvements to Western-driven liberal democracy; it just as often follows a very different dynamic. Similarly, the common tendency to elide the new activism with radical anticapitalist politics does a disservice to the complexity of current shifts in global civil society; modern activism sometimes adheres to this kind of identity but often does not.

The relationship between new civic activism and the much-debated surge in populism around the world is varied. In some instances, new activism has set itself squarely against the ascendant political style of illiberal populists. In other instances, new forms of civic activism are the bottom-up driving force behind populism.[6] This book has chronicled across many regions the rise of a right-wing activism that contests NGOs' standard, progressive identities. A deeply conservative civic activism is taking root in many parts of the world; if there is radicalism in the sweep of new civic activism, it is of the rightist as much as leftist variety. This conservative activism itself covers a wide spectrum, from the outright uncivil and violent through to more measured challenges to certain liberal values. Underlying much illiberal populism is a change in the way that citizens seek to engage with or against elites.

While these trends are far-reaching, it is important not to exaggerate. The new activism still involves a relatively modest percentage of the population, and in some cases it is not clear that it has greatly extended the number of engaged citizens beyond the numbers involved in the much-maligned professional NGO sector. Moreover, away from the novel and new groups that draw analysts' interest, much civil society activity is still of the traditional kind and has not undergone any qualitative change in recent years. The new activism is far from having entirely replaced the more traditional forms of NGO activity.

Protests

The ongoing increase in large-scale protests is significant. These protests represent a parallel process to the growth in new forms of civic organization, as revolts often grow out of the latter—although this is not always the case. Social protests have occurred at an unprecedented rate in the last decade. They have taken place in every region of the world and under all types of political regime. They have been triggered by a variety of driving factors. Some aim to throw out corrupt or undemocratic regimes; others seek a radical change in economic policies; others have more modest and specific goals. Such protests have become a staple feature of global politics.

The aims that animate protests overlap and differ among individual protesters. Nearly all mass mobilizations are made up of diverse elements, bringing together uneasy allies whose agendas and operational modes diverge significantly. While there is undoubtedly a degree of spontaneity to most protests, many are part of ongoing confrontation between reformers and state institutions that plays out in different forms in each national context.

A common view is that capitalism's or globalization's losers are the main drivers of today's protests.[7] This standard view works for some protests but not for others. There are those protests that demand formal democracy and those that dismiss such formal democracy as insufficient. Although analysis of protesters in the West habitually focuses on their skepticism toward formal democracy, protesters in authoritarian countries still fight for the kind of basic democratic rights that rich-world protesters now dismiss as hollow.

Most protests contain some mix of economic and political aims and some combination of very specific policy concerns with more generic antisystem discontent. Nearly all protests are ignited by a proximate cause: a particularly emblematic corruption case; a disaster that kills many people and can be traced back to government negligence. But they also emerge out of background grievances that fester for years, such as a slow decline in political freedoms or poor economic performance—or for rightists, a gradual rise in immigration and dilution of traditional or national values. As a general rule, protests erupt in dramatic fashion when both an immediate trigger and longer-term frustrations are powerfully present and interlock with each other.

Analytical implications flow from this: accounts of protests can often be incomplete because different groups of analysts focus on particular kinds of protests rather than the totality of the phenomenon. As noted, social movement experts tend to study antiglobalization and antiausterity mobilizations and neglect the significance of other driving factors and civic identities, especially those of a more conservative-nationalist hue. Democracy experts tend to focus on antiauthoritarian protests and leave an impression that this is an entirely different world of protest from the leftist anti-globalization movements. If anything, today's protests are characterized by an increasingly eclectic mix of dynamics, one that cautions against any single, uniform statement of what these revolts are "really about."

The results of protests and revolts have been mixed in recent years. There have been few outright successes, more cases of partial success, and some notable failures. Many of the factors normally suggested to explain why today's mass protests are either successful or ineffective do not entirely weather scrutiny. Indeed, it is difficult to boil down why some protests succeed and others fail to one or two simple variables.

While civic activism has been at the forefront of major political changes in many countries, it has usually not brought about long-term reform to the structures of governance. In the worst cases, protests have simply unleashed more draconian state repression and set back the causes for which they took place. Today's activists often compare their revolts to those of the Paris Commune in 1848, and as in that episode they have often suffered reprisals worse than the injustices that drove them to protest in the first place.

Beyond these worst cases, where protests achieve some positive change they often struggle to sustain innovative campaigns or to move effectively "from protest to politics." They have on occasion shown themselves potent in bringing down governments but not in constructing new ones. They can help kick-start democratic transitions but have often not helped keep these transitions on track over the long term. They have been good at pressing and cornering governments but less attuned to bringing constructive ideas for reform to the table. They are often good at confrontation but not at nuanced alliance building or making the necessary concessions to participate in broad governing coalitions.

These are all fairly standard criticisms made against the new activism. This book adds to existing debates by pointing out that such criticisms may be generally convincing but are not valid in all cases. Indeed, today such critiques look rather too sweeping. The foregoing chapters have presented a wide range of evidence that reveals cases where these often-commented-upon shortcomings do not apply, or at least where new tactics have mitigated such weaknesses. In some cases the new civic activism has been more conciliatory, more politically nuanced, and more constructive than it is habitually assumed to be. The emergent civic activism is far from being entirely disruptive, shallow, and contrarian. Some activists now make a point of insisting that they are actually "anti-antipolitics" and insist their core aim is to see more issues brought back into the political sphere from technocratic bodies. Contrary to conventional wisdom, some revolts do make a successful move from protest into normal politics.

Again, a caveat is in order: while the wave of protests has become an important and even defining dimension of global politics, it is important to retain a measured sense of perspective. Protests have become more numerous, more intense, more geographically widespread, and more explosively rapid and agile. Yet the spread of protests should not blind us to the reverse side of the coin: namely, the fact that in many contexts today's most pressing problem is not chaotic mobilization and ungovernability but citizens' inability to engage critically in any meaningful way to counter dysfunctional politics. Most civic activity is not protest. There is much pent-up discontent in authoritarian states that is still not expressing itself in protests. While the new wave of global protest is significant and unprecedented on many measures, it does *not* show that citizens have in all conditions or as a matter of course found the way or the will to protest systematically against nondemocratic regimes.

Explanations

The causal drivers of today's reshaped civic activism are both reactive and proactive. That is, the new activism is a reaction to deep-rooted problems of corruption, repression, economic injustice, the uncertainties of change, and governments' unresponsiveness to citizens' concerns, but it is in some cases proactive in discovering and designing new tactics and taking advantage of the enhanced resources and organizational options available within the civic sphere. New activism is born of both necessity and opportunistic creativity. Citizens seek alternative forms of activism because much of the wider, traditional civil society sphere has atrophied; yet, more positively, the new activism is sometimes also about deploying new tools and resources to add in a more complementary way to the work undertaken by standard NGOs.

The new civic activism is driven by a combination of opportunity and imperative. The common explanation that sees activism advancing when activists are able to mobilize resources is still pertinent. Yet today this still holds in places but has a less widespread relevance than may previously have been the case. It is a pattern that fits some of the emerging activism but not all of it.

Certainly, in many rising economies the newly empowered middle classes lead parts of the new activism, focusing on postmaterial grievances. On the back of economic growth and development, they have more resources and enhanced organizational capacity. Some research supports the view that civic activism rises in correlation with economic development.[8] For some authors this is part of what makes new civic activism so conservative, and in fact not focused on the kind of radical, emancipatory change that spurred activists in previous periods.[9]

Yet other areas of the emerging activism do not fit this model, as they involve poorer sectors of society and do not benefit from any obvious increase in organizational capacity. This strand of activism has emerged because problems are intensifying, not because of new material or political opportunities. It is a response to more acute hardships, organizational challenges, and social restrictions—almost the antithesis of the political-opportunity explanation for movement-based activism. World Values Survey data suggest that civic activism has in recent years intensified most notably in those countries most affected by backsliding toward authoritarian politics.[10]

Against the erstwhile focus on activism as a means of identity formation, many scholars interpret the new activism through an anticapitalist or antiglobalization lens and suggest that issues of class interests need to be brought back in as causal drivers. This tilt back toward material concerns is a significant shift given that many originally believed modern activism to be defined by nonmaterial issues.[11]

This conceptual adjustment is overdue but should not be taken too far. While many analysts see the phenomenon of civic activism as almost synonymous with anticapitalist protest, it is in truth a far broader and heterogeneous trend. In the developing world the shift is, if anything, in the other direction, toward activism targeted at a broader set of rights questions and away from purely economic and developmental questions. The idea—present at least implicitly in some Western literature—that the new activism is everywhere essentially a mimic of the US Occupy or European antiausterity movements is not accurate.

Overall, then, there are some explanations of the new activism that are to do with the nature of that activism itself and others that are related to political context. Countries' historically rooted structures of political order are different, and this conditions the context within which civic activism functions.[12] The question is whether activists have the strength to alter this in any meaningful fashion—that is, to override context-specific institutional features. The outcomes of recent protests are varied and inconclusive on this key question. Some have failed because their background context was so inauspicious, while others have succeeded in part because their context was more benign. Yet inverse examples are also plentiful: protests that had an impact in the most challenging contexts and those that failed where background conditions seemed ripe for change.

There is a final, more proximate explanatory driver of the new civic activism: a harsh wave of government attacks on civil society organizations. The era is one of both civil society empowerment and a stifling of civic organizations—and these two sides of the civil society coin are tightly interrelated. Regimes have become more brutal and clever in how they seek to constrict civil society freedoms. In some ways the new civic activism is an attempt to get around this, while government crackdowns are themselves a response to the new activism and an effort to prevent it gathering more steam.

The more limited space that now exists for civil society is surely not a temporary anomaly but is likely to be the new normal. The so-called closing-space problem is becoming a far broader phenomenon than most accounts of it suggest is the case. New types of activism offer some scope to evade the wave of reprisals against NGOs, but they cannot entirely escape the closing-space menace. The attack on global civil society can only be tempered through a wide range of more structural measures that address its root causes; it cannot be simply or entirely circumvented by new types of civic activism. For now it is unclear which has the upper hand, which is the more defining feature of the age: the new tide of empowered civic activism or regimes' assault on the free civic ethos.

Old versus new activism

In terms of the relationship between the old and new civic activism, the evidence points toward a similarly mixed picture. Some analysts and activists insist that the new activism is fundamentally antagonistic toward and in intense competition with traditional NGOs. At the other extreme, others believe there is nothing much genuinely new in the "new" activism to set it at odds with the older forms of civil society organization; these skeptics would probably dismiss the trends described in this book as little more than a continuation of previous or already existing civic activity. The evidence suggests that neither of these two perspectives provides an adequately nuanced portrait.

It is certainly the case that the new civic activism has often rubbed uneasily against more established NGOs. There remains much hostility between the two sets of civic actors, precisely because they are so different. But the new activism has not completely displaced the old; indeed, the two have melded together in many cases, and far more than has normally been assumed. This book has disaggregated the ways in which, in at least some instances, a more positive and complementary relationship between new civic activism and long-standing NGOs has taken root.

The most common situation is for established NGOs to be present but secondary players in today's protests, and for most protesters to be active neither in political parties nor in formal civil society bodies. NGOs play their part in trying to give more robust solidity to these revolts and translating explosive uprisings into longer-running civic campaigns; this role is useful and cannot be said to contradict protest aims, even if it is not normally the central dynamic or ethos of today's protests. There is some evidence that new and traditional civic activisms are just beginning to work out an effective division of labor. The record of recent years suggests that a judicious mix of competition and cooperation between new and old civic groups will imbue civic activism with its greatest influence over global politics.

There is not always an entirely sharp or qualitative distinction between emerging networks or movements and NGOs. New movements are not always the leaderless and structureless, nonorganized organizations of popular legend. For their part, NGOs can also be based in local communities doing grassroots development work and may be organized in a fairly informal way, grouping together a loose network of activists. Private-sector civic-tech start-ups and social entrepreneurship are other alternatives to NGOs that are emerging as vehicles for civic activism in challenging political contexts—this denoting another blurred line, in this case between civil society and the private sector. A broader implication for future research agendas follows from this: rather than focusing on social movements as homogenous organizational entities as such, research will need to examine activism that constantly crosses the divides between movements, NGOs, parties, and very ad hoc, spontaneous civic activity.

Criticisms of professional NGOs are merited, yet there is a degree of exaggeration in the now-standard line that these are uniquely unworthy forms of civic organization and that informal activism is intrinsically more legitimate, more effective, and more in tune with genuine citizen interests. This line overplays the divide between such NGOs and new civic forms, and it also somewhat overlooks the latter's own shortcomings. The informal networks that play a pivotal role in the new kinds of civic initiatives do not always or necessarily represent a form of benign politics undertaken by the ordinary citizen in pursuit of global commons—as evidenced by reactionary, even violent strands of the new activism. While new movements lacerate old NGOs for being little more than exclusionary cartels of vested interests, the new activists are themselves not entirely free of such blemishes.

The impact on democracy

This book has sought to tie together all the components and complexities of the new civic activism and to ascertain what they mean for democracy. Some aspects of the new activism are problematic for democratic quality, others more benign. Rather than reaching for a blanket, overarching judgment on whether this activism rescues or disassembles democracy, it is more instructive to unravel the ways in which it contributes toward a different *type* of democracy.

The new activism pushes toward a pluralism that is more erratic, with policy dynamics differing across policies and variations in democratic forms coming to the fore. It catalyzes shifts in the relationship between local accountability and national politics and leaves a profusion of civic forums vying for access to the democratic process. It also leads to a certain convergence of civic processes across different types of political regime, as looser forms of activism prosper in both established democracies and authoritarian states.

It is not yet entirely clear whether emerging forms of civic activism are ready and able to play constructive, democracy-building roles to the full—and more particularly, whether they are any better equipped in this regard than established NGOs. Indeed, in some of its guises the emerging civic activism involves ethnic and nationalist groupings pursuing nonliberal initiatives; it can no longer be so easily assumed as before that civic activism is largely synonymous with campaigns for progressive, liberal rights.[13]

This book has uncovered these contrasting impacts in one specific and central dimension of the new civic activism: digital technology. This is a core part of what makes the new civic activism tick and a crucial ingredient in its high-profile and potential effectiveness. But digital technology has a varied impact on civic activism. Digital activism brings with it many benefits for civic activists—but also increasingly apparent downsides. There are tensions between activists' use of information communications technology and their aim to get more citizens involved in practical civic action. New digital technologies have not yet enticed a significantly larger number of citizens into full political engagement. As digital activism moves into a new era, modifying some of the shortfalls of its formative phases of development, it will need to evolve in ways that enhance a wider range of democratic influence.

Challenges of supporting new activism

The changing face of civic activism around the world presents international aid donors with opportunities and challenges. These will have far-reaching ramifications for how international support is best delivered to civil society actors. The trends described in this book are not of merely analytical interest; nor are they only relevant to debates about political struggles within particular nation-state contexts. Rather, the trends in new civic activism pose profound questions for international diplomacy and for the very practical choices that governments, foundations, and multilateral organizations make when they support civil society—for developmental and political objectives.

In assessing the practical international policy ramifications of the new civic activism, this book has argued that a new generation of civil society assistance is needed but as yet lacks definition. Donors habitually argue that societies are healthier, more resilient, and more just when they have active civil societies. Yet changes to the nature of civic activism around the world mean that international support to civil society organizations needs to be rethought if the civic sphere is to get outside help to fulfil these functions.

The need for such a shift flows from a creeping marginalization of Western-supported NGOs in many countries experiencing roiling sociopolitical change. Donor-supported NGOs have not commonly been at the forefront of change in countries experiencing protest and major political disruption in recent years. The legitimacy of international NGO support has suffered as it has been caught up in the general antielite zeitgeist. The ease with which governments have marginalized prominent NGOs poses thorny questions about how well rooted donor-supported civil society groups are in their own societies. Their apparent lack of public support and their weak grassroots connections have accentuated their vulnerability to government-orchestrated marginalization. It would behoove the international community to reexamine the way it supports and conceptualizes global civil society.

While aid donors have begun to acknowledge the limits to supporting traditional NGOs, they remain circumspect in their support for the new civic activism. There are a number of reasons for this caution. In part it reflects donors' ambivalence over the new activists' political agendas and tactics; in part it is because of the practical difficulties of getting support through to relatively unstructured new organizations; in part it is related to activists' own lack of clarity about what kind of outside support they want. The international community's challenge is to devise novel initiatives that offer support for the new activism without undercutting new activists' autonomy or distinctive advantages over the old-style activism.

Donors could still gain significant advantages from a more systematic and generous focus on citizen movements and other innovative forms of activism outside the formal, organized NGO sector. A common view is that support to local activists would enhance donors' rights-based approach to development and reach out better to marginalized and grassroots sectors of the population. A deeper engagement with popular movements would help connect donors to grassroots actors and thus make aid more effective.[14]

All this points to the considerations that will determine whether civic activism has a healthy future. The new, looser forms of activism have both advantages and disadvantages and will likely complement rather than replace NGOs. While the international community would err if it simply redirected existing support from NGOs to this new activism, at present it is most commonly guilty of *under*playing the value of innovative activism. As the civic sphere evolves, a judicious balance will be needed between the new and the old civic activism, along with a more tailored focus on the most positive elements of the new activism. As shown throughout this book, where the old and new activisms work in tandem, they often have more chance of success. With multiple and varied protests still crowding onto the international agenda, this is surely a vitally important lesson for the future of civic politics.

Growing out of and extending previous periods of civic change, the current spike in civic activism appears firmly set to be more than a temporary blip, and the innovative changes that drive it promise far-reaching significance. A battery of new protests has erupted in 2018; citizen consultations are appearing across the European Union; new forms of local assemblies and community organization are multiplying from Brazil to Turkey, and from Ukraine to India. The analytical and policy issues covered in this book will condition the longevity of activism's current wave. And they will determine how far these forms of civic activism contribute to—or, more worryingly, detract from—democracy's much-needed regeneration. While optimists and pessimists may differ in their prognoses on this, it seems clear that a deep and balanced understanding of the new civic activism will be increasingly pertinent to the future of global politics.

NOTES

Chapter 1

1. The project is at http://carnegieendowment.org/specialprojects/civicresearchnetwork.
2. Definitive works in this vein include D. della Porta and M. Diani, *Social Movements: An Introduction*, 2nd ed. (Oxford: Blackwell, 2006), 18–20; S. Tarrow, *Power in Movement: Social Movements and Contentious Politics*, 3rd ed. (Cambridge: Cambridge University Press, 2011), 6; C. Tilly and S. Tarrow, *Contentious Politics*, 2nd ed. (Oxford: Oxford University Press, 2015), 11. For a collective overview of the social movement field, see J. Goodwin and J. Jasper, eds., *The Social Movements Reader*, 2nd ed. (Chichester, UK, and Malden, MA: Wiley-Blackwell, 2009).
3. See G. Martin, *Understanding Social Movements* (London: Routledge, 2015) for a good, recent overview of competing schools of social movement analysis.

Chapter 2

1. T. Beichelt, I. Hahn-Fuhr, F. Schimmelfennig, and S. Worschech, *Civil Society and Democracy Promotion* (London: Palgrave Macmillan, 2014); I. Krastev, *Democracy Disrupted* (Philadelphia: University of Pennsylvania Press, 2014).
2. International Civil Society Centre, *Riding the Wave* (Berlin: International Civil Society Centre, 2013).
3. B. Gnarig, "The Old World of Civic Participation Is Being Replaced," *openDemocracy*, 30 November 2016, https://www.opendemocracy.net/openglobalrights/burkhard-gn-rig/old-world-of-civic-participation-is-being-replaced.
4. Civicus, *State of Civil Society Report* 2015, https://www.civicus.org/index.php/socs2015, 70.
5. E. Lilja, "A New Ecology of Civil Society II," *Journal of Civil Society* 11, no. 4 (2015): 402–407, reporting on a major project funded by the Danish government.
6. P. Mair, *Ruling the Void* (London: Verso, 2013).
7. Edelman Trust Barometer 2017, https://www.edelman.com/trust2017/.
8. Compare p. 63 of the 2014 data in ISSP Research Group, *International Social Survey Programme: Citizenship II—ISSP* 2014 (Cologne: GESIS Data Archive, 2016) with p. 61 of the 2004 data in ISSP Research Group, *International Social Survey Programme: Citizenship II—ISSP* 2014 (Cologne: GESIS Data Archive, 2016). R. Dalton, *The Participation Gap* (Oxford: Oxford University Press, 2017) also uses the ISSP data to show the same trend.
9. International IDEA, *The Global State of Democracy: Exploring Democracy's Resilience* (Stockholm: International IDEA, 2017), 25, 78.
10. V-Dem Institute, *V-Dem Annual Report 2017: Democracy at Dusk?* (Gothenburg: V-Dem Institute at the University of Gothenburg, 2017).
11. Participedia is at https://participedia.net.

12. N. Pollock, B. Pressey, and T. Foreman, "Dolores Huerta's Life of Activism," *Atlantic*, video report, 18 April 2017, https://www.theatlantic.com/video/index/537165/dolores-huerta-wants-more-activism/.
13. R. Putnam, *Bowling Alone: The Collapse and Revival of American Community* (New York: Simon & Schuster, 2000).
14. M. Castells, *Networks of Outrage and Hope: Social Movements in the Internet Age* (Cambridge: Polity Press, 2012); P. Mason, *Why It's Still Kicking Off Everywhere: The New Global Revolutions* (Brooklyn, NY: Verso, 2011); C. F. Fominaya, *Social Movements and Globalization: How Protests, Occupations, and Uprisings Are Changing the World* (London: Palgrave Macmillan, 2014); K. Naidoo, "Boiling Point: Can Citizen Action Save the World?" *Development Dialogue* 54 (July 2010).
15. M. Kaldor and S. Selchow, *The Bubbling Up of Subterranean Politics in Europe* (London: LSE Civil Society and Human Security Unit, 2012), 18–19, 24.
16. F. Miszlivetz, "Lost in Transformation: The Crisis of Democracy and Civil Society," in *Global Civil Society 2012: Ten Years of Critical Reflection*, ed. S. Selchow, M. Kaldor, and H. Moore (London: Palgrave Macmillan, 2012), 62, 64.
17. J. Ekman and E. Amna, "Political Participation and Civic Engagement: Towards a New Typology," *Human Affairs* 22 (2012): 283–300.
18. D. Harvey, *Rebel Cities: From the Right to the City to the Urban Revolution* (London: Verso, 2013).
19. F. Polletta, "Social Movements in an Age of Participation," *Mobilization* 21, no. 4 (2016): 485–497.
20. F. Cavatorta, ed., *Civil Society Activism under Authoritarian Rule: A Comparative Perspective* (London: Routledge, 2013).
21. S. Hessel, *Indignez-Vous* (Montpelier: Indigène, 2010).
22. E. Clemens, "Commentary: The Many Paths from Protest to Politics," *Journal of Civil Society* 9, no. 1 (2013): 111–115.
23. P. Beaumont, "Global Protest Grows as Citizens Lose Faith in Politics and the State," *Guardian*, 22 June 2013, https://www.theguardian.com/world/2013/jun/22/urban-protest-changing-global-social-network.
24. P. Mishra, *Age of Anger* (London: Allen Lane, 2017).
25. Economist Intelligence Unit, *Rebels without a Cause: What the Upsurge in Protest Movements Means for Global Politics*, 2013, https://www.eiu.com/public/topical_report.aspx?campaignid=ProtestUpsurge.
26. J. Tully, *On Global Citizenship* (London: Bloomsbury, 2014).
27. D. della Porta and M. Diani, "Introduction: The Field of Social Movement Studies," in *The Oxford Handbook of Social Movements*, ed. D. della Porta and M. Diani (Oxford: Oxford University Press, 2015), 4.
28. A theme stressed in the different contributions to F. Rossi and M. von Bulow, eds., *Social Movement Dynamics: New Perspectives on Theory and Research from Latin America* (Farnham: Ashgate, 2015).
29. CitizensLab, *Mapping New Forms of Civic Engagement in Europe* (Berlin: MitOst e.V, 2017), 126, 136.
30. U. Beck, *Risk Society: Towards a New Modernity* (London: Sage, 1992).
31. G. Monbiot, *Out of the Wreckage: A New Politics for an Age of Crisis* (London: Verso, 2017) 76–77.
32. G. Monbiot, "This Is How People Can Truly Take Back Control: From the Bottom-Up," *Guardian*, 8 February 2017, https://www.theguardian.com/commentisfree/2017/feb/08/take-back-control-bottom-up-communities.
33. Home page, Building Change Trust website, accessed 12 February 2018, http://civicactivism.buildingchangetrust.org/.
34. CitizensLab, *Mapping New Forms of Civic Engagement*.
35. A. Smith, M. Fressoli, D. Abrol, E. Around, and A. Ely, *Grassroots Innovation Movements* (London: Routledge, 2016).
36. J. Bartlett, *Radicals: Outsiders Changing the World* (London: Heinemann, 2017).
37. F. Powell, *The Politics of Civil Society*, 2nd ed. (Bristol: Policy Press, 2013), 33.

38. A. Farro, "A New Era for Collective Movements: The Subjectivization of Collection Action," in *Reimagining Social Movements: From Collectives to Individuals*, ed. A. Farro and H. Lustiger-Thaler (London: Routledge, 2016), 17.
39. H. Anheier and N. Scherer, "Voluntary Actions and Social Movements," in della Porta and Diani, *Oxford Handbook of Social Movements*; A. Ishkanian, "Engineered Civil Society: The Impact of 20 Years of Democracy Promotion on Civil Society Development in Former Soviet Countries," in *Civil Society and Democracy Promotion*, ed. T. Beichelt, I. Hahn-Fuhr, F. Schimmelfennig, and S. Worschech (London: Palgrave Macmillan, 2014). For broader background, see the classic J. Keane, *Global Civil Society?* (Cambridge: Cambridge University Press, 2003); A.-M. Fechter, "Citizen Aid—and Why Ordinary People Are Founding Their Own Development Projects," *The Conversation*, 25 September 2017, https://theconversation.com/citizen-aid-and-why-ordinary-people-are-founding-their-own-development-projects-83665.
40. S. Tormey, *The End of Representative Politics* (Cambridge: Polity Press, 2015), 31.
41. Civicus, *State of Civil Society Report* 2018, https://www.civicus.org/index.php/state-of-civil-society-report-2018.
42. P. Kopecky and C. Mudde, *Uncivil Society? Contentious Politics in Post-Communist Europe* (London: Routledge, 2003).
43. M. Stephan and E. Chenoweth, "Why Civil Resistance Works: The Strategoc Logic of Nonviolent Conflict," *International Security* 33, no. 1 (2008); M. Stephan, "Responding to the Global Threat of Closing Civic Space," Congressional Testimony, 21 March 2017, https://www.usip.org/publications/2017/03/responding-global-threat-closing-civic-space-policy-options.
44. A. Mammone, E. Godin, and B. Jenkins, eds., *Mapping the Extreme Right in Contemporary Europe: From Local to Transnational* (London: Routledge, 2012).
45. G. Lazaridis, G. Campani, and A. Benveniste, eds., *The Rise of the Far Right in Europe: Populist Shifts and "Othering"* (Basingstoke: Palgrave Macmillan, 2016).
46. For a more detailed exploration of these themes, see R. Youngs, ed., *The Mobilization of Conservative Civil Society* (Washington, DC: Carnegie Endowment for International Peace, 2018).
47. M. Schulz, "A Longue Durée Approach to the Role of Civil Society in the Uprisings against Authoritarianism in the Arab World," *Journal of Civil Society* 11, no. 4 (2015): 424–439.
48. "How to Document, Train and Analyze Social Activism in the Arab Region," conference held at Asfari Institute for Civil Society and Citizenship, American University of Beirut, 31 March 2018.
49. I. Jebari, "Social Entrepreneurship among Algeria's Youth," *Carnegie Sada Journal*, 13 December 2016, http://carnegieendowment.org/sada/66429.
50. J. Beinin and F. Veirel, eds., *Social Movements, Mobilization, and Contestation in the Middle East and North Africa*, 2nd ed. (London: Routledge, 2013) 11.
51. Arab Reform Initiative, *Effervescent Egypt: Venues of Mobilization and the Interrupted Legacy of 2011* (N.p.: Arab Reform Initiative, 2018).
52. P. Becker and F. Stolleis, "The Crushing of Syria's Civil Actors," (Berlin: Stiftung Wissenschaft und Politik, 2016).
53. H. Al-Saidawi, "Preparing for the Aftermath," *Diwan* (Carnegie Middle East Center blog), 11 July 2018, http://carnegie-mec.org/diwan/76783.
54. A. Härdig, "Beyond the Arab Revolts: Conceptualizing Civil Society in the Middle East and North Africa," *Democratization* 22, no. 6 (2015): 1131–1153.
55. B. Özçetin and M. Özer, "The Current Policy Environment for Civil Society in Turkey," Johns Hopkins Comparative Nonprofit Sector Project Working Paper 53, January 2015, http://ccss.jhu.edu/wp-content/uploads/downloads/2015/02/Turkey_CNP_WP53_2015_FINAL.pdf, 9.
56. O. Zihnoglu, "Islamic Civil Society in Turkey," in Youngs, *The Mobilization of Conservative Civil Society*.
57. O. Zihnioglu, "Resuming Civic Activism in Turkey," Carnegie Endowment for International Peace, 13 December 2017, https://carnegieendowment.org/2017/12/13/resuming-civic-activism-in-turkey-pub-74987.

58. Zihnioglu, "Resuming Civic Activism in Turkey."
59. A. McManus, "Deliberative Street Politics and Sacralized Dissent: Morocco's 20 February Movement and the Jamaa Al Adl Wal Ihsane," *Social Movement Studies* 15, no. 6 (2016): 643–648.
60. S. Yerkes and M. Muasher, *Tunisia's Corruption Contagion: A Transition at Risk* (Washington, DC: Carnegie Endowment for International Peace, 2017).
61. M. J. Vijayan, "India: Innovation amid Adversity," in *Global Civic Activism in Flux*, ed. R. Youngs (Washington, DC: Carnegie Endowment for International Peace, 2017).
62. M. J. Vijayan, "The Rise and Rise of Conservative Civil Society in India," in Youngs, *The Mobilization of Conservative Civil Society*.
63. H. Gåsemyr, "Networks and Campaigns but Not Movements: Collective Action in the Disciplining Chinese State," *Journal of Civil Society* 12, no. 4 (2016): 394–410.
64. X. Yan and G. Xin, "Reforming Governance under Authoritarianism: Motivations and Pathways of Local Participatory Reform in the People's Republic of China," *Democratization* 24, no. 3 (2017): 405–424.
65. V. Nikitin, "The New Civic Activism in Russia," *Nation*, 20 October 2010, https://www.thenation.com/article/new-civic-activism-russia/; T. Vorozheikina et al., *New Forms of Civic Activism in Russia* (Moscow: Carnegie Moscow Center, 2008); S. Greene, *Moscow in Movement: Power and Opposition in Putin's Russia* (Stanford: Stanford University Press, 2014); A. Kolesnikov and D. Volkov, "Defending One's Backyard: Local Civic Activism in Moscow," Carnegie Moscow Center, 2 May 2017, http://carnegie.ru/2017/05/02/defending-one-s-backyard-local-civic-activism-in-moscow-pub-69822.
66. A. Ishkanian, 'Self-determined Citizens? New Forms of Civic Activism and Citizenship in Armenia," *Europe-Asia Studies* 67, no. 8 (2015): 1203–1227.
67. G. Nodia, "Nativists versus Global Liberalism in Georgia," in Youngs, *The Mobilization of Conservative Civil Society*.
68. N. Shapovalova, "The Two Faces of Ukraine's Conservative Civil Society," in Youngs, *The Mobilization of Conservative Civil Society*.
69. C. Tendolini, "Why Latin America Is a Hotbed of Political Innovation," Open Society Foundations, 1 February 2018, https://www.opensocietyfoundations.org/voices/why-latin-america-hotbed-political-innovation.
70. F. Da Silva, "State, Social Movements, and Democracy in the Andean Countries," *Journal of Civil Society* 11, no. 3 (2015): 259–270.
71. P. Fernando, "Working with Social Movements," in *Poverty Reduction and Pro-Poor Growth: The Role of Empowerment* (N.p: OECD Publishing, 2012), 256–268.
72. M. Sitrin and D. Azzellini, *They Can't Represent Us! Reinventing Democracy from Greece to Occupy* (London: Verso, 2014).
73. M. von Bülow, "What Happened to Brazil's Civic Activism?" Carnegie Endowment for International Peace, 19 December 2017, http://carnegieendowment.org/2017/12/19/what-happened-to-brazil-s-civic-activism-pub-75068.
74. A. Alemanno, *Lobbying for Change: Find Your Voice to Create a Better Society* (London: Icon, 2017).
75. E. Romanos, "Collective Learning Process within Social Movements: Some Insights into the Spanish 15-M/Indignados Movement," in *Understanding European Movements: New Social Movements, Global Justice Struggles, Anti-Austerity Protest*, ed. C. F. Fominaya and L. Cox (London: Routledge, 2013) 209.
76. M. Cillero, "What Makes an Empty Building in Naples a 'Common Good'?," *PoliticalCritique.org*, 25 April 2017, http://politicalcritique.org/world/2017/naples-common-good-empty-buildings/.
77. Home page, Bread Houses Network website, accessed 12 February 2018, https://www.breadhousesnetwork.org/.
78. E. McCormick, "The Rise of the Yimbys," *Guardian*, 2 October 2017, https://www.theguardian.com/cities/2017/oct/02/rise-of-the-yimbys-angry-millennials-radical-housing-solution.
79. C. Chwalisz, *Citizen Engagement in Politics and Policymaking: Lessons from the UK* (London: Populus and Westminster Foundation for Democracy, 2017).

80. Home page, CitizensUK website, accessed 12 February 2018, http://www.citizensuk.org/.
81. All these examples are taken from CitizensLab, *Mapping New Forms of Civic Engagement*.
82. The index can be found online at http://Index.fgu.bg/.
83. Jerphaas, "Bijna 17% van gemeenten gebruikt G1000 of vergelijkbare methodiek," G1000 blog, 13 June 2018, https://g1000.nu/blog/bijna-17-van-gemeenten-gebruikt-g1000-of-vergelijkbare-methodiek/.
84. S. Bengali, "Vigilantes Prowl Europe's Border with a Target: Muslim Migrants," *Los Angeles Times*, 14 March 2017.
85. J. Rosendahl and T. Forsell, "Anti-immigrant 'Soldiers of Odin' Raise Concern in Finland," Reuters, 13 January 2016.
86. D. Christopoulos, "The Golden Dawn Trial: A Major Event for Democracy in Greece and Beyond," *openDemocracy*, 26 January 2018.
87. P. Marczewski, "Freedom to Exclude: Conservative CSOs in Law and Justice Poland," in Youngs, *The Mobilization of Conservative Civil Society*.
88. A. Branch and Z. Mampilly, *Africa Rising: Popular Protest and Political Change* (London: Zed Books, 2015).
89. P. Mason, *Postcapitalism: A Guide to Our Future* (London: Penguin, 2016).
90. D. della Porta and S. Tarrow, eds., *Transnational Protest and Global Activism* (Lanham, MD: Rowman & Littlefield, 2005).
91. D. della Porta and A. Mattoni, eds., *Spreading Protests: Social Movements in Times of Crisis* (Colchester, ECPR, 2015); D. della Porta, *Mobilizing for Democracy: Comparing 1989 and 2011* (Oxford: Oxford University Press, 2014); D. della Porta, *Clandestine Political Violence* (Cambridge: Cambridge University Press, 2013).

Chapter 3

1. D. Meyer and S. Tarrow, eds., *The Social Movement Society* (Oxford: Rowman & Littlefield, 1998).
2. K. Leetaru, "Did the Arab Spring Really Spark a Wave of Global Protests?" *Foreign Policy*, 30 May 2014.
3. Economist Intelligence Unit, *Rebels without a Cause: What the Upsurge in Protest Movements Means for Global Politics*, 2013, https://www.eiu.com/public/topical_report.aspx?campaignid=ProtestUpsurge.
4. The ACLED data set. For background, see C. Raleigh et al., "Introducing ACLED—Armed Conflict Location and Event Data," Journal of Peace Research 47, no. 5 (2010: 651–660.
5. Figures and data based on the GDELT Project data set; see "GDELT 1.0 Event Data" at https://www.gdeltproject.org/. The GDELT figures are based on how frequently media sources report protest events. The program recorded a dramatic rise from 4,418 protests in 1991 to 146,678 in 2016. As it has increased the number of sources it tracks per year, this translates into a more modest rise in "protest intensity" (the number of protests divided by the number of media stories covered) from 4 to 5 percent over this period. For details on the coding for these figures, see P. A. Schrodt, "CAMEO Conflict and Mediation Event Observations: Event and Actor Codebook v. 1.1b3," 2012, http://data.gdeltproject.org/documentation/CAMEO.Manual.1.1b3.pdf.
6. E. Chenoweth, J. Pinckney, and O. A. Lewis, "NAVCo Data Project," University of Denver, 2017, cited in Rhize, Understanding Activism: How International NGOs, Foundations and Others Can Provide Better Support to Social Movements (Washington, DC: Atlantic Council, 2017), p. 2.
7. I. Ortiz et al., World Protests, 2006–2013, IPD/FES Working Paper (New York: Initiative for Policy Dialogue and Friederich-Ebert-Stiftung, 2013).
8. Civicus, "A Year in Civil Society—Citizen Action to the Fore," in *State of Civil Society Report 2014*, https://www.civicus.org/index.php/socs2014, 2.
9. World Values Survey 2014 and 2016, www.worldvaluessurvey.org.
10. International Labour Organization, *World Employment and Social Outlook: Trends* 2017, http://www.ilo.org/global/research/global-reports/weso/2017/WCMS_541211/lang--en/index.htm.

11. M. Boduszytiski, "Iraq's Year of Rage," Journal of Democracy 27, no. 4 (2016) 110–124.
12. Y. Mounsif, *Human Rights Action and Social Movements in Morocco*, Arab Reform Initiative research paper, February 2018, https://www.arab-reform.net/en/node/1239, 10.
13. A. Sahbani, ed., Social Protests in Tunisia, Year: 2015 (Tunis: OST/FTDES, 2016), 58–63.
14. Y. Cherif, "Why Are Tunisans Protesting?: *Al Jazeera*, 14 January 2018, http://www.aljazeera.com/indepth/opinion/tunisians-protesting-180114082908910.html.
15. For an overview of the MENA region, see F. Gerges, ed., Contentious Politics in the Middle East: Popular Resistance and Marginalised Activism beyond the Arab Uprisings (New York: Palgrave Macmillan, 2015).
16. A. Ishkanian, "A Revolution of Values: Freedom, Responsibility, and Courage in the Armenian Velvet Revolution," LSE EUROPP blog, 3 May 2018, http://blogs.lse.ac.uk/europpblog/2018/05/03/a-revolution-of-values-freedom-responsibility-and-courage-in-the-armenian-velvet-revolution/.
17. E. Marat, "Kazakhstan Had Huge Protests, but No Violent Crackdown. Here's Why," *Washington Post*, 6 June 2016, https://www.washingtonpost.com/news/monkey-cage/wp/2016/06/06/kazakhstan-had-big-protests-without-a-violent-crackdown-heres-why/?utm_term=.0da9a53d5128.
18. D. Achilov, "When Actions Speak Louder than Words: Examining Collective Political Protests in Central Asia," Democratization 23, no. 4 (2016) 699–722.
19. M. Gabowitsch, Protest in Putin's Russia (Cambridge: Polity Press, 2015).
20. Yevgenia Kuznetsova, "Center for Economic and Political Reform: Protests on Rise in Russia," *Russian Reader*, 10 July 2017, https://therussianreader.com/2017/07/12/center-for-economic-and-political-reform-protests-on-rise-in-russia/.
21. O. Onuch and G. Sasse, "The Maidan in Movement: Diversity and the Cycles of Protest," Europe-Asia Studies 68, no. 4 (2016).
22. V. Pekar, "Why the Reforms in Ukraine Are So Slow?" *New Eastern Europe*, 19 July 2017, http://neweasterneurope.eu/2017/07/19/why-the-reforms-in-ukraine-are-so-slow/.
23. V. Hui, "The Protests and Beyond," Journal of Democracy 26, no. 2 (2015): 111–121.
24. S. Chaudhuri and S. Fitzgerald, "Rape Protests in India and the Birth of a New Repertoire," Social Movement Studies 14, no. 5 (2015): 622–628.
25. L. Djani and O. Törnquist, "Insight: Overtaking Right-wing Populism in Indonesia?" *Jakarta Post*, 10 March 2017.
26. H. Gåsemyr, "Networks and Campaigns but Not Movements: Collective Action in the Disciplining Chinese State," Journal of Civil Society 12, no. 4 (2016): 397; T. Phillips, "Hundreds Take Part in Rare Protest in Beijing over Migrant Crackdown," *Guardian*, 11 December 2017, https://www.theguardian.com/world/2017/dec/11/hundreds-take-part-rare-protest-beijing-migrant-crackdown.
27. "10 Killed as Ethiopia Forces Clash with Protestors in Oromia," *Africanews*, 26 October 2017, http://www.africanews.com/2017/10/26/deaths-reported-as-ethiopia-elite-forces-clash-with-protesters-in-oromia//.
28. A. Branch and Z. Mampilly, *Africa Rising: Popular Protest and Political Change* (Chicago: Zed Books, 2015).
29. A. Larok, "Uganda's New Civic Activism," Carnegie Endowment for International Peace, 24 July 2017, http://carnegieendowment.org/2017/07/24/uganda-s-new-civic-activism-beyond-egos-and-logos-pub-71600.
30. S. Booysen, Fees Must Fall: Student Revolt, Decolonisation, and Governance in South Africa (Johannesburg, Wits University Press, 2016).
31. J. Formina and J. Kucharczyk, "Populism and Protest in Poland," Journal of Democracy 27, no. 4 (2016): 58–68.
32. I. Ortiz et al., *World Protests 2006–2013*, Initiative for Policy Dialogue Working Paper 24, http://policydialogue.org/publications/working-papers/world-protests-2006-2013/.
33. A. Ishkanian and M. Glasius, Reclaiming Democracy in the Square? Interpreting the Movements of 2011–12 (London: LSE, 2013), 19.
34. D. Eriskson, "The Rise of the African Street," *American Interest*, 26 March 2015, https://www.the-american-interest.com/2015/03/26/the-rise-of-the-african-street/.

35. H. Chen, "Why Middle Class Activism Surprises Economists," *LSE Business Review*, 13 October 2017, http://blogs.lse.ac.uk/businessreview/2017/10/10/why-middle-class-activism-surprises-economists/.
36. D. Graeber, *The Democracy Project: A History, a Crisis, a Movement* (London: Penguin, 2017).
37. J. Ahlquist and M. Levi, *In the Interest of Others: Organizations and Social Activism* (Princeton, Princeton University Press, 2013).
38. O. Cisar, "Social Movements in Political Science," in *The Oxford Handbook of Social Movements*, ed. D. della Porta and M. Diani (Oxford: Oxford University Press, 2015).
39. B. Brownlee and M. Ghiabi, "Passive, Silent and Revolutionary: The 'Arab Spring' Revisited," Middle East Critique 25, no. 3 (2016): 299–316.
40. C. Cakmak, *The Arab Spring, Civil Society, and Innovative Activism* (London: Palgrave Macmillan, 2017).
41. For an account of these balances between national frames and transnational links, see R. Feenstra, "Rethinking Global Civil Society and the Public Sphere in the Age of Pro-Democracy Movements," Journal of Civil Society 13, no. 3 (2014): 337–348, as well as other articles in this special edition on antiausterity social activism.
42. L. Parks, *Social Movement Campaigns on EU Policy: In the Corridors and in the Streets* (London: Palgrave Macmillan, 2015).
43. D. Brancati, *Democracy Protests: Origins, Features, and Significance* (Cambridge University Press, 2016), 25; H. Anheier, "Civil Society Research: Ten Years On," Journal of Civil Society 10, no. 4 (2014): 335–339.

Chapter 4

1. P. J. Ganesh, "Protesting against Populism Is an Ineffectual Parade of Principles," *Financial Times*, 24 January 2017.
2. L. Bosi, M. Giugni, and K. Uba, "The Consequences of Social Movements: Taking Stock and Looking Forward," in *The Consequences of Social Movements*, ed. L. Bosi, M. Giugni, and K. Uba (Cambridge: Cambridge University Press, 2016), 22.
3. J. Sombatpoonsiri, "Thailand: Politically Divided Civic Activism," in *Global Civic Activism in Flux*, ed. R. Youngs (Washington, DC: Carnegie Endowment for International Peace, 2017).
4. A. Oloo, *Kenya's 2017 Election and New Wave of Activism* (Washington DC, Carnegie Endowment for International peace, 2018).
5. N. Ketchley, "Elite-Led Protest and Authoritarian State-Capture in Egypt," POMEPS Studies 20 (2016).
6. J. Yarwood, "The Power of Protest," Journal of Democracy 27, no. 3 (2016) 51–60.
7. M. Dizolele, "Waiting for Democracy in Congo," *Foreign Affairs*, September–October 2018.
8. M. Yahya, *The Summer of Our Discontent: Sects and Citizens in Lebanon and Iraq* (Washington, DC: Carnegie Endowment for Internationl Peace, 2017).
9. M. Gabowitsch, *Protest in Putin's Russia* (Cambridge: Polity Press, 2017).
10. D. Brancati, *Democracy Protests: Origins, Features, and Significance* (Cambridge University Press, 2016), 25.
11. I. Ortiz et al., World Protests, 2006–2013, IPD/FES Working Paper (New York: Initiative for Policy Dialogue and Friederich-Ebert-Stiftung, 2013).
12. E. Chenowath, "How Social Media Helps Dictators," *Foreign Policy*, 16 November 2016.
13. C. Cakmak, *The Arab Spring, Civil Society, and Innovative Activism* (London: Palgrave Macmillan, 2017).
14. This is shown in relation to some past cases of democratization in Central and Eastern Europe, in D. della Porta, *Where Did the Revolution Go? Contentious Politics and the Quality of Democracy* (Cambridge: Cambridge University Press, 2016).
15. Civicus, *State of Civil Society Report 2015*, https://www.civicus.org/index.php/socs2015, 37.
16. Z. Tufekci, *Twitter and Tear Gas* (New Haven: Yale University Press, 2017).

17. C. F. Fominaya, Social Movements and Globalization: How Protests, Occupations, and Uprisings Are Changing the World (London: Palgrave Macmillan, 2014), 195.
18. G. Martin, Understanding Social Movements (London: Routledge, 2015), 55.
19. A similar point was made earlier in the seminal D. Meyer and S. Tarrow, eds., The Social Movement Society (Oxford: Rowman & Littlefield, 1998).
20. A. Ishkanian and M. Glasius, Reclaiming Democracy in the Square? Interpreting the Movements of 2011–12 (London: LSE, 2013).
21. S. Popovic, A. Milivojevic, and S. Djinovic, Nonviolent Struggle: 50 Crucial Points (Belgrade: Centre for Applied Nonviolent Action and Strategies, 2006); S. Popovic, Blueprint for Revolution: How to Use Rice Pudding, Lego Men, and Other Nonviolent Techniques to Galvanize Communities, Overthrow Dictators, or Simply Change the World (New York: Spiegel & Grau, 2015).
22. S. Crawshaw, Street Spirit: The Power of Protest and Mischief (London: Michael O'Mara, 2017).
23. Tufekci, Twitter and Tear Gas.
24. D. Graeber, The Democracy Project: A History, a Crisis, a Movement (London: Penguin, 2017), 148.
25. C. Boulding, NGOs, Political Protest, and Civil Society (Cambridge: Cambridge University Press, 2014), 190.
26. D. Ritter, The Iron Cage of Liberalism: International Politics and Unarmed Revolutions in the Middle East and North Africa (Oxford: Oxford University Press, 2015).
27. M. Levitin, "The Triumph of Occupy Wall Street," Atlantic, 10 June 2015.
28. A. Feuer, "Occupy Sandy: A Movement Moves to Relief," New York Times, 9 November 2017.
29. P. Beinart, "The Rise of the Violent Left," Atlantic, September 2017.
30. F. Santos, "At the Southern Border, a Do-It-Yourself Tack on Security," New York Times, 21 December 2016.
31. L. Kauffman, "We Are Living through a Golden Age of Protest," Guardian, 6 May 2018, https://www.theguardian.com/commentisfree/2018/may/06/protest-trump-direct-action-activism.
32. E. Gay, "The Women's March Inspired Them to Run. Now They're Unseating GOP Men," Huffington Post, 10 November 2017, https://www.huffingtonpost.com/entry/womens-march-inspired-democrats-unseating-gop-men_us_5a03099de4b06ff32c91cb55.
33. S. Nasiripour, "Colleges Face Student Protests over Fossil Fuel Investments," Huffington Post, 25 April 2016, https://www.huffingtonpost.com/entry/college-student-protests-fossil-fuel-investments_us_571e27cce4b0d912d5ff16ed.
34. O. Milman, "March for Science Puts Earth Day Focus on Global Opposition to Trump," Guardian, 22 April 2017, https://www.theguardian.com/environment/2017/apr/22/march-for-science-earth-day-climate-change-trump.
35. E. Yong, "What Exactly Are People Marching for When They March for Science?" Atlantic, 7 March 2017.

Chapter 5

1. Z. Williams, Why We Deserve Better Politics (London: Hutchinson, 2015).
2. Civicus, "Executive Summary," in State of Civil Society Report 2015, https://www.civicus.org/index.php/socs2015, 6.
3. C. Bee and R. Guerrina, "Framing Civic Engagement, Political Participation and Active Citizenship in Europe," Journal of Civil Society 10, no. 1 (2014): 1–4.
4. M. White, "Without a Path from Protest to Power, the Women's March Will End Up like Occupy," Guardian, 22 January 2017, https://www.theguardian.com/world/2017/jan/19/womens-march-washington-occupy-protest.
5. S. Chayes, Fighting the Hydra: Lessons from Worldwide Protests against Corruption (Washington, DC: Carnegie Endowment for International Peace, 2018).
6. J. Lim, "Video Blogging and Youth Activism in Malaysia," International Communication Gazette 75, no. 3 (2013): 300–321.

7. J. Beinin and F. Vairel, eds., Social Movements, Mobilization, and Contestation in the Middle East and North Africa 2nd ed. (Stanford: Stanford University Press, 2013).
8. A. Bendaña, NGOs and Social Movements: A North/South Divide? Civil Society and Social Movements Programme Paper 22 (Geneva: United Nations Research Institute for Social Development, 2006).
9. A. Branch and Z. Mampilly, *Africa Rising: Popular Protest and Political Change* (Chicago: Zed Books, 2015), chapters 5–8.
10. S. Alvarez et al., eds, Beyond Civil Society: Activism, Participation, and Protest in Latin America (Durham, NC: Duke University Press, 2017).
11. M. Glasius and A. Ishkanian, "Surreptitious Symbiosis: Engagement between Activists and NGOs," Voluntas 26, no. 6 (2015).
12. S. Tarrow, Power in Movement: Social Movements and Contentious Politics, 3rd ed. (Cambridge: Cambridge University Press, 2011).
13. D. della Porta and M. Diani, Social Movements: An Introduction, 2nd ed. (Oxford: Blackwell, 2006).
14. A. Boubekeur, The Politics of Protest in Tunisia: Instrument in Parties' Competition vs. Tool for Participation (Berlin: Stiftung Wissenschaft und Politik, 2015).
15. O. Zihnioglu, "Resuming Civic Activism in Turkey," Carnegie Endowment for International Peace, 2017, https://carnegieendowment.org/2017/12/13/resuming-civic-activism-in-turkey-pub-74987.
16. Arab Reform Initiative, *Effervescent Egypt: Venues of Mobilization and the Interrupted Legacy of 2011* (N.p.: Arab Reform Initiative, 2018).
17. Alvarez et al., *Beyond Civil Society*.
18. C. Boulding, NGOs, Political Protest, and Civil Society (Cambridge, Cambridge University Press, 2014).
19. H. Aliyev, "Examining the Use of Informal Networks by NGOs in Azerbaijan and Georgia," Journal of Civil Society 11, no. 3 (2015): 317–332.
20. D. Brancati, Democracy Protests: Origins, Features, and Significance (Cambridge University Press, 2016), 18.
21. A. Ishkanian and M. Glasius, *Reclaiming Democracy in the Square? Interpreting the Movements of 2011–12* (London: LSE, 2013), 24.
22. L. Bosi, M. Giugni, and K. Uba, "The Consequences of Social Movements: Taking Stock and Looking Forward," in *The Consequences of Social Movements*, ed. L. Bosi, M. Giugni, and K. Uba (Cambridge, Cambridge University Press, 2016), 22.
23. "Why Apolitical," Apolitical, accessed 14 February 2018, https://apolitical.co/why-apolitical/.
24. T. Skocpol, "Voice and Inequality: The Transformation of American Civic Democracy," APSA Presidential Address, 1 February 2004, https://scholar.harvard.edu/files/thedaskocpol/files/skocpol.pdf.
25. International IDEA, The Global State of Democracy: Exploring Democracy's Resilience (Stockholm: International IDEA, 2017), 121.
26. C. Chwalisz, "En March: From a Movement to a Government," Carnegie Endowment for International Peace, 6 April 2018, https://carnegieeurope.eu/2018/04/06/en-marche-from-movement-to-government-pub-75985.
27. K. Pishchikova and O. Ogryzko, Civic Awakening: The Impact of Euromaidan on Ukraine's Politics and Society, Working Paper 124 (Madrid: FRIDE, 2014).
28. For more on these examples, see N. Shapovalova, "Civic Volunteerism and the Legacy of Euromaidan," in *Global Civic Activism in Flux*, ed. R. Youngs (Washington, DC: Carnegie Endowment for International Peace, 2017); and T. Ash et al, The Struggle for Ukraine, Chatham House Report (London: Chatham House, 2017) 62, 64, 69.
29. I. Rachidi, "Protests Continue in Morocco Despite Crackdown," *Al-Monitor*, 24 July 2017, https://www.al-monitor.com /pulse/home.html.
30. E. Cheng and W.-Y. Chan, "Explaining Spontaneous Occupation: Antecedents, Contingencies and Spaces in the Umbrella Movement," Social Movement Studies 16 (2017).
31. M. P. Kaeding, "The Rise of 'Localism' in Hong Kong," Journal of Democracy 28, no. 1 (2017): 157–171.

32. M. Ho, "The Activist Legacy of Taiwan's Sunflower Movement," Carnegie Endowment for International Peace, 2018, https://carnegieendowment.org/2018/08/02/activist-legacy-of-taiwan-s-sunflower-movement-pub-76966).
33. G. Yovanovich and R. Rice, eds., Reimagining Civil Society and Community in Latin America and the Caribbean (London: Routledge, 2017).
34. A. Ishkanian, "Self-determined Citizens? New Forms of Civic Activism and Citizenship in Armenia," Europe-Asia Studies 67, no. 8 (2015): 1203–1227.
35. M. Savage, "Jon Lansman: 'To Keep Labour's New Members Engaged, We Must Give Them Power,'" *Guardian*, 15 July 2017, https://www.theguardian.com/politics/2017/jul/15/jon-lansman-momentum-give-labour-members-power.
36. D. della Porta and M. Diani, "Introduction: The Field of Social Movement Studies," in *The Oxford Handbook of Social Movements*, ed. D. della Porta and M. Diani (Oxford: Oxford University Press, 2015), 14; see also introduction to special edition of *Mobilization*: N. Eggert and E. Pavan, "Researching Collective Action through Networks: Taking Stock and Looking Forward," Mobilization 19, no. 4 (2014): 363–368.
37. Civicus, "A Year in Civil Society—Citizen Action to the Fore," in *State of Civil Society Report 2014*, https://www.civicus.org/index.php/socs2014, 24.
38. A. Bebbington, Poverty Reduction and Social Movements: A Framework with Cases, prepared for UNRISD, 2009, http://gsdrc.org/document-library/poverty-reduction-and-social-movements-a-framework-with-cases/, 7.
39. B. Gnarig, "The Old World of Civic Participation Is Being Replaced," *openDemocracy*, 30 November 2016, https://www.opendemocracy.net/openglobalrights/burkhard-gn-rig/old-world-of-civic-participation-is-being-replaced.
40. S. Parker, Taking Power Back: Putting People in Charge of Politics (Bristol, Policy Press, 2015).
41. Bendaña, *NGOs and Social Movements*.

Chapter 6

1. C. Sirkey, Here Comes Everybody: The Power of Organizing without Organisation (London: Penguin, 2009).
2. L. Diamond, "Liberation Technology," Journal of Democracy 21, no. 3 (2010): 71.
3. J. Penny, The Citizen Marketer: Promoting Political Opinion in the Social Media Age (Oxford: Oxford University Press, 2017).
4. L. Bernholz and R, Reich, "Civic Crowdsourcing 101: Democracy, Institutional Design, and Technologies of Expertise," *Medium*, 15 March 2016, https://medium.com/the-digital-civil-society-lab/civic-crowdsourcing-101-e460ef37c461#.ejuefco3v.
5. C. Sidar, "How Technology Can Restore Our Trust in Democracy," *Foreign Policy*, 3 August 2016.
6. U. Dolata and J. Schrape, "Masses, Crowds, Communities, Movements: Collective Action in the Internet Age," Social Movement Studies 15, no. 1 (2016): 1–18.
7. W. Bennett and A. Segerberg, The Logic of Connective Action: Digital Media and the Personalization of Contentious Politics (Cambridge: Cambridge University Press, 2013.
8. "About Us," Accela, accessed 14 February 2018, https://www.accela.com/company.
9. Home page, DemocracyOS, accessed 14 February 2018, http://democracyos.org/.
10. "Civi," DemTools, accessed 14 February 2018, https://www.dem.tools/civi.
11. Alanna, "How OuiShare Is Scaling a Shared Vision across Countries," *Loomio Blog*, 21 January 2016, http://blog.loomio.org/2016/01/21/ouishare/.
12. E. Rekosh, *Rethinking the Human Rights Business Model* (Washington, DC: CSIS, 2017), 18–19.
13. T. Peixoto and M. Sifry, Civic Tech in the Global South (Washington, DC: World Bank, 2017), 37–39.
14. J. Earl, "Protest Online: Theorizing the Consequences of Online Engagement," in *The Consequences of Social Movements*, ed. L. Bosi, M. Giugni, and K. Uba (Cambridge: Cambridge University Press, 2016), 377.

15. T. Mawarire, I. Pousadela, and C. Gilbert, Civil Society Watch Report, Civicus, 2016, https://www.civicus.org/images/CSW_Report.pdf, 3.
16. E. Smith, "In Central Africa, Citizens Are Using Social Media to Build Democracy. Here's How," *Washington Post*, 6 April 2016, https://www.washingtonpost.com/news/monkey-cage/wp/2016/04/06/in-central-africa-citizens-are-using-social-media-to-build-democracy-heres-how/?noredirect=on&utm_term=.f7bb1f477ecc
17. A. Breuer, T. Landman, and D. Farquhar, "Social Media and Protest Mobilization: Evidence from the Tunisian Revolution," Democratization 22, no. 4 (2015): 764–792.
18. K. Ruijgrok, "From the Web to the Streets: Internet and Protests under Authoritarian Regimes," Democratization 24, no. 3 (2017): 498–520.
19. H. Margetts, P. John, S. Hale, and T. Yasseri, Political Turbulence: How Social Media Shape Collective Action (Princeton, Princeton University Press, 2016).
20. Margetts et al., Political Turbulence.
21. Diamond, "Liberation Technology," 71.
22. T. Carothers et al., "Why Has Technology Not Delivered More Democracy?" *Foreign Policy*, 3 June 2015.
23. F. Polimeni, "From the Assembly to the Party, and Back. The Network Party in Argentina, Five Years On," *openDemocracy*, 21 February 2017, https://www.opendemocracy.net/democraciaabierta/florencia-polimeni/form-assembly-to-party-and-back-network-party-five-years-on.
24. D. Vittori and M. Candia, "From Online Participation to Offline Consensus? The Declining Appeal of Web-Democracy to Five Star Movement Supporters." *LSE EUROPP blog*, 11 January 2018, http://blogs.lse.ac.uk/europpblog/2018/01/11/five-star-movement-decline-online/.
25. Civicus, "Executive Summary," in State of Civil Society Report 2015, https://www.civicus.org/index.php/socs2015, 6.
26. Y. N. Harari, Homo Deus: A Brief History of Tomorrow (London: Vintage, 2016).
27. J. Farwell, "The Media Strategy of ISIS," Survival 56, no. 6 (2014):. 49–55; J. M. Berger, "The Metronome of Apocalyptic Time: Social Media as Carrier Wave for Millenarian Contagion," Perspectives on Terrorism 9. no. 4 (2015).
28. P. Neumann, Radicalized: New Jihadists and the Threat to the West (London: I. B. Tauris, 2016)
29. M. Haig, "I Used to Think Social Media Was a Force for Good. Now the Evidence Says I Was Wrong," *Guardian*, 6 September 2016, https://www.theguardian.com/commentisfree/2017/sep/06/social-media-good-evidence-platforms-insecurities-health.
30. A. Smith, Civic Engagement in the Digital Age (Washington, DC: Pew Research Center, 2013).
31. U. Serdult, M. Germann, M. Harris, F. Mendez, and A. Potenier, "Who Are the Internet Voters?" in *Electronic Government and Electronic Participation*, ed. E. Tambouris et al. (Amsterdam: IOS Press, 2015)
32. Peixoto and Sifry, *Civic Tech in the Global South*.
33. M. Miller and P. Soira, "Les 'Civic tech' ou la démocratie en version start-up," *Le Monde*, 14 March 2017.
34. L. Diamond, "Liberation Technology," 80.
35. V. Polonski, "'he Biggest Threat to Democracy? Your Social Media Feed," World Economic Forum, 4 August 2016, https://www.weforum.org/agenda/2016/08/the-biggest-threat-to-democracy-your-social-media-feed/.
36. T. Berners-Lee, "Three Challenges for the Web, according to Its Inventor," Web Foundation, 12 March 2017, https://webfoundation.org/2017/03/web-turns-28-letter/.
37. "E-Government Development Index," UN E-Government Knowledgebase, accessed 14 February 2018, https://publicadministration.un.org/egovkb/Data-Center.
38. T. Pogrebinschi, "Digital Innovation in Latin America," *openDemocracy*, 6 June 2017, https://www.opendemocracy.net/democraciaabierta/thamy-pogrebinschi/digital-innovation-in-latin-america-how-brazil-colombia-mexico-.
39. S. Kelly et al., Freedom on the Net 2017: Manipulating Social Media to Undermine Democracy (Washington, DC: Freedom House, 2017).

40. R. MacKinnon, "China's 'Networked Authoritarianism,'" Journal of Democracy 22, no. 2 (2011): 41, quoted in S. Oates, Revolution Stalled: The Political Limits of the Internet in the Post-Soviet Sphere (Oxford: Oxford University Press, 2013).
41. A. Denisova, "Democracy, Protest and Public Sphere in Russia after the 2011–2012 Anti-Government Protests: Digital Media at Stake," Media, Culture & Society 39, no. 7 (2017): 976–994.
42. These paragraphs are based on Kelly et al., *Freedom on the Net 2017: Manipulating Social Media to Undermine Democracy*, which includes chapters on the different countries mentioned.
43. J. Sombatpoonsiri, "Growing Cyber Activism in Thailand." Carnegie Endowment for International Peace, 14 August 2017, http://carnegieendowment.org/2017/08/14/growing-cyber-activism-in-thailand-pub-72804.
44. S. Kalathil and T. Boas, Open Networks, Closed Regimes: The Impact of the Internet on Authoritarian Rule (Washington, DC: Carnegie Endowment for International Peace, 2003), 39.
45. E. Chenowath, "How Social Media Helps Dictators," *Foreign Policy*, 16 November 2016.
46. J. Behrend and L. Whitehead, "The Struggle for Subnational Democracy," Journal of Democracy 27, no. 2 (2016): 155–169.
47. B. Goodman and K. Willits, "How We Spent $1 Million for Digital Rights in 2017: Empowering the Grassroots across the Globe," Access Now, 22 December 2017, https://www.accessnow.org/spent-1-million-digital-rights-2017-empowering-grassroots-across-globe.
48. E. Brattberg and T. Mauer, "Russian Election Interference: Europe's Counter to Fake News and Cyber Attacks," Carnegie Endowment for International Peace, 2018, https://carnegieendowment.org/2018/05/23/russian-election-interference-europe-s-counter-to-fake-news-and-cyber-attacks-pub-76435.
49. For example, see J. Bartlett, *The People vs Tech* (London: Ebury Press, 2018)
50. Earl, "Protest Online."
51. Peixoto and Sifry, *Civic Tech in the Global South*.
52. Z. Tufekci, *Twitter and Tear Gas* (New Haven: Yale University Press, 2017).
53. "How to Document, Train and Analyze Social Activism in the Arab Region," conference held at Asfari Institute for Civil Society and Citizenship, American University of Beirut, 31 March 2018.
54. R. Gibson, M. Cantijoch, and S. Galandini, The Third Sector and Online Citizen Empowerment: The Case of mySociety (Manchester: Report for the ESRC Knowledge Exchange Programme and Project Partner *mySociety*, 2014), https://www.mysociety.org/files/2014/12/manchester.pdf.
55. A. Mandelbaum, "Online Tools for Engaging Citizens in the Legislative Process," *Opening Parliament*, 28 February 2014, http://blog.openingparliament.org/post/78098143764/online-tools-for-engaging-citizens-in-the.
56. W. Puckett, "What Makes 38 Degrees a Powerful Voice for Change?" *Guardian*, 8 April 2011, https://www.theguardian.com/society/joepublic/2011/apr/08/38-degrees-nhs-campaign.
57. P. Wesełowicz, M. Wilgocki, and R. Wójcik, "'Wolne sądy, wolne wybory, wolna Polska': Protesty w całym kraju [Zapis relacji]," *Wyborcza.pl*, 25 November 2017, http://warszawa.wyborcza.pl/warszawa/14,87090,22695123.html.
58. N. Hull and P. Ireland, "Transforming Activism: Digital Era Advocacy Organizations," *Stanford Social Innovation Review*, 6 July 2016, https://ssir.org/articles/entry/transforming_activism_digital_era_advocacy_organizations.

Chapter 7

1. R. Jilali, "Financing Empowerment? How Foreign Aid to Southern NGOs and Social Movements Undermines Grass-Roots Mobilization," Sociology Compass 7, no. 1 (2013): 63.
2. D. della Porta, Mobilizing for Democracy: Comparing 1989 and 2011 (Oxford: Oxford University Press, 2014).

3. D. Brancati, Democracy Protests: Origins, Features, and Significance (Cambridge: Cambridge University Press, 2016).
4. M. Sitrin and D. Azzellini, They Can't Represent Us! Reinventing Democracy from Greece to Occupy (London: Verso, 2014).
5. D. Held, Models of Democracy (Cambridge: Polity Press, 1982), 263–271, 307.
6. C. Chwalisz, The People's Verdict: Adding Informed Citizen Voices to Public Decision-Making (London: Policy Network, 2017).
7. J. Keane, The Life and Death of Democracy (New York: Simon & Schuster, 2009).
8. S. Tormey, The End of Representative Politics (Cambridge: Polity Press, 2015), 2, 6.
9. D. della Porta, Can Democracy Be Saved? Participation, Deliberation and Social Movements (Cambridge: Polity Press, 2013).
10. J. Talpin, "Democratic Innovations," in The Oxford Handbook of Social Movements, ed. D. della Porta and M. Diani (Oxford: Oxford University Press, 2015).
11. See the special edition: J. Fishkin and J. Mansbridge, eds., "The Prospects and Limits of Deliberative Democracy," Daedalus 146, no. 3 (2017), articles by C. Sunstein; H. Landemore; B. Manin; and N. Curato et al. See also J. Dryzek, Global Deliberative Politics: Discourse and Democracy in a Divided World (Cambridge, Polity Press, 2006).
12. "Legal Designs," Navigator to Direct Democracy, accessed 15 February 2018, http://www.direct-democracy-navigator.org/legal_designs.
13. D. Altman, Direct Democracy Worldwide (Cambridge: Cambridge University Press, 2010).
14. R. S. Suss and A. Kolioulis, "Circularity: A New Strategic Horizon," openDemocracy, 15 January 2018, https://www.opendemocracy.net/rahel-sophia-s-alessio-kolioulis/circularity-new-strategic-horizon.
15. For more on this debate, see R. Youngs, The Puzzle of Non-Western Democracy (Washington DC: Carnegie Endowment for International Peace, 2015).
16. J. Bohman, Democracy across Borders: From Demos to Demoi (Cambridge, MA, MIT Press, 2007); Dryzek, Global Deliberative Politics.
17. For a flavor of these debates, see A. Kioupkiolis and G. Katsambekis, eds., Radical Democracy and Collective Movements Today (Ashgate: Routledge, 2016).
18. P. Aslanidis, "Populism and Social Movements," in The Oxford Handbook of Populism, ed. C. R. Kaltwasser et al. (Oxford: Oxford University Press, 2017).
19. P. Aslanidis, "Populism and Social Movements."
20. A. Maleki and F. Hendriks, "The Relation between Cultural Values and Models of Democracy: A Cross-National Study," Democratization 22, no. 6 (2015): 981–1010.
21. J. Fomina and J. Kucharczyk, "The Specter Haunting Europe: Populism and Protest in Poland," Journal of Democracy 27, no. 1 (2016): 6.
22. See, for example, J-W. Müller, What Is Populism? (Philadelphia: University of Pennsylvania Press, 2016).
23. International IDEA, The Global State of Democracy: Exploring Democracy's Resilience (Stockholm: International IDEA, 2017), 57.
24. J. Talpin, "Democratic Innovations."
25. A. Badiou, The Rebirth of History: Times of Riots and Uprisings (London: Verso, 2012).
26. S. Žižek and B. Ramm, "Slavoj Žižek on Brexit, the Crisis of the Left, and the Future of Europe," openDemocracy, 1 July 2016, https://www.opendemocracy.net/can-europe-make-it/slavoj-zizek-benjamin-ramm/slavoj-i-ek-on-brexit-crisis-of-left-and-future-of-eur.
27. F. Cavatorta, ed., Civil Society Activism under Authoritarian Rule: A Comparative Perspective (London: Routledge, 2013).
28. M. Vargas Llosa, "El ciudadano rabioso," El Pais, 27 November 2016, https://elpais.com/elpais/2016/10/27/opinion/1477572688_830439.html.
29. A. C. Grayling, Democracy and Its Crisis (London: One World, 2017); J. Brennan, Against Democracy (Princeton, Princeton University Press, 2016).
30. S. Huntington, Political Order in Changing Societies (New Haven, Yale University Press, 1968).
31. One of the best of the more critical takes is I. Krastev, Democracy Disrupted (Philadelphia: University of Pennsylvania Press, 2014). For gentler and more balanced critiques, see M. Saward, Democracy (Cambridge: Polity Press, 2003); and P. Ginsborg, Democracy:

Crisis and Renewal (London: Profile Books, 2008); as well as material from "Unruly Politics," Institute for Development Studies/University of Sussex, accessed 15 February 2018, http://www.ids.ac.uk/idsresearch/unruly-politics; A. Khanna, "Seeing Citizen Action through an 'Unruly' Lens," Development 55, no. 2 (2012).
32. L. Phillips, "Kick 'Em All Out? Anti-Politics and Post-Democracy in the European Union," Statewatch Journal 23, no. 1 (2013): 9–19.
33. P. Rosanvallon, Counter-Democracy: Politics in an Age of Distrust (Cambridge: Cambridge University Press, 2008); Z. Bauman, The Individualized Society (Cambridge: Polity Press, 2001).
34. R. Dalton, The Participation Gap (Oxford: Oxford University Press, 2017).
35. L. Way, "The Maidan and Beyond: Civil Society and Democratization," Journal of Democracy 25, no. 3 (2014): 35–43.
36. See the special edition: J. Fishkin and J. Mansbridge, eds., "The Prospects and Limits of Deliberative Democracy," Daedalus 146, no. 3 (2017), articles by A. Lupia and A. Norton; C. Lafont; and I. Shapiro.
37. S. Chayes, Fighting the Hydra: Lessons from Worldwide Protests against Corruption (Washington, DC: Carnegie Endowment for International Peace, 2018).
38. G. Baiocchi and E. Ganuza, Popular Democracy: The Paradox of Participation (Stanford: Stanford University Press, 2016).
39. L. Bherer, P. Dufour, and F. Montambeault, "The Participatory Democracy Turn: An Introduction," Journal of Civil Society 12, no. 3 (2016): 227–228; and F. Polletta, "Participatory Enthusiasms: A Recent History of Citizen Engagement Initiatives," Journal of Civil Society 12, no. 3 (2016): 231–246.
40. A. Bächtiger and D. Hangartner, "When Deliberative Theory Meets Empirical Political Science: Theoretical and Methodological Challenges in Political Deliberation," Political Studies 58, no. 10 (2010).
41. Krastev, Democracy Disrupted.
42. Tormey, The End of Representative Politics, 87.
43. N. Belyaeva, "Citizen Plenums in Bosnia Protests: Creating a Post-Ethnic Identity," in Non-Western Social Movements and Participatory Democracy: Protest in the Age of Transnationalism, ed. E. Arbatli and D. Rosenberg (New York: Springer, 2017): 115–138.
44. L. Bosi, M. Giugni, and K. Uba, "The Consequences of Social Movements: Taking Stock and Looking Forward," in The Consequences of Social Movements, ed. L. Bosi, M. Giugni, and K. Uba (Cambridge: Cambridge University Press, 2016), 22.

Chapter 8

1. C. Agg, Trends in Government Support for Non-Governmental Organizations: Is the "Golden Age" of the NGO Behind Us? Civil Society and Social Movements Programme Paper 23 (Geneva: United Nations Research Institute for Social Development, 2006).
2. Civicus, "Executive Summary," in State of Civil Society Report 2015, https://www.civicus.org/index.php/socs2015.
3. Oxfam, The Power of People against Poverty: Oxfam Strategic Plan, 2013–2019, 2013, https://www.oxfam.org/en/countries/oxfam-strategic-plan-2013-2019-power-people-against-poverty, 9.
4. R. Jenkins, "Mistaking 'Governance' for 'Politics': Foreign Aid, Democracy and the Construction of Civil Society," in Civil Society: History and Possibilities, ed. S. Kaviraj and S. Khilnani (Cambridge, Cambridge University Press, 2001), 265.
5. Ministry for Foreign Affairs of Denmark, Support to Civil Society Engagement in Policy Dialogue, Joint Evaluation—Synthesis Report, 2012, http://www.netpublikationer.dk/um/11193/index.htm, 12, 14, 16.
6. J. Johansen, "Analyzing External Support to Nonviolent Revolutions," in Experiments with Peace: Celebrating Peace on Johan Galtung's 80th Birthday, ed. J. Johansen and J. Y. Jones (Oxford: Pambazuka Press, 2010), 105.
7. M. McFaul, "Ukraine Imports Democracy: External Influences on the Orange Revolution," International Security 32, no. 2 (2007): 73.

8. L. Wild and M. Foresti, *Support to Political Parties: A Missing Piece of the Governance Puzzle*, ODI Briefing Paper 66 (London, Overseas Development Institute, 2010), 1.
9. S. Wolff, "EU Religious Engagement in the Southern Mediterranean: Much Ado about Nothing?" *Mediterranean Politics* 23, no. 1 (2018).
10. O. Richmond, *Peace Formation and Political Order in Conflict Affected Societies* (Oxford: Oxford University Press, 2016), 179.
11. USAID, *USAID Strategy on Democracy, Human Rights and Governance* (Washington, DC: USAID, 2013).
12. USAID, "Small Grants Program Report to Congress," 2015, https://www.usaid.gov/sites/default/files/documents/1865/SGP.ReportforCongress.pdf.
13. USAID, *USAID Forward Progress Report* 2013 (Washington, DC: USAID, 2013).
14. "What We Do," Making All Voices Count, accessed 15 February 2018, http://www.makingallvoicescount.org/about/.
15. National Endowment for Democracy, 2012 *Strategy Document*, https://www.ned.org/docs/strategy/2012StrategyDocument.pdf.
16. "Global 2017," National Endowment for Democracy, https://www.ned.org/region/global-2017/; "About MOVEMENTS," Movements.org, accessed 16 February 2018, https://movements.org/en/movements/about-movements/about-movements/.
17. The other 75 percent is devoted to health, disaster relief, education, and multisector efforts. DFID, *Department for International Development: Annual Report and Accounts* 2015–16, https://www.gov.uk/government/publications/dfid-annual-report-and-accounts-2015-16; "Development Tracker," DFID, accessed 16 February 2018, https://devtracker.dfid.gov.uk/.
18. Foreign and Commonwealth Office, *Human Rights and Democracy: The* 2014 *Foreign & Commonwealth Office Report*, https://www.gov.uk/government/publications/human-rights-and-democracy-report-2014; Foreign and Commonwealth Office, "Human Rights and Democracy Programme: Frequently Asked Questions," 2014, https://www.gov.uk/government/news/call-for-bids-human-rights-and-democracy-programme-fund; Foreign and Commonwealth Office, *Human Rights and Democracy: The* 2017 *Foreign & Commonwealth Office Report*, https://www.gov.uk/government/publications/human-rights-and-democracy-report-2017
19. "Making All Voices Count: A Grand Challenge for Development Programme," DFID, accessed 16 February 2018, https://devtracker.dfid.gov.uk/projects/GB-1-202628.
20. Foreign and Commonwealth Office, *Human Rights and Democracy:* 2014.
21. "Results Strategy for Special Initiatives for Human Rights and Democratisation for the Period 2014–2017," Swedish Institute, 15 May 2014, https://si.se/app/uploads/2017/10/results-strategy-for-special-initiatives-20142017.pdf.
22. "Indigenous Peoples' Organizations (UNFPA)—Organisation of Indigenous Peoples," Openaid.se, accessed 16 February 2018, http://openaid.se/activity/SE-0-SE-6-5107006801-BOL-15160/.
23. "Villagers Influence Their Local Development through Knowledge," Sida, 27 June 2014, http://www.sida.se/English/where-we-work/Africa/Kenya/examples-of-results/David-Wambua/?id=128400; "About PENKenya," Poverty Eradication Network, accessed 16 February 2018, http://www.penkenya.org/index.php/about-us.
24. "Openness and Transparency," Sida, 5 December 2016, http://www.sida.se/English/how-we-work/approaches-and-methods/openness-and-transparency/.
25. "Applying for Funding through an Organisation with Framework Agreement," Sida, 14 October 2016, http://www.sida.se/English/partners/our-partners/Civil-society-organisations/How-to-cooperate/Applying-for-funding-through-an-organisation-with-framework-agreement/; Ministry for Foreign Affairs of Denmark, *Support to Civil Society Engagement in Policy Dialogue.*
26. Ministry for Foreign Affairs of Denmark, *Support to Civil Society Engagement in Policy Dialogue.*
27. BMZ, *Participating, Engaging, Making a Difference: Strategy on Working with Civil Society in German Development Policy*, BMZ Strategy Paper 8, 2013, https://www.bmz.de/en/publications/archiv/type_of_publication/strategies/Strategiepapier337_08_2013.pdf.
28. BMZ, *Participating, Engaging, Making a Difference.*

29. "Project Data," GIZ, accessed 16 February 2018, https://www.giz.de/projektdaten/index.action?request_locale=en_EN.
30. "EU-Project 'Environmental Empowerment for Grassroots and Non-State Actors in Thailand,'" Konrad-Adenauer-Stiftung, accessed 18 February 2018, http://www.kas.de/thailand/en/pages/14600/.
31. "Partners," Konrad-Adenauer-Stiftung Ghana Office, accessed 16 February 2018, http://www.kas.de/ghana/en/about/partners/.
32. Institut fur Europaische Politik, Civic School for Sound EU Practice project, supported by the Auswärtiges Amt, http://cisep.eu/.
33. BMZ, *Promoting Resilient States and Constructive State-Society Relations*, 2009, http://www.bmz.de/en/publications/archiv/type_of_publication/strategies/spezial168.pdf.
34. For more about the political foundations supported by BMZ, including the links to their websites, see "Political Foundations," BMZ, accessed 16 February 2018, http://www.bmz.de/en/what_we_do/approaches/bilateral_development_cooperation/players/political_foundations/index.html.
35. "Policy for Danish Support to Civil Society," Danida, 2014, http://amg.um.dk/en/policies-and-strategies/policy-for-support-to-danish-civil-society/.
36. C. Coventry, *Evaluation of Danish Support to Civil Society* (Copenhagen: Ministry of Foreign Affairs of Denmark, 2013); "Non-Governmental Organisations (NGOs) and Civil Society," Danida, accessed 16 February 2018, http://openaid.um.dk/en/organisations/20000.
37. "Policy for Danish Support to Civil Society," Danida.
38. European Endowment for Democracy, *Annual Report 2017: Supporting People Striving for Democracy*, 2018, https://www.democracyendowment.eu/annual-report-2017/.
39. "Project: The Future Sports Leadership Education, Tunisia," Danida, accessed 16 February 2018, http://openaid.um.dk/en/projects/DK-1-216585.
40. "Results Based Management," Danida, accessed 16 February 2018, http://um.dk/en/danida-en/results/results-based-management/; "Data from Programmes and Projects," Danida, accessed 16 February 2018, http://um.dk/en/danida-en/about-danida/Danida-transparency/data-from-programmes-and-projects/.
41. Government of the Netherlands, *Policy Memorandum of the Netherlands on Civil Society Organisations: Cooperation, Customisation, and Added Value* (The Hague: Government of the Netherlands, 2009); Ministry of Foreign Affairs of the Netherlands, *Human Rights Policy—Justice and Respect for All*, 2013, https://www.government.nl/documents/policy-notes/2013/06/14/justice-and-respect-for-all; Ministry of Foreign Affairs of the Netherlands, *A World to Gain: A New Agenda for Aid, Trade and Investment*, 2013, https://www.government.nl/documents/letters/2013/04/05/global-dividends-a-new-agenda-for-aid-trade-and-investment.
42. "KAI Islamic Female Preachers," Openaid.nl, last updated 1 February 2018, https://www.openaid.nl/projects/XM-DAC-7-PPR-29645?tab=summary.
43. Ministry of Foreign Affairs of the Netherlands, *A World to Gain*.
44. European Commission, *The Roots of Democracy and Sustainable Development: Europe's Engagement with Civil Society in External Relations*, Communication from the Commission, 9 December 2012, https://ec.europa.eu/europeaid/roots-democracy-and-sustainable-development-europes-engagement-civil-society-external-relations_en.
45. Council of the European Union, *EU Action Plan on Human Rights and Democracy*, 2015, https://eeas.europa.eu/sites/eeas/files/eu_action_plan_on_human_rights_and_democracy_en_2.pdf.
46. The CivicTech4Democracy website is at https://civictech4democracy.eu/.
47. C. Hackenesch, *Good Governance in EU External Relations: What Role for Development Policy in a Changing International Context?* (Brussels: European Parliament, 2016), 24.
48. European Commission, *Report on EU Engagement with Civil Society*, Staff Working Document, 2017, https://ec.europa.eu/europeaid/report-eu-engagement-civil-society_en.
49. Solidaire's website is at www.solidaire.org.
50. "Movement Innovation Lab," Rhize, accessed 16 February 2018, http://www.rhize.org/movement-innovation-lab/.

51. Civil Society Europe, *Civil Society Paper on Budgetary Control of Funding NGOs from the EU Budget*, 2016, https://civilsocietyeuropedoteu.files.wordpress.com/2016/11/civilsocietypaperbudgetarycontrolngofunding.pdf.
52. R. Jilali, "Financing Empowerment? How Foreign Aid to Southern NGOs and Social Movements Undermines Grass-Roots Mobilization," *Sociology Compass* 7, no. 1 (2013): 65.
53. P. Fernando, "Working with Social Movements," in *Poverty Reduction and Pro-Poor Growth: The Role of Empowerment* (N.p: OECD Publishing, 2012), 258.
54. H. Haider, *Helpdesk Research Report: Donor Engagement with Social Movements* (Birmingham: Governance and Social Development Resource Centre, 2009), 1.
55. L. Whitehead, "International Democracy Promotion as Political Ideology: Upsurge and Retreat," *Journal of Political Ideologies* 20, no. 1 (2015): 10–26.
56. L. Nader and J. G. de Campos, "Five Reasons to Fear Innovation," *Sur: International Journal on Human Rights* 23 (2016); see the blog at www.liquidworld.info, reporting on their Solid Organizations in a Liquid World project.
57. M. Miller-Dawkins, *Understanding Activism: How International NGOs, Foundations and Others Can Provide Better Support to Social Movements*, Rhize report on behalf of Atlantic Council (Washington, DC: Atlantic Council, 2017), 3.
58. M. E. Hansen, *Country CSO Roadmaps: How EU Delegations Can Strengthen Engagement with Civil Society*, (Brussels: Concord Europe, 2013), 9.
59. S. Nossel, "Pushing Back against the Tyrants: How to Counter the Alarming Authoritarian Assault on Civil Society Groups," *Democracy: A Journal of Ideas* 41 (2016), https://democracyjournal.org/magazine/41/pushing-back-against-the-tyrants/.
60. Fernando, "Working with Social Movements," 263.
61. Civicus, *State of Civil Society Report* 2015, 163.
62. Fernando, "Working with Social Movements," 263–264.
63. B. Masters and T. Osborne, "Social Movements and Philanthropy," *Foundation Review* 2 (2010): 16–17.
64. Masters and Osborne, "Social Movements and Philanthropy," 18–19.
65. Masters and Osborne, "Social Movements and Philanthropy," 21.
66. C. Saavedra, "Five Ways Funders Can Support Social Movements," *Stanford Social Innovation Review*, July 2018.
67. D. Mitlin, *The Role of Collective Action and Urban Social Movements in Reducing Chronic Urban Poverty*, Working Paper 64 (London: Chronic Poverty Research Centre, 2006), 58.
68. Masters and Osborne, "Social Movements and Philanthropy," 12.
69. P. Fernando, "Working with Social Movements," 260–261.
70. E. Rekosh, *Rethinking the Human Rights Business Model* (Washington, DC: CSIS, 2017).

Chapter 9

1. Civicus, "Message from the Civicus Secretary-General," 2015, http://www.civicus.org/images/SOCS2015SGForeword.pdf.
2. T. Mawarire, I. Pousadela, and C. Gilbert, *Civil Society Watch Report*, Civicus, 2016, https://www.civicus.org/images/CSW_Report.pdf; "Civil Society Rights Violated in 96 Countries," Civicus, 18 June 2015, https://www.civicus.org/index.php/media-resources/news/962-new-civicus-report-civil-society-rights-violated-in-96-countries.
3. D. Rutzen, "Civil Society under Assault," *Journal of Democracy* 26, no. 4, 2015.
4. Brechenmacher, *Civil Society under Assault*; "Briefing on Shrinking Space for Civil Society in Russia," Human Rights Watch, presented at the Carnegie Center, 23 February 2016, https://www.hrw.org/news/2017/02/24/briefing-shrinking-space-civil-society-russia.
5. A. Rashid, "Pakistan's NGO Ban Strengthens Extremist Groups," *Financial Times*, 20 December 2017, https://www.ft.com/content/72b3c858-e184-11e7-8f9f-de1c2175f5ce.
6. I. Butler, "Participatory Democracy under Threat: Growing Restrictions on the Freedoms of NGOs in the EU," Civil Liberties Union for Europe, 2017, https://www.liberties.eu/en/news/participatory-democracy-under-threat-summary/12755.

7. European Union Agency for Fundamental Rights, *Challenges Facing Civil Society Organisations Working on Human Rights in the EU*, 2017, http://fra.europa.eu/en/publication/2018/challenges-facing-civil-society-orgs-human-rights-eu, 13.
8. Front Line Defenders, *Annual Report on Human Rights Defenders at Risk* 2016, (Dublin: Front Line Defenders, 2016).
9. Civicus, "Executive Summary," in *State of Civil Society Report* 2015, https://www.civicus.org/index.php/socs2015, 6–7.
10. Rachel Cox, "New Data Reveals 197 Land and Environmental Defenders Murdered in 2017," Global Witness blog, 2 February 2018, https://www.globalwitness.org/en/blog/new-data-reveals-197-land-and-environmental-defenders-murdered-2017/.
11. A. O'Reilly, "Report: Brazil Becomes Most Dangerous Country in World for Environmental Activists," Fox News, 20 June 2016, http://www.foxnews.com/world/2016/06/20/report-brazil-becomes-most-dangerous-country-in-world-for-environmental.html.
12. L. Baydas and S. Green, eds., *Counter-terrorism Measures and Civil Society* (Washington, DC: Center for Strategic and International Studies, 2018); Civicus, *State of Civil Society Report* 2016, https://www.civicus.org/index.php/socs2016, 58.
13. *Report of the Special Rapporteur on the Rights to Freedom of Peaceful Assembly and of Association*, A/HRC/35/28 (Geneva: UN Human Rights Council, 2017), 15.
14. S. Brechenmacher and T. Carothers, eds., *Examining Civil Society Legitimacy* (Washington, DC: Carnegie Endowment for International Peace, 2018), 35–36.
15. S. Brechenmacher, *Civil Society under Assault: Repression and Responses in Russia, Egypt, and Ethiopia* (Washington, DC: Carnegie Endowment for International Peace, 2017).
16. A. Hamzawy, "Egypt's Resilient and Evolving Social Activism," Carnegie Endowment for International Peace, 5 April 2017, http://carnegieendowment.org/2017/04/05/egypt-s-resilient-and-evolving-social-activism-pub-68578.
17. H. Halawa, "Egypt and the Middle East: Adapting to Tragedy," in *Global Civic Activism in Flux*, ed. R. Youngs (Washington, DC: Carnegie Endowment for International Peace, 2017).
18. UN High Commissioner for Human Rights, "Practical Recommendations for the Creation and Maintenance of a Safe and Enabling Environment for Civil Society, Based on Good Practices and Lessons Learned," 11 April 2016, https://digitallibrary.un.org/record/841791?ln=en.
19. *Report of the Special Rapporteur*.
20. See the home page at www.csolifeline.org.
21. "Awarded Grants Search," National Endowment for Democracy database, http://www.ned.org/region/middle-east-and-northern-africa/egypt-2015/.
22. European Union, *Shared Vision, Common Action: A Stronger Europe*, 2016, https://europa.eu/globalstrategy/en/shared-vision-common-action-stronger-europe.
23. European External Action Service, "Ensuring Protection—European Union Guidelines on Human Rights Defenders," 2008, https://eeas.europa.eu/sites/eeas/files/eu_guidelines_hrd_en.pdf.
24. "Innovative Support to the Civil Society," Sida, 23 July 2104, http://www.sida.se/English/partners/our-partners/Civil-society-organisations/How-to-cooperate/civil-society-nnovation-program/.
25. Front Line Defenders, Reporters without Borders; World Organisation against Torture; International Federation for Human Rights (FIDH); Economic, Social and Cultural Rights Network; International Gay and Lesbian Association; Urgent Action Fund for Women's Human Rights; Protection International; Peace Brigades International; Euro-Mediterranean Foundation of Support to Human Rights Defenders; Forum-Asia; East and Horn of Africa Human Rights Defenders Project.
26. "Sivil Düşun," European Union website, accessed 16 February 2018, https://indd.adobe.com/view/419a6f1b-2c43-4e99-a063-d0068cd47eb9.
27. "Project: Global Equality Fund (Phase I)," Danida, accessed 16 February 2018, http://openaid.um.dk/en/projects/DK-1-223413.
28. Ministry of Foreign Affairs of the Netherlands, *A World to Gain: A New Agenda for Aid, Trade and Investment*, 2013, https://www.government.nl/documents/letters/2013/04/05/global-dividends-a-new-agenda-for-aid-trade-and-investment.

29. For more about the Civic Space Monitor, see http://civic-forum.eu/en/civic-space/.
30. T. Carothers, "The Closing Space Challenge: How Are Funders Responding?" Carnegie Endowment for International Peace, 2 November 2015, http://carnegieendowment.org/2015/11/02/closing-space-challenge-how-are-funders-responding-pub-61808, 24.
31. J. Watts, "Kenya Forest Death: Activists Blame EU for Ignoring Human Rights Warnings,' *Guardian*, 19 January 2018, https://www.theguardian.com/environment/2018/jan/19/kenya-forest-death-activists-blame-eu-for-ignoring-human-rights-warnings
32. Ariadne, International Human Rights Funders Group, and European Foundation Centre, *Challenging the Closing Space for Civil Society: A Practical Starting Point for Funders*, 2015, http://www.ariadne-network.eu/wp-content/uploads/2015/03/Ariadne_ClosingSpaceReport-Final-Version.pdf, 23.
33. International Center for Not-for-profit Law, *Effective Donor Responses to the Challenge of Closing Civic Space*, 2018, http://www.icnl.org/news/2018/Effective%20donor%20responses%20FINAL%201%20May%202018.pdf.
34. Brechenmacher, *Civil Society under Assault*.
35. See, for example, Human Rights and Democracy Network, *Promoting and Protecting Civil Society Space*, report from 17th EU-NGO Human Rights Forum in Brussels, 2016, http://hrdn.eu/2016/03/15/report-protecting-promoting-civil-society-space-15-march-2016/, 16. The Human Rights and Democracy Network says the EU is guilty of "mixed messages" in this sense.
36. S. Nossel, "Pushing Back against the Tyrants: How to Counter the Alarming Authoritarian Assault on Civil Society Groups," *Democracy: A Journal of Ideas* 41 (2016), https://democracyjournal.org/magazine/41/pushing-back-against-the-tyrants/.
37. M. J. Stephan, S. Lakhani and N. Naviwala, *Aid to Civil Society: A Movement Mindset* (Washington, DC: United States Institute of Peace, 2015).
38. B. Leather, T. Webster and T. McEvoy, *Protecting Our Space: Human Rights Defender Strategies to Protect Civil Society Space* (Geneva: International Service for Human Rights, 2016).

Chapter 10

1. M. Diani and D. McAdam, eds., *Social Movements and Networks: Rational Approaches to Collective Action* (Oxford: Oxford University Press, 2003); H. Johnston, *What Is a Social Movement?* (Cambridge: Polity Press, 2014), 4.
2. F. Powell, *The Politics of Civil Society*, 2nd ed. (Bristol: Policy Press, 2013).
3. H. Anheier, M. Kaldor, and M. Glasius, "The Global Civil Society Yearbook: Lessons and Insights 2001–2011," in *Global Civil Society 2012: Ten Years of Critical Reflection*, ed. S. Selchow, M. Kaldor and H. Moore (London: Palgrave Macmillan, 2012).
4. C. F. Fominaya, *Social Movements and Globalization: How Protests, Occupations, and Uprisings Are Changing the World* (London: Palgrave Macmillan, 2014), 194; E. A. Fogarty, "After the Halcyon Days: The Anti-/Alterglobalization Movement and International Organizations, 1996–2011," *Journal of Civil Society* 12, no. 1 (2016): 57–81.
5. C. Froissart, "The Ambiguities between Contention and Political Participation: A Study of Civil Society Development in Authoritarian Regimes," *Journal of Civil Society* 10, no. 3 (2014): 219–222.
6. P. Aslanidis, "Populist Social Movements of the Great Recession," *Mobilization* 21, no. 3 (2016) 301–321.
7. N. Konak and R. Ö. Dönmez, eds., *Waves of Social Movement Mobilizations in the Twenty-First Century* (London: Lexington Books, 2015).
8. C. Butcher and I. Svensson, "Manufacturing Dissent: Modernization and the Onset of Major Nonviolent Resistance Campaigns," *Journal of Conflict Resolution* 60, no. 2 (2016): 311–339.
9. C. Hoeft et al., "Protesting without the 'Underclass,'" *Journal of Civil Society* 10, no. 4 (2014): 393–407.
10. International IDEA, *The Global State of Democracy: Exploring Democracy's Resilience* (Stockholm: International IDEA, 2017), 96.

11. One example being D. della Porta, *Social Movements in Times of Austerity: Bringing Capitalism Back into Protest Analysis* (Cambridge: Polity Press, 2015). See also D. della Porta and M. Diani, "Introduction: The Field of Social Movement Studies," in *The Oxford Handbook of Social Movements*, ed. D. della Porta and M. Diani (Oxford: Oxford University Press, 2015), 10.
12. F. Fukuyama, *The Origins of Political Order: From Prehuman Times to the French Revolution* (New York, Farrar, Straus & Giroux, 2011).
13. Della Porta and Diani, "Introduction: The Field of Social Movement Studies," 11.
14. P. Fernando, "Working with Social Movements," in *Poverty Reduction and Pro-Poor Growth: The Role of Empowerment* (N.p: OECD Publishing, 2012), 254.

INDEX

1848 uprisings 31, 151
1960s movements 10
Abdullah II, King 54
Access Now 95
Africa 20–24, 55–57, 72
al-Abadi, Haider 54
al-Bashir, Omar 24, 57
al-Sadr, Moqtada 31–32, 54
al-Sisi, Abdel Fattah 56
Aliyev Ilham 35
Amazon 94–97
Anarchist movements 12
ANC 55
Apple 94–97
Arab spring 15–16, 29–30, 49
Argentina 40, 85, 88
   Net Party 85, 88
Armenia 35, 53
   Electric Yerevan 35
   Nagorno-Karabakh 35
Article 19 95
Assad, Bashar 16
Astroturfing 92–93
Austria 21
Azerbaijan 35, 74

Bahrain 57
Bakiyev, Kurmanbek 53
Bangladesh 42
Basuki Tjahaja Purmana (Ahok) 41
Beck, Ulrich 12
   sub-politics 12
Belarus 35–36, 57–58
Bellingcat 95
Ben Ali, Zine el-Abidine 33, 53
Benetech 95
Berners-Lee, Tim 90
Bolivia 20, 39–40, 76–77

Bongo, Ali 43
Bosnia and Herzegovina 109
Brazil 20, 37–39, 53
   Olympic Games 37–39
   Workers Party 37–39
   World Cup 37–39
Bulgaria 21
   Civic participation index 21
Burkina Faso 52–53, 74
Burundi 55–57

Cambodia 42, 54
Cambridge Analytica 94–97
Cameroon 44–45
Campaoré, Blaise 52–53
Carnegie Endowment for International
   Peace 5
Catalonia 46–47, 78, 86
   Barcelona en Comú 86
   Catalan National Assembly (CAN) 78
   Popular Union Candidacy (CUP) 78
Chávez, Hugo 39
Chile 39–40
China 18, 41–42, 93
   50 Cent party 93
Ciampi, Annalisa 138
Circular democracy 102–103
Citizen assemblies 90
Citizen reporting 11
Civic practice 9–10
Civic Research Network 5
Civic-tech 82
Civicus 9–10, 14, 29–30, 88, 95, 114,
   130, 139–141,
Civocracy 86
Closing civic space 129–145
Coalition against Unlawful Surveillance Exports
   (Cause) 95

Communing 13
Community of Democracies 138
Congo (Brazzaville) 55–57
Connective action 84
Conservative movements 9, 14–15
Creative commons 9
Croatia 21
Crowdpac 84
Crowdsourcing 83, 137
Cuba 51

Deliberative democracy 102
Democracy festivals 21
DemocracyOS 84, 88
Democratic Republic of the Congo 44–45, 57
Democratization 101–102
Denmark 9, 114–115, 119–121, 139–141
    Danida 119–121
Desalegn, Haliemariam 42–43, 52–53
Digital activism 82–100
Digital Defenders Partnership 95
Digital exclusion 91
Digital Rights Watch 95
Direct democracy 102–103

E-Participation Index 91
Economist Intelligence Unit 28
Egypt 16, 31, 52, 71–72, 74, 89, 132–133
    Muslim Brotherhood 56
    Tahrir Square 31
    Wael Ghonim 89
Electronic Frontier Foundation 88, 95
Enabling environment 125
Engine Room 95
Erdoğan, Recep Tayyip 17, 34, 55
Estonia 99
    Deliberation Day 99
Ethiopia 42–43, 52–53
    Oromia 42–43
Eurasia 19, 35–37, 77
European Civic Forum 139–141
European Endowment for Democracy 113, 139
European Union 114–115, 122–122, 139–140
    European Commission 122–123
    European Instrument for Democracy and Human Rights 140

Facebook, 83, 94–95
Fake news 92–93, 97
Far-right 14, 21, 104
Fearless cities 13
Fico, Robert 53
Finland 21
First Draft News 95

Five Star Movement 88
Flash activism 86
France 21, 45, 58, 75–76, 86, 90, 99
    La République en Marche 75–76
    Nuit Debout 45, 58
    Paris participatory budget 86, 90
Freedom House 92–93
Friedrich Ebert Stiftung 28
Frontline Defenders 95, 133
Fujimori, Alberto 40
Fund for Global Human Rights 139–141

G20 summit Hamburg 49–50, 147–148
Gabon 43
Gambia 43, 52–53
GDELT 28
    regional graphs 28–31
Georgia 19, 37, 74
    Georgian March 19
Germany 21, 119
    PEGIDA 21
    BMZ 119
Global ethics 25–26
Global south 72, 121–122, 125
Global Witness 133
Gnassingbé, Faure 44–45, 55–57
Google 94–97
Greece, 21, 45, 58
    Golden Dawn 21
Guatemala 39–40, 53
Gulf states 51

Hacktivism 82
Haiti 54
Hariri, Rafik 33
Hariri, Saad 33
Honduras 39–40
Hong Kong 40–41, 58, 76
    Demosistō 76
    Umbrella movement 40–41, 58
Horizontality 11
Huerta, Dolores 10–11
Hun Sen 54
Hungary 21, 41

Ice Bucket Challenge 88
Iceland 46–47
Identitarian movements 89
Inácio da Silva, Luís 37–39
India 18, 40, 77
    anti-Romeo movement 18
    Common Man Party 77
Indonesia 41, 93–94
    Muslim Cyber Army, 93–94

Information Communication Technology
    (ICT) 82–100
Information Safety and Capacity 95
Initiative for Policy Dialogue 28
International Aid Transparency
    Initiative 118–121
International Civil Society Centre 9, 80
International IDEA 10
International Labor Organization 30–31
International Social Survey Programme 10
Iran 32, 57, 85
    Green Movement 32, 57
    My Stealthy Freedom 85
Iraq 31–32, 54
IserveU 85
Islamic State 31–32, 89

Jammeh, Yahya 43, 52–53
Japan 42
Jonathan, Goodluck 43
Jordan 54

Kabila, Joseph 44–45, 57
Kazakhstan 36
Keane, John 102
    monitory democracy 102
Kenya 24, 44–45, 54, 85
    Flour movement 24
    Ushahidi 85
Kenyatta, Uhuru 54
Kuczyinski, Pedro Pablo 40, 53
Kyrgyzstan 53

Latin America 20, 37–40, 72, 74, 76–77, 115
    Atlas Network 20
Lebanon 16, 33, 57, 77
    March 14 alliance 33
    Tahaluf Watani 77
    You Stink 33, 57
Libya 16–18
Liquid democracy 84
Local ownership 125
Loomio 84
Lukashenko, Alexander 35–36, 57–58

Macedonia 37
Macron, Emmanuel 75–76
Madrid 21, 78, 86, 98–99
    Decide Madrid 86, 98–99
Maduro, Nicolás 59
Mair, Peter 10
    stakeholder politics 10
Malaysia 54–55, 71, 74

Black 505 movement 74
Medvedev, Dimitri 36–37
Mexico 20, 39–40
Microsoft 94–97
Middle East and North Africa 31–35, 57, 60,
    71–72, 115–116
Mnangagwa, Emmerson 44
Modi, Narendra 18
Moldova 37, 77
Morales, Evo 20
Morocco 16–18, 32–33, 55, 76
    February 20 movement 16–18, 32–33, 55, 76
    Rif protests 32–33
Morsi, Mohammed 56
MoveOn 85
Mubarak, Hosni 31, 60
Mugabe, Robert 44, 55
Museveni, Yoweri 43–44, 57
Mutualism 7, 25
Myanmar 77, 89

Naples 13, 21
Navalny, Alexei 36–37
Nepal 42
Netherlands 21
    Rotterdam 21
Netherlands 121–122
Networked governance 25
NGO-ization 80, 113, 127–128
Nicaragua 40
Nieto, Enrique Pena 39–40
Nigeria 24, 43, 72
    Boko Harem 24
Nonobedience 15–16
Norway 21

Oak Foundation 139–141
Obama, Barack 139
Occupy movement 30–31, 60, 67, 71
OECD 124, 126
Open Society Foundations 139–141
Orban, Viktor 46–47
Ortega, Daniel 40
OuiShare 84

Palestine 16–18, 71–72
    Gaza 16–18, 71–72
    Palestinian Authority 16–18
Paraguay 40
Park Geun-Hye 53
Participative democracy 102, 107
Participatory budgeting 13–14, 91–92
Participatory commons 86
Participidia 10

Party movements 75
Pashinyan, Nikol 35
Personal Democracy Forum 85
Peru 40, 53
Pew Research Center 90
Poland 21, 45–46, 58
   Defence of Democracy (KOD) 45–46
   Law and Justice (PiS) 45–46
Populism 15, 104, 149
Portugal 21
Postrepresentative democracy 102
Pre-figurative 25
Protection International 95
Putin, Valdimir 36–37, 57–58
Putnam, Robert 10–11

Qadafi, Muammar 16–18
Qurium 95

Reykjavik 21
Rhize 123
Right to the city 13
Romania 46
Rouhani, Hassan 32
Rousseff, Dilma 20, 37–39, 53
Russia 18–19, 36–37, 57–58, 93, 131
   foreign agent law 129
   March of Millions 36
   Night Wolves 18–19

Saakashvili, Mikhail 38
Salafists 14
Saleh, Ali Abdullah 34–35, 53
Sanders, Bernie 77
Sargsyan, Serzh 35, 53
Second-generation activism 13
Senegal 52–53
Serbia 37
sharing-economy 25
Shinawatra, Yingluk 53, 74
Sigrid Rausing Trust 123, 139–141
Singapore 41
Slacktivism 87–88
Slovakia 53
Slovenia 21, 53
Smart cities 91
Social movements theories 7, 152–153
Solidaire 61, 123
Sousveillance 86
South Africa 44–45, 55
South Korea 42, 53
Spain 46–47, 78
   Ahora Madrid 78
   Podemos 78

Sudan 24, 44–45, 57
Swarming 12
Sweden 118–119
   Sida 118–119
Syria 16, 57

Tactics Technology Collective 95
Taiwan 42, 76, 98
   Sunflower movement 42, 76, 98
   vTaiwan 98
Telegram messaging 89
Thailand 53, 74, 94
Togo 44–45, 55–57
Transnational collective action 25–26
Trolls 92–93
Tunisia 16–18, 33–34, 53, 71–74
Turkey 17, 34, 55, 74, 93–94
   AK Hearths 17
   AK Party 17
   Gezi Park 17, 34, 55
   Ottoman Hearths 17
   TESEV 17
   Vote and Beyond 17
Twitter 83, 95

Uganda 24, 43–44, 57, 72
   Black Monday 24
   Jobless Brotherhood 43–44
   Walk to work 43–44
UK 21, 77, 117–118
   Citizens UK 21
   DfID 117–118
   Labour Party 77
   Magna Carta Fund for Human Rights and Democracy 117–118
   Momentum 77
   Peoples Plan for Greater Manchester 21
   Scotland 21
Ukraine 19–20, 38, 53, 76
   Automaidan 76
   Donbas 19–20, 38
   Maidan 38, 76
   pro-Zorra 19–20, 76, 85
   Reanimation Package of Reforms 76
   Right Sector 19–20
   SOS Crimea 76
   SOS Donbas 76
Uncivil society 14
Unconventional action 10–11
United Nations 113–114, 116, 138
   United Nations Development Program 116
United States 67, 77, 98, 116–117, 138
   AntiFa 67
   Arizona Border Recon 67

Black Lives Matter 67
Challenge.gov 98
Crowd Counting Consortium 67
March for Science 67
March for Our Lives 67
National Endowment for Democracy 117
Oath Keepers 67
Patriot Movement 67
Tea Party 77
USAID 116–117
Women's March 67

Vargas Llosa, Mario 105
Varieties of Democracy project 10
Venezuela 20, 39, 59, 93–94

Wade, Abdoulaye 52–53
Women's marches 147–148
World Human Rights Cities Forum 13
World Social Forum 13

Yanukovych, Viktor 38, 53
Yemen 34–35, 53
Yimby 9, 67

Zimbabwe 24, 44, 55, 75
   ZANU-PF 44, 55
   WOZA 24
Žižek, Slavoj 105
Zuma, Jacob 55

www.ingramcontent.com/pod-product-compliance
Ingram Content Group UK Ltd.
Pitfield, Milton Keynes, MK11 3LW, UK
UKHW021250180426
11946UKWH00003B/66